THE
AMERICAN SOLDIER

THE AMERICAN SOLDIER

U.S. Armies in uniform, 1755 to the present

Philip Katcher

MILITARY PRESS
New York

HALF-TITLE PAGE: US Marines in Vietnam, heavily burdened with flak jackets and extra ammunition bandoliers, carry to the rear captured Communist 12.7mm anti-aircraft machine guns. [*US Marine Corps*]

TITLE PAGE: Fine study of a US Army rifle squad leader in autumn 1950: Corporal Carroll Vogles of the 35th RCT, based on the 35th Infantry from 25th Division. No unit or rank insignia are worn in the field. He carries the M1 rifle, and a triple-pocket grenade pouch (left) and first aid pouch are attached to his rifle belt. The extra bandoliers are typical enough – but one suspects that the grenades, rather precariously attached by slipping their spoons into pockets, were the photographer's idea . . . in combat they would be rather more securely attached to the equipment. [*US Army via Shelby Stanton*]

BELOW: Members of the 5th SFGA1 pictured in February 1962. The flashes were made by gluing a piece of black felt on to a larger white piece, explaining the variation in the width of the borders. At this time officers still wore the Special Forces distinctive insignia, rather than their rank insignia, on the flash. [*US Army*]

JACKET FLAP: A captain of the Women's Army Corps, pictured from 1944. The shoulder-patch is that of SHAEF (Supreme Headquarters Allied Expeditionary Force), where many WACs were employed. The shoulder-bag, beige stockings and brown buckled shoes are all regulation.

© Osprey Publishing Limited

This 1990 edition published by Military Press and distributed by Outlet Book Company, Inc., a Random House company, 225 Park Avenue South, New York, New York 10003

ISBN 0–517–01481–5

Printed and bound in Hong Kong

87654321

Compiled and edited by **Richard Widdows**

Designed by **Janette Widdows**

CONTENTS

COLOR ILLUSTRATORS

Gerry Embleton: 12–13, 38–41, 98–103
Michael Roffe: 14–23
Bryan Fosten: 26–29, 204–211
Paul Hannon: 32–35, 182–185
Ron Volstad: 44–51, 56–77, 80–95, 130–139, 158–167, 190–201, 214–224, back cover
Jeffrey Burn: 108–115
Chris Collingwood: Front cover, 120–127
Andy Carroll: 142–151
Mike Chappell: 154–155, 172–179
Angus McBride: Jacket flap [from MAA 100: *Women at War 1939–45*, Jack Cassin-Scott (1980)]

To Ann, who finds it funny to see the name Katcher in bookstores.

Acknowledgements
Many people have contributed generously with their time, knowledge and help in gathering much of what is found in this book. Thanks for all their help over the years are due to Thomas Arliskas, William T. Barrante, Paul Braddock, Richard Carlisle, Robert Cassidy, Philip Cavanaugh, Rene Chartrand, Richard Claydon, Robert Crisman, Gary Christopher, John Elting, Gerry Embleton, John Ertzgaard, Mike Hilbner, David Horn, Don Johnson, Lee Johnson, Lee Joyner, David A. Katcher, Vincent J-R Kehoe, Fritz Kirsch, John Lyle, Michael J. McAfee, John McIlhenny, H. Michael Madaus, Benedict R. Maryniak, Bernie Mitchell, John A. Morrow, Chris Nelson, George C. Neumann, David Oswalt, Sheperd Paine, Herb Peck Jr., Ernie Peterkin, Russ Pritchard, Bill Printz, Harry Roach, Gerry Rolph, David Scheinmann, John Sickles, Judith Stillwell, David L. Sullivan, Dr. Thomas Sweeney, Tim Terrell, Don Troiani, Richard Tibbals, Lee A. Wallace Jr., Richard Widdows, Martin Windrow, Mike Winey, George Woodbridge, William Yarborough, Kevin R. Young, Marko Zlatich, and especially to my wife Rebecca. What's helpful in this book is largely due to them; any errors are my fault.

The material in this book is derived mainly from the following titles in the MEN-AT-ARMS (MAA) and ELITE military series, published by Osprey:

MAA 18: *George Washington's Army*, text by Brig. Peter Young (first published 1972)
MAA 48: *Wolfe's Army*, Robin May (1974) [*reprinted 1989*]
MAA 56: *The Mexican–American War 1846–48*, Philip Katcher (1976) [*reprinted 1990*]
MAA 63: *The American Indian Wars 1860–90*, Philip Katcher (1977) [*reprinted 1990*]
MAA 70: *The US Army 1941–45*, Philip Katcher, (1984)
MAA 104 *Armies of the Vietnam War 1962–75*, Philip Katcher (1980)
MAA 143: *Armies of the Vietnam War (2)*, Lee E. Russell (1983)
MAA 157: *Flak Jackets: 20th-Century Military Body Armor*, Simon Dunstan (1984)
MAA 159: *Grenada 1983*, Lee E. Russell & M. Albert Mendez (1985)
MAA 168: *US Cavalry on the Plains 1850–90*, Philip Katcher (1985)
MAA 170: *American Civil War Armies (1): Confederate Artillery, Cavalry & Infantry*, Philip Katcher (1986)
MAA 173: *The Alamo & the War of Texan Independence 1835–36*, Philip Haythornthwaite (1985)
MAA 174: *The Korean War 1950–53*, Nigel Thomas & Peter Abbott (1986)
MAA 177: *American Civil War Armies (2): Union Artillery, Cavalry & Infantry*, Philip Katcher (1986)
MAA 179: *American Civil War Armies (3): Staff, Specialist & Maritime Services*, Philip Katcher (1986)
MAA 190: *American Civil War Armies (4): State Troops*, Philip Katcher (1987)
MAA 205: *US Army Combat Equipment 1910–88*, Gordon L. Rottman (1989)
MAA 207: *American Civil War Armies (5): Volunteer Militia*, Philip Katcher (1989)
MAA 214: *US Infantry Equipments 1775–1910*, Philip Katcher (1989)
MAA 226: *The American War 1812–14*, Philip Katcher (1974) [*reprinted 1990*]
MAA 230: *The US Army 1890–1920*, Philip Katcher (1978) [*reprinted 1990*]

ELITE 2: *The US Marine Corps since 1945*, Lee E. Russell (1984)
ELITE 4: *US Army Special Forces 1952–84*, Gordon L. Rottman (1985)
ELITE 13: *US Army Rangers & LRRP Units 1942–87*, Gordon L. Rottman (1987)
ELITE 20: *Inside the US Army Today*, Gordon L. Rottman (1988)

INTRODUCTION

Citizens of the United States of America do not consider themselves warlike, yet the US Army has engaged in wars both large and small just about once every decade of its existence. In most instances, such as in 1898 for the Spanish–American War and in 1861 for the Civil War, conflict was widely welcomed. Sometimes, such as in 1846 for the Mexican–American War and in the 1960s for the Vietnam War, there was considerable opposition.

In each case, however, the Army and public entered each war anew. Because of fears of a professional military and the threat such an organization poses to civilian liberties, the US Army has always been small and under civilian control. A civilian head – until after World War 2 the Secretary of War and thereafter the Secretary of the Army – is and always has been in charge.

Moreover, because of the small size of the traditional peacetime US Army, civilians have had to reinforce its ranks during any major war. These civilians have joined the Army either as individuals volunteering or by being drafted into the Army or as whole militia, volunteer or National Guard units. Only the high-ranking professional officers and a scattering of senior non-commissioned officers have maintained any sense of Army continuity.

It was said during the Vietnam War, when each officer and enlisted man served only one year before being rotated back to the States, that the Army there didn't fight one war for ten years – it fought ten wars for one year each. In much the same way, the Army may have been said to have fought each of its wars as new body. Volunteer units which fought in the Mexican–American War didn't fight in the Civil War 13 years later, although many veterans did return to the colors.

The result, generally, has been a similar pattern to America's major wars. Initial defeat (Bunker Hill in 1775, Detroit in 1812, First Manassas in 1861, Kasserine Pass in 1942), leads to a swell of enthusiasm and renewed dedication which eventually overcomes the enemy. True, small wars such as the Mexican–American, Spanish–American and Grenada were wholly successful, with nothing but victories until final conquest. Vietnam, where a string of small victories ended in eventual defeat, was different; but since that was a civil war in which Americans intervened, the situation was quite different from other American wars – as was the result.

Today the US Army makes an attempt to maintain traditions of past unit glories. However, because of the frequent transfer of officers and men within its ranks, there is little real US Army unit pride stemming from past wars.

This is not true of the US Marine Corps which, though not a part of the Army, appears in these pages. The Marine Corps is proudly traditional, with an independence demonstrated by the fact that its commandant sits with the Joint Chiefs of Staff, even though he is technically under Naval command. Nevertheless many of American's wars were fought with joint Army/Marine units, such as the 2nd Infantry Division of World War 1, which was led by a Marine general officer and included both soldiers and Marines.

PHILIP KATCHER
Devon
Pennsylvania

October 1990

THE COLONIAL WARS,

On 18 May 1754 a small band of Virginians attacked a French party on the colony's western frontier and plunged North America into war. This was, however, a war not to be contained to one continent. Eventually the Seven Years War, as it was generally known, or the French and Indian War, as it was locally known, involved the armies of Great Britain, France, Prussia, Austria, Russia and the states of the Holy Roman Empire.

Under ordinary circumstances regular British troops, with only minor colonial military unit participation, would have been sufficient to defend the 13 British colonies along the Atlantic coast. As it was, Britain had to spread its army across the world to fight the Seven Years War. In 1760, for example, the British Army had 23 foot regiments in Britain, 17 in Ireland, one in Jersey, six in Gibraltar, 16 in Germany, six in the West Indies, two in Africa and four in the East Indies; only 21 could be spared for North America itself, and much of the war there would be fought by North American natives.

The British North American Colonials actively aided in the war against the French in three ways, in addition to providing money and logistical support for the Regulars. First, some Colonials joined Regular British Army units. Second, some joined new Regular Army units created in America. Indeed the 62nd, later 60th (Royal American) Regiment of Foot was raised in 1756 from German settlers in Pennsylvania under native Swiss and German officers.

Ranging companies were also raised, sometimes under British officers with Colonials in the ranks, to aid the British Army. The most famous such company was His Majesty's Independent Company of Rangers, better known as Rogers' Rangers. Other ranging companies were wholly Colonial in membership, originating as local, informal bands that hunted Indians in the woods and took their scalps for bounty money. Later they became formalized with their commander's names forming their titles; an example would be Hezekiah Dunn's Company of Rangers from New Jersey, which saw action in New York in 1756–60.

Third, the Colonies raised, equipped and uniformed their own complete Provincial regiments. These were above and beyond the standing militia to which virtually every man in the Colonies belonged. These new combat units were, in Colonial eyes, established on the same footing as Regular units of foot and horse. Indeed many of these units were like Regular ones in virtually every detail: in 1758, for example, the New Jersey Regiment had 1,000 totally uniformed, equipped and well-drilled officers and men, complete with a grenadier company.

There was a difference between Provincial and other units. Unlike other units with Colonials in their ranks, which largely had British officers, Provincial units had Colonial officers. These officers were as jealous of their authority and place in life as British officers were slighting of them.

Although many early battles went against the British and Colonials, on 17 September 1759 Quebec, French North America's leading city, fell. The British and

BELOW: Major Robert Rogers wears the uniform of his battalion of Rangers in this contemporary mezzotint. He carries a fusil and wears a cap probably cut down from an issue tricorne. [*John Ross Robertson Collection, Metropolitan Toronto Central Library*]

BELOW RIGHT: Standing Orders, Rogers' Rangers—cards bearing the original 1759 orders are still given to today's Ranger students. [*US Army*]

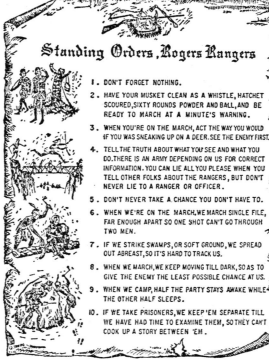

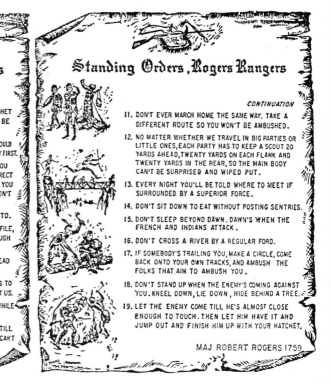

Standing Orders, Rogers Rangers

1. DON'T FORGET NOTHING.

2. HAVE YOUR MUSKET CLEAN AS A WHISTLE, HATCHET SCOURED, SIXTY ROUNDS POWDER AND BALL, AND BE READY TO MARCH AT A MINUTE'S WARNING.

3. WHEN YOU'RE ON THE MARCH, ACT THE WAY YOU WOULD IF YOU WAS SNEAKING UP ON A DEER. SEE THE ENEMY FIRST.

4. TELL THE TRUTH ABOUT WHAT YOU SEE AND WHAT YOU DO. THERE IS AN ARMY DEPENDING ON US FOR CORRECT INFORMATION. YOU CAN LIE ALL YOU PLEASE WHEN YOU TELL OTHER FOLKS ABOUT THE RANGERS, BUT DON'T NEVER LIE TO A RANGER OR OFFICER.

5. DON'T NEVER TAKE A CHANCE YOU DON'T HAVE TO.

6. WHEN WE'RE ON THE MARCH, WE MARCH SINGLE FILE, FAR ENOUGH APART SO ONE SHOT CAN'T GO THROUGH TWO MEN.

7. IF WE STRIKE SWAMPS, OR SOFT GROUND, WE SPREAD OUT ABREAST, SO IT'S HARD TO TRACK US.

8. WHEN WE MARCH, WE KEEP MOVING TILL DARK, SO AS TO GIVE THE ENEMY THE LEAST POSSIBLE CHANCE AT US.

9. WHEN WE CAMP, HALF THE PARTY STAYS AWAKE WHILE THE OTHER HALF SLEEPS.

10. IF WE TAKE PRISONERS, WE KEEP 'EM SEPARATE TILL WE HAVE HAD TIME TO EXAMINE THEM, SO THEY CAN'T COOK UP A STORY BETWEEN 'EM.

Standing Orders, Rogers Rangers

CONTINUATION

11. DON'T EVER MARCH HOME THE SAME WAY. TAKE A DIFFERENT ROUTE SO YOU WON'T BE AMBUSHED.

12. NO MATTER WHETHER WE TRAVEL IN BIG PARTIES OR LITTLE ONES, EACH PARTY HAS TO KEEP A SCOUT 20 YARDS AHEAD, TWENTY YARDS ON EACH FLANK AND TWENTY YARDS IN THE REAR, SO THE MAIN BODY CAN'T BE SURPRISED AND WIPED OUT.

13. EVERY NIGHT YOU'LL BE TOLD WHERE TO MEET IF SURROUNDED BY A SUPERIOR FORCE.

14. DON'T SIT DOWN TO EAT WITHOUT POSTING SENTRIES.

15. DON'T SLEEP BEYOND DAWN. DAWN'S WHEN THE FRENCH AND INDIANS ATTACK.

16. DON'T CROSS A RIVER BY A REGULAR FORD.

17. IF SOMEBODY'S TRAILING YOU, MAKE A CIRCLE, COME BACK ONTO YOUR OWN TRACKS, AND AMBUSH THE FOLKS THAT AIM TO AMBUSH YOU.

18. DON'T STAND UP WHEN THE ENEMY'S COMING AGAINST YOU. KNEEL DOWN, LIE DOWN, HIDE BEHIND A TREE.

19. LET THE ENEMY COME TILL HE'S ALMOST CLOSE ENOUGH TO TOUCH. THEN LET HIM HAVE IT AND JUMP OUT AND FINISH HIM UP WITH YOUR HATCHET.

MAJ ROBERT ROGERS 1759

1755–1783

Colonials successfully stood off French attempts to recapture Quebec, going on the attack to capture Montreal on 8 September 1760. On 10 February 1763 the Treaty of Paris was signed, leaving all of eastern North America in British hands.

There was no longer any pressing French threat to the Colonies. Even so, the British government felt that it should continue to station troops in North America. Moreover, it considered that the Colonials should bear part of the burden of their defence by paying taxes collected through stamps required on legal documents or other means.

The Colonials, many of whom had not recovered from slights on their Seven Years War service, understandably felt otherwise. They saw little reason for the British Army to defend North America; their own Provincial regiments could again be raised and would be, they felt, sufficient for any future defence—if any were to be needed.

Tensions grew. The Stamp Act had to be repealed when Colonials burned sheets of the hated stamps and threatened tax collectors. A mob threatening a squad of the 29th Foot in Boston in March 1770 led to shots being fired and five dead Colonials. Another mob stormed a ship with East India Company taxed tea in Boston harbor on 16 December 1773 and threw the cargo overboard.

The Boston garrison was enlarged so that by the beginning of 1775 it contained some 4,500 Regular Army troops. The inhabitants no longer saw these troops as serving in their defence, but as oppressing the local population. Residents began gathering weapons for their own defence.

Finally, in mid-April 1775, the garrison sent a party towards the western town of Concord to seize the weapons, shot and powder known to be stored there. The Colonials resisted, forming a line of battle at the Concord Bridge and then sniping at the battered Regulars as they returned to Boston.

It was now open war between North Americans and Britons, and Boston was besieged. Other colonies re-raised their Provincial, now called Continental, units for their defence.

That the Colonies felt that their new regiments were simply continuations of the regiments of the Seven Years War can be seen in their uniforms. Pennsylvania's 1st Battalion of 1758, for example, wore green coats with red collars, cuffs and lapels (called 'facings'). The first battalion Pennsylvania raised in 1775, which became the 1st Continental Regiment, wore identically colored coats. In the same way New Jersey's first unit wore blue coats with red facings in both wars; Connecticut's first unit in both wars wore red coats; and South Carolina's first unit wore blue coats.

The Colonial effort went further than it had in the

A Continental musketman as seen by a contemporary British cartoonist. [*Metropolitan Museum of Art*]

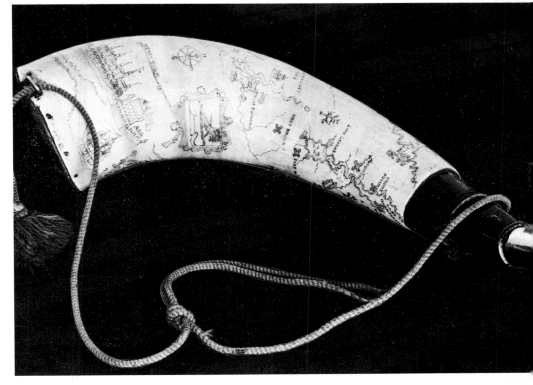

BELOW: The average Colonial rifleman carried his own powder horn, in which he kept loose powder. Most of these were engraved by their owners with scenes from their campaigns or various symbols. [*Philip Katcher*]

RIGHT: Saddlebags are hung
on the rear of this saddle.
Across the front is a pair of
bearskin-covered holsters. The
carbine-jacket hangs below the
holster.

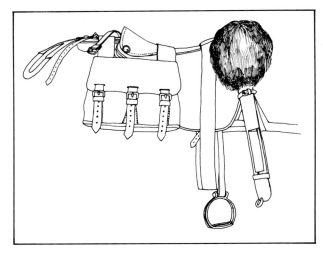

BELOW: The iron head of a
typical six-foot pontoon.
[*Philip Katcher*]

RIGHT: The rifleman on the
left wears the usual white linen
rifle dress of the War of
Independence. Although he
wears a cartridge box, he does
not carry a bayonet since they
were not fitted to rifles. The
infantryman he faces,
apparently from the
Pennsylvania Line, wears a
white shoulder belt for his
bayonet scabbard and another
to support his cartridge box.
[*Anne S. K. Brown Military
Collection, Brown University
Library*]

Seven Years War, however, in that a central government, the Continental Congress, ran the overall war effort. Congress put the various state units under one command as a national army. Beyond that it created units of its own – including, on 10 November 1775, the Continental Marines which were to serve on the new nation's ships.

Eventually the central government standardized the Army, doing away with much of the states' authorities over their own units. On 4 November 1775 Congress ordered all Continental troops to wear brown coats with different facings for the different regiments. Before that, each unit had dressed as its colonel pleased or as the state provided.

Congress also authorized infantry regiments of 728 officers and men at the same time. On 8 October 1776 Congress called for each soldier serving in its army to receive two linen hunting shirts, two pairs of gaitered trousers and a leather or wool waistcoat. On 2 October 1779 it would issue orders putting all its men into blue coats, with white facings for New Englanders, buff facings for those from New York and New Jersey, red facings for those from Pennsylvania, Delaware, Maryland and Virginia, and blue facings with white lace for Southerners.

Congress also helped shape the face of an American Army that grew to 33,535 officers and men at its largest in January 1779. In 1777 it authorized a Regiment of Artillery Artificers and at various other times authorized Corps of Continental Artillery and Light Dragoons, an Engineer Department (16 June 1775), an Invalid Corps, made up of soldiers no longer able to take to the field (20 June 1777), and a Corps of Pioneers (26 March 1782).

For the staff, Congress sanctioned an Adjutant General's Department (June 1775), a Clothier General's Department (December 1776), a Field Department and a Geographer's Department (both 1782). It also authorized a Hospital Department, later Medical Department (July 1775), an Inspector General's Department (1778), a Judge Advocate General's Department (June 1775), a Commissary of Military Stores (1776), a Commissary of Musters, a Paymaster General's Department and Quartermaster General's Department (all 16 June 1775), and a Provost Troop of Light Dragoons (early 1778).

The new Continental Army and Marines began to differ from the British Army and Marines in other ways, too. Their battle tactics and drill came from a half-pay Prussian captain, Baron von Steuben, and the French Army musket, lighter and stronger than the British model, was adopted as the American standard. American frontiersmen brought the rifle into the Army as a combat weapon, and while it never wholly replaced the smoothbore musket, it still played an important part in many campaigns.

Again, once France entered the war on the American side, Britain had to fight a worldwide war. A hard-pressed empire held on to Gibraltar and gained ground in India – but lost its North American holdings with the signing of the Treaty of Paris in 1783.

At the war's end the new American government, fearful of professional, standing armies such as the British one they had just driven from their shores,

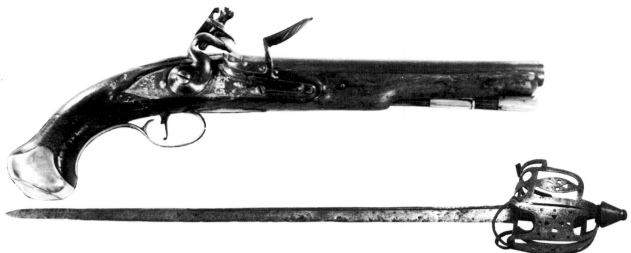

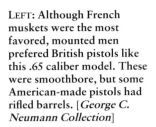

LEFT: Although French muskets were the most favored, mounted men preferred British pistols like this .65 caliber model. These were smoothbore, but some American-made pistols had rifled barrels. [*George C. Neumann Collection*]

LEFT: Scottish iron-hilted broadswords were highly popular as Continental dragoon sabres. [*Philip Katcher*]

disbanded the Continental Army and Marines, with only a small company of men left to guard public property. But the lessons of the Colonial Wars had been learned and a core of battle-hardened veterans remained to be ready if ever needed again in America's defence. On 2 June 1784 Congress reduced its army to 80 enlisted men and several officers, the top ranking one being a captain. West Point, with its government stores, was to have a garrison of 55 men, while the rest were sent to Fort Pitt, Pennsylvania.

Moreover, the practices established in the late war would affect the US Army in later years. Many of the various staff organizations and departments established as early as 1775 remained as staff officers, then saw life again as the country enlarged its Army to meet Indian and other threats. Many of them, such as the Inspector General's Department and the Quartermaster General's Department, exist today under the same names they adopted in 1775.

Many of the practices of the modern US Army date from the Colonial era. The Special Forces and Rangers of today trace their ancestry, even their basic standing orders, to Ranging Companies of the Seven Years War, and many existing Army National Guard units started during that period; Troop A, 104th Cavalry Regiment, Pennsylvania Army National Guard, for example, was founded as the First Troop, Philadelphia City Cavalry in 1774.

The First Troop points up another American military practice that dates from the colonial era–the dependence on volunteers, rather than a standing army, for national defense. During the peaceful years, the US has traditionally allowed its armed forces to stay small, and when war breaks out the modest army has been supplemented with volunteers, either as wholly formed units of the militia, National Guard or Reserves, or as individuals joining regular and other units.

Finally, though the last Continental Marine was discharged in September 1783, today's US Marine Corps cites 10 November 1775 as its founding date and has built on the basic traditions begun in the Continental Marines.

George Washington when serving as President of the United States. At the end of the war it had been seriously proposed that he be made king. Washington regarded the suggestion 'with abhorrence', and when he was able to retire in 1783, he told Congress: 'I resign with satisfaction the appointment I accepted with diffidence.' His familiarly odd expression was caused by ill-fitting false teeth. [*National Portrait Gallery, London*]

1

2

3

1. RANGER, HIS MAJESTY'S INDEPENDENT COMPANIES OF AMERICAN RANGERS, 1758

The most famous of these renowned units were Rogers' Rangers—originally the Ranger Company of Blanchard's New Hampshire Regiment—later expanded into His Majesty's Independent Companies of American Rangers. With a maximum strength of seven companies, they were neither Regulars nor Provincials, but were paid by the King. Some attempt was made at a uniform dress, varying within each company. Some, at least, of Rogers' men are known to have worn short green frieze jackets—made up by Messrs. Thos. and Benjamin Forseys of Albany—from 1758.

2. RANGER, LATE 1750s

Although Rogers' men attracted most of the publicity, then and since, there were other companies of Rangers serving with the British Army in America. Major Gorham's Company of Rangers in 1761 wore red coats with brown linings and facings (so that the coat could be reversed, brown faced red, in the field), brown waistcoats, and leather 'jockey' caps with an oakleaf or branch painted on the left side.

This Ranger wears a cap made from a cut-down cocked hat with a part of the brim retained and hooked up—it could be dropped as a peak to shade the eyes at will. This 'cut-hat' was popular among both Provincials and Regulars. He wears Indian leggings and British Army equipment, with the sword replaced by a hatchet or tomahawk. Note the straight haft—the curved shape did not develop until the 19th century.

3. RANGER, LATE 1750s

In 1759 Captain John Knox of the 43rd Foot described Rangers wearing 'black rateen'—a coarse frieze cloth—lapeled and cuffed with blue, a sleeved waistcoat, a short jacket without sleeves, white metal buttons, canvas or linen 'drawers', and a short 'petticoat' or kilt made with a waistband and one button, open in front, black 'leggins' which buttoned on the calf, and Highland bonnets. The very Scottish character of this costume seems to confirm the influence among Rangers recruited from recently settled Scots immigrants. This Ranger has a quilled and tufted Indian pouch, a British Army tin canteen, and carries his kit rolled in a blanket and slung Indian-style by a 'tumpline'.

1. SOLDIER OF THE INDEPENDENT COMPANIES, 1755

Various Independent Companies were formed and sent on garrison duty to the Colonies, and these units are known to have been stationed in the West Indies, Georgia and New York, among other places. There is little firm evidence of their uniforms in the 1750s. In the 1730s they were ordered to wear red coats faced and lined green; and those serving in the West Indies (then rather a vague term used to cover many overseas stations) were to have their coats lined with brown linen, which showed when the skirts were hooked back for ease of marching.

The number of companies in North America varied as new ones were raised and others transfered or re-formed. The constant changes must have led to great variations in uniform.

2. PRIVATE, JERSEY BLUES, 1755–62

While many militiamen fought in civilian clothes, and were offered cash bounties if they brought their own guns, some states provided items of equipment and even complete uniforms. The 'Jersey Blues' were probably the best known of the Provincial regiments raised, though their colors of blue with red facings were shared by troops from Massachusetts and Virginia. This man's colors are the same as those of his colonel, Philip Schuyler, painted in his full regimental uniform, but his coat has been bobbed after the Highland manner, as ordered. He is holding a fringed smock which, unlike the typical linen hunting shirt, is buttoned at the cuff and uncaped.

3. OFFICER, 2ND CONNECTICUT REGIMENT, 1758

The costume of this well-dressed officer is based largely on a portrait of Colonel Nathan Whiting, who commanded a Provincial battalion at Ticonderoga in 1758. He is dressed as for a parade. His regimentals are of fashionable cut, a scarlet coat with slashed cuffs of yellow, a yellow waistcoat with silver lace and scarlet breeches. He wears the usual insignia of commissioned rank – a silver gorget suspended round his neck on a ribbon of facing color (yellow in this case) and a crimson silk net sash over the shoulder. He wears a liberally powdered wig of the popular contemporary style known as a 'pigeon-winged toupée'; the powder frosting his shoulders was quite acceptable socially, and appears in several portraits.

1. PRIVATE, 1ST CONTINENTAL LIGHT DRAGOONS, 1778

This unit was formed around some Virginia light dragoon volunteer troops and was taken into Congress' army in January 1777. Renamed the 1st Legionary Corps in 1781, when infantry was added to its ranks, the last members were discharged at the end of the war.

This figure, pictured from 1778, wears a brown coat with green facings, though previously the unit had worn blue coats with red facings—and by 1780 blue coats with green facings seem to have been standard. Fully equipped, he sports a carbine, sword and two pistols. By 23 September 1777 the Continental supplier in Philadelphia had issued the unit 266 coats, 266 vests, 266 pairs of breeches, 268 pairs of shoes, 258 shirts and 177 pairs of boots. Through 1 January 1778 they would receive even more of all these, plus 624 pairs of stockings, 192 hats and 43 blankets.

2. PRIVATE, 1ST CONTINENTAL REGIMENT OF FOOT, 1776

Lapels of regimental coats were made to button over in cold weather, as is being done by this soldier of the first regiment raised in Pennsylvania, as Thompson's Rifle Battalion, in the spring of 1775. It was reorganized as the 1st Continental around January 1776. Besides the red-faced green coats, the men wore buckskin breeches. The musket is a French one, probably a relic of the previous conflict.

1. PRIVATE, CONTINENTAL MARINES, 1777

Nicholas' Battalion of Continental Marines was stationed with the main Continental Army from December 1776 until the fall of Fort Mifflin. The men's uniforms are believed to have been captured British ones intended to have been issued to Provincials. The extra buttons on each cuff are the traditional ones in seafaring men's coats of that period. The brim of the three-cornered hat has been cut down, bound with tape and turned up on one side. Red facings have replaced the white ones as worn initially (though white remained more common) and light-colored cloth breeches are worn here in place of white.

2. OFFICER OF HORSE, CHARLES DABNEY'S VIRGINIA STATE LEGION, 1782

The Legion was comprised of remnants of the 3rd State Regiment, Major Nelson's Corps of Cavalry, Captain John Rogers' dismounted Illinois dragoons and Captain Christopher Roan's artillery; and at first the men wore the clothing of their former units. The first State issue of clothing was cloth for the coats, which were blue with facings of the same color, lined with white serge. The addition of red facings could be afforded only by a few officers, of whom this man is one. He wears also a white, long-sleeved waistcoat, leather boots and breeches, and a brown cloth cloak lined with white corduroy. Equipment carried on the horse included deerskin holsters, carbine and sword.

3. OFFICER, BAYLOR'S DRAGOONS, 1777

In January 1777 Colonel George Baylor was authorized to raise a regiment of horse, and for some time it was inevitably known as Baylor's Dragoons rather than its more formal title of The 3rd Continental Regiment of Light Dragoons. Knowledge of the uniform is scanty, except that the rifle-shirt is well-known and examples have survived. The hunting-shirt was a comfortable and serviceable field dress. The body was made of a single piece of linen, an opening out for the neck and the front, and the cape stitched on. The buttons were of bone or cloth-covered wood. Fringes were made by cutting strips of linen and pulling out the threads on both edges. His only badge of rank is his crimson silk sash, rarely worn by Continental officers. His helmet is boiled leather and decorated with horsehair. Note the obsolete abbreviation of 'Unites States' on the wooden canteen.

1. RIFLEMAN, THOMPSON'S PENNSYLVANIA RIFLE BATTALION, 1775

The favored hunting shirt of the rifleman. A journal of the time describes Thompson's Battalion as 'stout and hardy men, many exceeding six feet in height. They are dressed in white frocks, or rifle shirts, and round hats. These men are remarkable for the accuracy of their aim.' Clearly shown here are the powder horn and the tomahawk; often there would be a large hunting knife as well. The rifle was spectacularly more accurate than the musket, and the men who used them acquired a special glamor which has, however, caused historians to overrate its importance. Its disadvantages were its slowness of loading and its lack of a bayonet, leaving the men defenseless against the sort of charge at which the British excelled.

2. PRIVATE, 13TH ALBANY MILITIA, 1777

Like any other militia unit, the 13th Albany were not professional soldiers; they wore civilian clothing and were normally as badly equipped as they were trained. They turned out at moments of crisis (and did particularly well against Burgoyne's advance), then returned to their farms and shops. The only 'uniform' shown here is musket, cross belt, cartridge pouch and knapsack. Each man was required to provide his own musket and bayonet or short sword. His hat was a safe place to carry his fragile clay pipe.

3. MUSKETMAN, PENNSYLVANIA STATE REGIMENT, 1778

The musket battalion had blue coats with red facings, white waistcoats and stockings, and buckskin breeches. The bicorne hats were bound with yellow. The blanket roll was a common substitute for a regular knapsack. In August 1776 their colonel reported that his men were without shirts, breeches or stockings; and in 1778 the commander was compelled to write to the President of Pennsylvania: 'My hopes of getting the Regiment genteelly and well clothed this campaigne are vanished unless your Excellency and the Council will assist me in it.' Nevertheless, the regiment did not suffer the lack of supply which afflicted some other units in the army. The uniform was very like that of some of the Hessians in British pay, which led to their being fired on by their own side on at least two occasions.

1. TROOPER, 3RD CONTINENTAL DRAGOONS, 1779
This soldier wears a white coat with blue facings and white metal buttons, and buff breeches, tight in front and loose-fitting behind. The helmet, a decorated leather jockey cap, is ornamented with a fox-tail and a red turban. The sabre is suspended from a waist-belt. The private's set of plain leather saddlebags would contain all his spare clothing.

2. PRIVATE, 6TH SOUTH CAROLINA REGIMENT, 1777
This is the uniform issued to the 6th in late 1777–blue coat, red facings, pewter buttons, white waistcoat, white equipment– and he wears an early version of the 'overalls' (see page 20). At his left side he carries a water-canteen, cartouche pouch and bayonet, and on his back a brown knapsack containing rolled blanket and all his personal possessions.

3. BRIGADIER GENERAL, 1780
The pipe-smoking officer sports blue coat, gold lace, buff facings and linings, yellow buttons and buff breeches and waistcoat. The close-fitting breeches are probably of buckskin. The distinguished rank of brigadier general is denoted by the single silver star on each gold epaulette and the white hat-plume or feather.

1. CORPORAL, 3RD PENNSYLVANIA BATTALION, 1776

Coat with white facings and silver lace were shared with the 2nd Canadian Regiment, some of whose members come from Pennyslvania. The green epaulette on his right shoulder is his badge of rank; a sergeant would be distinguished by an epaulette of red. The knapsack is of white linen, and the canteen is made of wood.

2. PRIVATE, 5TH PENNSYLVANIA REGIMENT, 1781

The illustration features the famous hunting shirt of the revolution. Made of linen or any other homespun cloth, it was loose and comfortable, easily mended and maintained. It could be dyed almost any color according to regimental requirements. Some hunting shirts were pulled over the head; others, like this, opened down the front. Originally worn only by rifle units, their popularity caused them to spread throughout the Continental Army during the war.

3. OFFICER, WASHINGTON'S BODYGUARD, 1782

He sports blue coat, white facing and overalls, gold lace. The cocked hat is edged with yellow and bears the standard black cockade on the left side. This man follows the convention among some officers of wearing the turned-up brim almost flat across at the front instead of bent around the crown. The uniform is inaccurate in that it is a 1790–style 'rise and fall' collar style not in use at the time.

TROOPER, 1ST CONTINENTAL LIGHT DRAGOONS, 1777

Detailed regimental orders of April 1777, set forth by the unit commander Colonel Theodorick Bland, prescribed brown coats with green lapels, cuffs and collar, and leather breeches; so far the man is properly dressed. But few men were wholly correctly dressed: his waistcoat should be green, the buttons gilt or yellow instead of pewter; and one can only guess where he acquired that helmet, which should be of black leather with a green turban. The pair of large pistols are standard issue, probably of British pattern.

OFFICER, LIGHT HORSE OF THE CITY OF PHILADELPHIA, 1779

Among the oldest United States military units in continuous existence, the Philadelphia Light Horse was founded by 28 young men of wealth and social distinction on November 17, 1774. Each man agreed to mount, arm and equip himself at his own expense. One of them, Benjamin Randolph, noted his subsequent purchase—a carbine, a broadsword, belt, cartridge box, pair of pistols, saddle, gun bucket, saddle bags, saddle cloth and a 'sute' of clothes and cap—in his copy of *Father Abraham's Pocket Almanack* 1775.

The Troop's organization included a captain, first lieutenant, second lieutenant, cornet, quartermaster, two sergeants and two corporals. A veteran soldier was hired as sword master and riding master; and a trumpeter and a farrier likewise were retained to accompany the Troop on active service.

Volunteering its services early in the Revolution, the Troop's first recorded duty was to escort General George Washington from Philadelphia to New Rochelle on his ride to assume command of the American Army. Throughout the war, detachments of the Troop served as escorts for supply trains and prisoners. In the fall of 1776, the Troop (25 officers and men, plus their trumpeter) was among the Pennsylvania units which reinforced Washington's defeated army on the south bank of the Delaware River. It served with distinction throughout the ensuing Trenton-Princeton campaign, both on reconnaissance missions and several spirited little shock actions. In January 1777, Washington discharged them with sincere thanks. Later, the Troop served in the 1777–1778 operations around Philadelphia.

This officer wears the prescribed uniform of brown coat with white facings and waistcoat. He has discarded the tight-fitting breeches for overalls, a garment covering the entire leg and lower torso, adopted by most regiments after 1775; they were woollen in winter, linen in summer. Like the British officers of the day he wears a scarlet sash around his waist. The dragoon helmet is of hard black leather with a fox-tail; his hair is tied in a queue. The lack of saddlebags or pistol holsters show that he is not on campaign.

Today, officially, the unit is called the First Troop, Philadelphia City Cavalry, but both Philadelphia Light Horse (an earlier title) and First City Troop are also correct.

1. PRIVATE, LIGHT INFANTRY, 1780

This soldier has blue coat, white facings and smallclothes, pewter buttons and black spatterdashes; plus black leather helmet trimmed with fur—a very smart soldier by the standards of the army at the time. With his musket at half-cock, and pan open, he is biting off the top of the cartridge to release the powder. He will pour a little into the pan, the rest down the barrel, drop the bullet after it and ram the ball down firmly against the powder with his ramrod.

2. LIEUTENANT COLONEL, 5TH PENNSYLVANIA REGIMENT, 1777

His campaign trunk is made of leather, bound with iron and studded with brass tacks. The only observable differences between his uniform and that of other senior officers illustrated are the half-boots and the silver bullion epaulettes.

3. LIEUTENANT, 5TH PENNSYLVANIA REGIMENT, 1779

The original uniform was blue with white facings, but by February 1778 suitable white cloth was unobtainable in Philadelphia and the facings were changed to red. The regiment's first commanding officer wrote: 'I thought on an expedient of reducing the heterogeneous old, new, cock'd & floped hats & pieces of hats, to Infantry Caps, in which we succeeded very well—by making three decent caps out of one tolerable and two very ordinary hats, to which we added by way of embellishment a white plume and a comb of red hair.' The spontoon is not only a badge of rank but, unlike the sergeant's halberd, also an efficient weapon. Washington was very keen on spontoons: they were generally between 6 feet and 6½ feet, but the styles of head varied considerably. The simple shape illustrated is the one standardized by 1778.

1

2

3

1. ARTILLERYMAN, 1779

The Continental artillery regiments were to have the most elaborate uniform ordered for any Continental unit. A few early artillery units used different color schemes—including black and brown coats faced with red, with plain yellow buttons—but dark blue faced red and laced with yellow was the most popular and officially ordered by Washington for the Corps in 1779. Artillerymen carried full infantry accoutrements and muskets for personal defense.

2. FIFER, VIRGINIA MILITIA, 1778

The lad pictured is typical of many Virginia militia units except that he has adopted the brown coat, with green facings and pewter buttons, of the 9th Virginia Regiment. There are few other concessions to uniformity, except for the buff equipment and the short hanger.

3. DRUMMER, 3RD NEW JERSEY BATTALION, 1779

This drummer wears blue coat and breeches, red facings and pewter buttons of the 'Jersey Blues'. Like the fifer, he is enough to break the heart of any respectable drum-major. His colonel has not even managed to have any regimental device painted on the drum. Both men are wearing regular line coats but the colors should have been reversed—that is, this drummer would wear a red coat with blue facings.

GENERAL GEORGE WASHINGTON, 1780

A Virginian aristrocrat, Washington became a military surveyor at the age of 16 and Adjutant-General of Virginia militia with the rank of major before he was 21. He saw fighting in the Seven Years War and was on Braddock's staff when he was defeated and killed on the Monongahela in 1755. When in June 1755 Washington took over command of his host of 15,000 armed civilians he had not led troops for 20 years. When selected he said: 'I this day declare with the utmost sincerity, I do not think myself equal to the command I am honored with.' For six years he labored through hardships, shortages, discouragement, treachery, minor victories and some severe defeats to keep his army in being.

Not unlike General Eisenhower in World War 2 he had the personal courage and quiet determination to bring the best out of a team—a balance of qualities rather than any specialized genius. It is said that he personally stopped the rout of Charles Lee's men at Monmouth, one of the few occasions when the calm and steady voice gave way to 'foolish and profane cursing and swearing'. Despite his detractors—and they were many—Washington led the American revolutionary forces to victory and guided the destinies of the United States of America during its first 20 years.

Here he wears the parade uniform of a general officer of the style prescribed by a General Order of June 1780. On 14 July 1775 Washington ordered that the Commander-in-Chief wear a light blue ribband, worn across his breast, between his coat and waistcoat, which he wears here. Other generals wore pink ribbands; aides, green ones.

THE WAR OF 1812

Brass shako-plate of the 1st Rifle Regiment. [*Illustration by Rebecca Katcher*]

The Treaty of Paris did not end friction between Britain and its late American colonies, now the United States. A large number of Americans who had stayed loyal to the Crown fled to the British colony of Canada in 1783, and Americans felt threatened by them. Moreover, British Army units were slow leaving western frontier posts promised to the Unites States, while Indians supported by British officials continued to threaten the shaky frontier peace.

The spark that caused another war was, however, none of these things: it was the insistence that the Royal Navy could stop any ship under American flag and remove men it felt had been in, and still should be in, the Royal Navy. Indeed, many of these men had been Royal Navy deserters but now had legal American passports.

The American government declared war on Great Britain on 18 June 1812, but their Army was not able to fight a huge enemy. Luckily, the British had more pressing matters on their hands in the form of Napoleon, and the US Army leaders reckoned they could successfully capture Canada.

The basic Army structure was the same as the earlier war's Continental Army, and most of its senior officers in 1812 had been junior officers back in 1783. It was basically a foot force with mostly heavy artillery, infantry and a regiment of riflemen. A regiment of ten companies of light artillery, with every man mounted, had been authorized in 1808, but only one company, Captain George Peter's company, had been actually equipped as field artillery in 1812. A regiment of light dragoons had also been authorized in 1808 but they were serving as light infantry when war broke out, since Congress declined to spend money for horses for the unit. In all, the Army had a little over 6,500 officers and men in 1812, although 35,604 had been authorized.

The French Army, by now conqueror of most of Europe, was the model for the American Army's practices. It continued to use a copy of the French infantry musket, and its infantry drill and tactics manual was an adoption of the French system produced by William Duane. The period cavalry tactics, training and discipline manual was also produced by him, and the new artillery drill was also French in origin. American artillerymen, while retaining British tube designs and calibers, adopted the French Gribeauval gun carriage designs almost completely.

There were, however, some items that were unique to the American military experience. The élite Rifle Regiment was equipped with a handsome, brass-mounted, 1803 model rifle. Instead of having the short, heavy barrels used by European armies, the M1803 had a long barrel more like the rifles civilian woodsmen used on the American frontier.

By October 1814 the Secretary of War reported that 'the present military establishment [consisted of] 62,448 men.' Congress had been forced to create a general staff, something that had not previously ever existed, on 3 March 1813. The staff departments, according to the Army's 1 May 1813 regulations, included the Adjutant General's Department, the Inspector General's Department, the Quartermaster General's Department, the Ordnance Department, the Purchasing Department, Topographical Engineers and the Hospital and Medical Department.

The war also saw the creation of three additional rifle regiments, set aside as élite units, and a second regiment of light dragoons. Some of the Light Artillery Regiment's companies became heavy artillery companies, while others were equipped as field artillery companies. Sea Fencibles, responsible for the defense of

The Battle of Queenston Heights, above the Niagara River in October 1812, drawn by an eye-witness. [*Public Archives of Canada*]

1. SERGEANT, THE US REGIMENT OF LIGHT ARTILLERY, 1812

Although the Regiment of Light Artillery, to include ten companies, had been authorized in 1808, only one company had been equipped as field artillery by 1812. When the war began, the Army recruited some horse (with every man mounted) and some field (some men walked) artillery companies. Both types served in the field rather than in fortifications.

2. CORPORAL, PIONEERS, 25TH INFANTRY REGIMENT, 1814

The 25th, one of Winfield Scott's Brigade units, was one of the first in the US Army to organize pioneers. Ten men, one from each company, with a corporal commanding, formed the regimental pioneer squad. Each man wore a linen apron. Four pioneers were equipped with a felling axe and spade, two with a spade and pick axe, and four, 'necessary tools in due proportions'. Scott's Brigade wore gray kersey roundabout jackets but did receive the new 1813 model leather shakos.

3. SERGEANT, 22ND US INFANTRY REGIMENT, 1813

The 22nd, recruited in Pennsylvania in 1812, was typical in that the regulation uniform was unavailable for its recruits. Officers, who supplied their own uniforms, would have worn the regulation dark blue with red facings and silver lace. The 22nd too did not receive cap plates, which were in short supply, or buff equipment belts. The regiment served along the Niagara frontier.

1. LIEUTENTANT, BALTIMORE UNITED VOLUNTEERS, 1814

This unit served during the British attack on Baltimore, as the 4th Company, 5th Regiment, Maryland Volunteer Infantry. The unit was so elegant that its privates all wore engraved sterling silver shoulder belt plates. The uniform, however, conforms to period regulation Maryland State dress rules.

2. PRIVATE, RIFLE COMPANY, LEGIONARY CORPS, MILITIA OF THE TERRITORY OF MICHIGAN, 1812

Michigan's 'Legionary Corps' was formed in 1805 and was to contain cavalry (red coats faced black), artillery (blue coats faced red), light infantry (blue coats faced buff) and riflemen. The cavalry and riflemen served in the Detroit campaign, surrendering in 1812. Although the rifle company had used rifles when in Federal service in 1807, in 1812 the company apparently received smoothbore muskets.

3. MAJOR GENERAL, US ARMY, 1813

Generals wore essentially the Army's staff uniform, except that they could have embroidered buttonholes—though few did. The Commissary General of Ordnance, Adjutants, Inspectors, Quartermasters General, and the Commissary General of Purchases were allowed embroidery only on collar buttonholes. Blue pantaloons were worn in winter. Yellow-hilted straight swords were worn by all but officers of the Adjutant, Inspector and Quartermaster Generals' officers, who had sabres. Hospital staff officers wore the same uniform save that they wore pocket flaps, black buttons and four vertical black buttons on each cuff.

1. PRIVATE, 5TH US INFANTRY REGIMENT, 1815

In 1816 Charles Hamilton Smith, a British subject, drew several US soldiers while visiting the country. His are some of the few period drawings of the new uniform approved in 1813 which was to be plain blue with white lace trim. This figure is closely based on one of his sketches.

2. PRIVATE, US REGIMENT OF LIGHT DRAGOONS, 1814

Although a number of volunteer militia mounted units served during the war, only two regular regiments of light dragoons were raised. They were largely wasted in scouting, courier and escort work and the regiments were combined into one regiment in early 1814. On 3 March 1815 even this regiment was abolished as being too costly to maintain.

3. MASTER WORKMAN, US CORPS OF ARTIFICERS, 1814

The Corps, made up of masons, carpenters, blacksmiths, armorers, saddle and harness makers, ships carpenters, boatbuilders and laborers, was authorized in April 1812 and mustered out on 3 March 1815. The unit was commanded by a superintendent, with assistants and master workmen under him who, in turn, supervised workmen and laborers. Yellow lace was worn by the latter two grades; the higher grades wore gold with red wings. The superintendent wore three stars on each wing; assistants, two; and master workmen, one.

A contemporary engraving of Antonio López de Santa Anna, President of Mexico and Commander-in-Chief of the Army of Operations in Texas. He entered the territory on 16 February 1836.

Americans started moving west from the moment they first set foot on the continent, and by the 1820s they were pushing into Mexican territory which, at that time, extended far north into what is now the United States. Mexico itself was in a constant state of turmoil, having gone through several governments after gaining its independence in 1821. In April 1823 the Mexican government ruled that Americans could settle in their northern territory of Texas and the following year the Mexicans adopted a liberal constitution, modeled on the US one. Within 12 years, almost 28,000 Americans had moved to Texas.

There were constant conflicts between the Americans, now calling themselves Texians or Texicans, and the native Mexicans. The Americans were Protestant Anglo-Americans with a legal upbringing based on English law; the Mexicans were Hispanic Roman Catholics, with a legal system based on the Code Napoleon, despite the adoption of the constitution of 1824. Finally, in April 1830, the Mexican government forbade further American immigrants from coming into Texas.

Their action was like trying to hold back the wind with straw. Americans continued to pour into Texas, and in 1832 Sam Houston, a soldier in 1812 and afterwards a Governor of Tennessee, entered Texas with plans for either independence or a union with the US. Other pro-Americans who came to this new promised land included Jim Bowie of the knife fame, William Barret Travis of South Carolina and Davy Crockett of Tennessee.

On 3 November 1835 Texans gathered for a convention to decide to abide by the 1824 Mexican constitution, which had been put aside by Mexico's military dictator Santa Anna, or declare the state's independence. They chose the latter.

Pleas went back to the United States for equipment, arms and men. Volunteer companies, long the core of all American military efforts, were raised. Most of them came from the South; while the rest of the country looked on with polite interest but little enthusiasm, states such as Georgia, Alabama, Kentucky, Tennessee, South Carolina and Louisiana provided most of the American volunteer units in Texas.

Again, volunteers proved to be something less than wholly ideal for military purposes. Texas companies were totally democratic, not making one move without a vote to decide what to do. Two companies from nearby Louisiana, the New Orleans Greys, came to San Antonio, which was being besieged by Texans, but as winter drew closer the Louisiana companies voted to give up their efforts and return home. As one of their officers wrote, they had not come to Texas to 'lie three or four months in the colonies'.

Sam Houston, rising to the top of the local leaders, attempted to raise a 'Regular Army of Texas'. According to Houston the Army's 'pay, rations, clothing &c. will be the same that was allowed during the last war with the U. States,' the War of 1812. The Army of Texas was to consist of one infantry and one artillery regiment, each to consist of two battalions. Each infantry battalion was to have a full complement of officers and five companies of 56 men each. The artillery regiment was to have the same with four more field officers and an additional lieutenant per company. In all, the Texas Army would in theory consist of 1,120 officers and men.

The reality was something different. One enlistee in March 1836 noted that the Texas Army consisted of three companies of volunteer and three regular infantry companies, all on foot, and some 20 volunteer infantry companies which were mostly mounted. On the march the practice was for the mounted men to ride together,

Alamo cannons, excavated from the site of the defenses and deliberately damaged before being buried, almost certainly by the Mexican Army in 1836. The cannon in the background is probably the Alamo's famous 18-pounder: note how the cascabel has been smashed off. [Kevin R. Young]

INDEPENDENCE, 1835–1836

regardless of company, while the dismounted men maintained company structures.

The US military influence was total. The infantry was drilled with the manual produced by the US Army's commanding general, Winfield Scott, whose drill system had replaced Duane's manual as the US Army's standard on 10 April 1835. The main difference between it and earlier systems was the use of only two, rather than three, ranks of infantry as a line of battle.

Drill masters to the Texas forces were a US Military Academy drop-out, Joseph M. Chadwick, who had seen service during the Black Hawk War in Illinois in 1832, and an ex-US Marine, John S. Brooks. Even the look of the rank and file was greatly affected by the US Army. A US Army officer sent into Texas to reclaim deserters saw some 200 men still in their old US Army uniforms. Most of them refused to return to the United States.

The US was also the main source of supplies for the Texas Army. Not only were uniforms ordered from New Orleans and other such sources, but weapons and equipment came from there as well. For example, in January 1836 the Texas government received a shipment of 440 US Army muskets, 100 carbines, 200 pistols, 150 sabres, 200 cartridge boxes and belts, 432 canteens and 18 US Army drill manuals. Even the Republic of Texas

military buttons were made in Waterbury, Connecticut.

Not every man would be able to receive a set of US Army equipment and weapons, however. The first Texas volunteers were to provide their own weapons, usually hunting rifles and shotguns. Others received weapons captured from the Mexican Army, whose basic infantry longarm was the British India Pattern Brown Bess. Indeed, most of the artillery the Texans had was captured Mexican weaponry, but often it was of poor quality or not suitable for the task at hand. Mexican naval tubes saw use mounted on garrison and even field carriages.

It is difficult to imagine that such a motley clad and equipped force, disciplined as poorly as it was, could beat the large, professional force Mexico could theoretically field. However, years of chaos at the top had taken its toll on Mexico's Army. Its men, although magnificently adorned, were poorly led, equipped, trained and fed. Although the Mexicans captured a small Texas band at the Alamo, when they met the Texas Army at San Jacinto in April 1836 they were totally beaten in an 18-minute battle. Santa Anna was captured and forced to recognize Texan independence. Yet, sporadic hostilities continued along the border between the two countries during an uneasy peace.

'Travis defends the wall of the Alamo': a typical example of how the Alamo has been portrayed in later art, and how it has come to be regarded in some quarters as the very symbol of liberty. Some later reconstructions exhibit considerable inaccuracy, especially in the costume of the Mexican Army. This is one of the better examples of the genre – a painting by Ruth Conerly Zachrisson.
[*The Alamo Museum*]

TEXAN VOLUNTEERS, 1835

The three figures wear their civilian clothes, as did the majority of the Texan forces. One is dressed as a frontiersman, with a 'hunting frock' or 'hunting shirt', a common garment of fabric or buckskin, usually with a yoke across the shoulders and fringed edges, with buckskin Indian leggings and moccasins. Another has 'store clothes': a frock coat and the common 'round hat'. The third wears working clothes, with a haversack as a 'hold-all'.

Weaponry varied from Kentucky rifles to shotgun fowling pieces and even old blunderbuss-type firearms useful only at close range. Personal equipment was a matter of choice or availability, though the ideal was probably that described by one of the Kentucky Mustangs: a 'good Kentucky rifle', shot pouch, powder horn, tomahawk, butcher knife and knapsack, later augmented by a Mexican blunderbuss. Those experienced with the Kentucky rifle could achieve fine marksmanship. These long-barreled weapons, characterized by the elegant proportions of a stock often incorporating a decorative brass-lidded patch box, were in fact developed from German *jäger* rifles made by early immigrants to Pennsylvania—but the 'Kentucky' nickname has stuck. They had up to four times the effective range of a common musket and were remarkably accurate even at 300 yards.

Shown here is the Gonzales cannon known as 'Come and Take It' (from the legend on the flag which flew over the gun when the Mexicans tried to repossess it). It consisted of an old 22in. iron barrel which fired grapeshot, mounted on a home-made wooden carriage with four-inch-thick slices of tree-trunk as wheels; though it presumably answered its original function of frightening Indians, militarily its only use was a symbol of defiance and rallying point. Drawn by a yoke of oxen, it was soon abandoned by the Texans.

1. COLONEL DAVID CROCKETT

The most famous of frontiersmen, 'Davy' Crockett (1786–1836), an uneducated Tennesseean, established so great a reputation as a hunter, fighter, raconteur and general 'character' that he was half a legend even before his death. He served three terms in the US House of Representatives (two as Democrat, one as Whig), and only went to Texas when defeated in 1835.

Crockett is shown wearing a hunting frock over more conventional shirt and legwear, with the coonskin cap which has become part of the Crockett legend, and which Mrs Dickinson noted lying beside his body just after the battle. His rifle in Texas was his old hunting weapon known as 'Betsy', not the ornate 'Pretty Betsy' presented to him by the Whigs.

2. LIEUTENANT COLONEL WILLIAM BARRET TRAVIS

The South Carolinan lawyer who had been a member of the 'war party' agitating for independence as early as 1832, William B. Travis (1809–36) was a flamboyant character, who in civilian life had favored a white hat and red trousers. He appears to have entertained a conviction that he was destined for immortality—completing his autobiography at the age of 23!

Travis is shown wearing a typical 'round hat' of the period and a civilian tail-coat; he had ordered a uniform for himself—but apparently was killed before he could receive it. The Mexican Sgt. Nuñez, who appropriated his coat after the battle, said that it was of home-made Texas jeans.

3. COLONEL JAMES BOWIE

Though commissioned a colonel in the Texan Army in December 1835 and appointed to command the volunteers in the Alamo, Jim Bowie (1796–1836) was famous principally as a duelist and entrepreneur.

A living legend who literally carved his reputation with his famous knife—which may, in fact, have been invented by a brother—he had reputedly made fortunes from land deals and even from slave trading with the pirate Lafitte. He was a courteous, even polished man, and his quiet bearing made him appear even more potentially lethal than his string of famous fights suggested. Though a Mexican citizen from 1830, and married to the daughter of the Vice-Governor, he was a leading figure in the early independence movement, and had been involved in several skirmishes in 1835.

1. PRIVATE, ALABAMA RED ROVERS

The Red Rovers were a volunteer company about 60 strong, formed by Dr John Shackelford around Courtland, Alabama. The women of the community made their uniforms: 'linsey woolsey' hunting shirts, fringed on the sleeves and shoulders and dyed bright red (one source also mentions 'brown and green checks'), from which the unit took its name. Their 'full dress' consisted of a cap and jacket of red velvet, white trousers and a blue sash. Equipment of knapsack, haversack, canteen, cartridge box and blanket, and US muskets, were furnished by the Alabama State Arsenal. Leaving in December 1835, the Rovers joined Fannin at La Bahía and went into the Lafayette Battalion. Almost all died when the prisoners at La Bahía were shot, though Dr. Shackelford was spared to treat Mexican casualties.

2. VOLUNTEER IN US ARMY UNIFORM

This figure wears items of US uniform, taken with him when deserting from the US Army to join the Texans. Considerable numbers of US deserters swelled the Texan ranks, attracted by the prospect of bounty or action, or from a desire to assist their countrymen in a campaign which was doubtless more attractive than the guerrilla war against the Seminoles in Florida.

The man illustrated wears a dress coatee of the US artillery, minus epaulettes—though troops on the frontier would have made greater use of the sky-blue kersey undress jacket and trousers of a style not unlike that of the New Orleans Grays. He wears the 1833 leather forage cap (as may conceivably have been worn by the Grays), constructed so as to fold flat; but apart from his musket, the remainder of his 'equipment' is privately acquired.

3. PRIVATE, NEW ORLEANS GRAYS

Two companies of New Orleans Grays were enrolled, under Capts. Thomas H. Breece and Robert C. Morris (later William G. Cooke, who served as Houston's aide at San Jacinto). Composed of 'mostly athletic mechanics', it was one of the best-equipped volunteer corps from the US. According to a German recruit, Herman Ehrenberg (late of the University of Jena), Breece's company at least wore 'gray, made-for-service-in-the-prairie-fitting uniforms, which we found ready-made in the numerous magazines' of New Orleans, before their departure for Texas.

1. SAM HOUSTON

The illustration depicts Sam Houston (1793–1863) in a costume which might have been worn by any Texan officer: civilian dress with the addition of a sash (not an official badge of rank), and a sabre and belt of US pattern. Houston's dress during the war was described by witnesses: Zuber noted him as '... a large, plainly dressed man riding a large, stout, clumsy-looking gray horse... He wore plain coarse jeans, a white wool hat, and mud boots ... not-withstanding his coarse attire. I thought that he was the noblest-looking man that I had ever seen.'

2. VOLUNTEER STANDARD BEARER

This figure wears typical civilian costume with the addition of the full US Army equipment (cartridge box, bayonet belt, musket and canteen) with which many Texans were equipped at San Jacinto. Attached to the top of the staff was a lady's long, white kid glove, presented to the company as a good luck mascot on the eve of their departure for Texas.

3. TEXAN VOLUNTEER OFFICER

These details are based on the uniform reputedly worn by Lt. Col. Sidney Sherman at San Jacinto, which may have been 'restored', together with a straw hat of a type not uncommon in Texas. The frock coat has black facings, including wide lapels, and gold lace; a reconstruction by J. Hefter shows rank bars on the shoulders—which, though they feature in portraits of Texan commanders painted after the war, were probably not worn at the time. J. H. Kuykendall saw Sherman in the San Jacinto campaign wearing a blue 'round jacket' laced silver, and carrying a 'handsome dress sword' with 'a trim and military appearance'. Edward Burleson he described wearing a simple blue homespun 'round jacket' and pantaloons, and armed only with a brace of pistols in his belt.

4. TEXAN CAVALRY SCOUT

This figure wears typical frontier costume, representing Houston's trusted scout or 'spy', Erastus 'Deaf' Smith. This noted scout was married to a Mexican and so versed in their language and customs that he could easily pass as Mexican. In addition to the common 'round hat' and buckskin jacket, he wears Indian-style leather leggings which covered the upper part of the foot.

THE MEXICAN-AMERICAN

A Model 1842 issue percussion pistol claimed to be the best martial pistol of its time. However, its time was virtually past, and Texas Rangers, officers and others were precuring Colt six-shot revolvers.

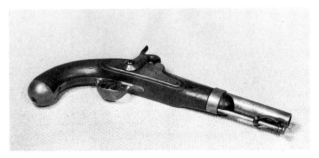

Some 75,000 Americans moved into the new Republic of Texas during the decade after its independence was recognized, bringing the Anglo population to 125,000. At the same time tensions with Mexico continued as Texas unsuccessfully sent troops at various times into New Mexico.

From the beginning, however, Texans wanted to join the United States, a move rebuffed initially since Northerners did not want another slave state in the Union. James J. Polk campaigned for the office of President in 1844 on a platform of annexing Texas into the US; he won, and asked the Congress to approve making Texas part of the nation. On 4 July 1845 the Texas Convention voted 55 to one for annexation, and on 29 December 1845 Texas became part of the Union.

Mexico was not amused. As early as 1843 its government had warned that a US takeover of Texas would be the 'equivalent to a declaration of war against the Mexican Republic'. As Texas entered the Union both sides rushed troops to the Rio Grande, the river border between Texas and Mexico.

Not that the US had all that many troops to rush. The country had only 6,562 men of all ranks in its Army. Moreover, it had to defend posts in Florida, along the East Coast, on the Western frontiers and the Canadian border. In all, the Army included two regiments of dragoons, four artillery regiments and eight infantry regiments.

Nevertheless, troops were dispatched to Texas and on 25 April 1846 a skirmish between Mexican and US cavalry took place. On 8 and 9 May the battles of Palo Alto and Resaca de la Palma were fought, and both won by the Americans. On 11 May President Polk sent a war message to Congress; Congress declared war and asked for 50,000 volunteers to augment the Regular Army.

As before, Congress also authorized new Regular Army units. These included the Regiment of Mounted Riflemen, a third regiment of dragoons, nine new regiments of infantry, the Regiment of Voltigeurs or Foot Riflemen, and a company of enlisted engineer soldiers. In all, vigorous recruiting brought 22,180 new recruits into the Regular Army between 1 October 1846 and 30 September 1847. At that point, the Regular Army has swollen to 30,350 officers and men.

At the same time the Army's volunteer units, enlisted for the duration of the war, included 5,055 mounted officers and men, 354 foot artillery officers and men and 28,762 infantry officers and men. Another 2,119 officers and men who had volunteered for only one year's service were also present.

The war's first battles were fought, to the dismay of the volunteers and pleasure of the regulars, by Regular Army units, and the units that gained the most prestige from these battles were the new light, or horse, artillery companies. Each man in these companies was mounted, and the companies' weapons were six-pound bronze guns based on a new tube-and-carriage system devised by Alfed Mordecai—the Army's first truly integrated artillery system.

At the war's outbreak there was one light company in each artillery regiment (K in the 1st, A in the 2nd, C in the 3rd, and D in the 4th). These companies dashed about the field, stopping Mexican advances and blowing holes in the Mexican lines for the rest of the Army to pass through. Following their successes an additional company per regiment was designated a light company on 3 March 1847. Only I of the 1st, E of the 3rd and G of the 4th actually were so equipped and trained by the war's end, however.

Other Army branches also worked towards greater efficiency and professionalism. The Medical Department, for example, tried developing an ambulance to replace the hit-or-miss methods of getting wounded soldiers from the field to the hospital. Efforts were made towards enlisting intelligent enlisted medical personnel, called hospital stewards, who would be responsible to the Medical Department. Indeed, Inspector General Ethan Allen Hitchcock complained in Mexico that some hospital stewards, who were given no regulation insig-

The Mormon Battalion halts for water. After the expedition to Santa Fé, the battalion was sent to California. Composed almost entirely of members of the Church of Jesus Christ of the Latter Day Saints, and raised in Iowa in July 1846, it was one of the best volunteer regiments. [*Church of Jesus Christ of the Latter Day Saints Historical Department*]

WAR, 1846–1848

nia, 'are wearing lace upon their shoulders & adopting fancy dresses of all kinds' as a sign of their improved status.

The Ordnance Department's 36 officers were especially busy since the Mexican War came at a time when fundamental changes were being made in basic armaments. A new system of sea coast artillery had been adopted in 1844 and the Mordecai field artillery system, with its bronze instead of iron tubes, had been adopted three years earlier. And, most basic, an infantry longarm system based on the copper percussion cap rather than the old flintlock system had been adopted with the model 1841 rifle and the 1842 musket.

This new system could function in the rain and ensure a shot every time the trigger was pulled—something no flintlock could do. But it brought new problems: not only were cartridges required, but now Ordnance officers has to make sure caps were available, too. Moreover, the men had somehow to keep the small copper caps safe.

Even with these problems, the new longarms quickly became standard. On 30 June 1847, for example, Co. A, 4th US Artillery reported that it was equipped with 87

Fatigue cap worn by Captain James Duncan, commanding Company A, 2nd US Artillery. Officers' caps do not seem to have been made with ear flaps. [*West Point Museum Collections, United States Military Academy*]

percussion muskets and only 14 old-style flintlocks.

Thus armed and organized, the US Army, Regulars and Volunteers, defended the Texas border, seized Mexican provinces of California, New Mexico and Arizona, drove deep into both Northern and Central Mexico—and captured Mexico City. The Mexican government, fighting not only the Americans but a civil war of its own with Native Americans on the Yucatan, fell apart, and for several months after capturing the capital the US Army was the only responsible Mexican government. Finally, a government was organized and on 2 February 1848 the Treaty of Guadalupe Hidalgo was signed between the two countries.

An original Daguerreotype showing General Wool and his staff in the streets of Saltillo in 1847. A dragoon on the extreme right appears to have a colored band on his forage cap, a regimental distinction of the 2nd US Dragoons. [*Yale University Library*]

1. CAPTAIN, 2ND US ARTILLERY

Most of the artillery served as infantry–and served very well. Artillery dress and fatigue uniforms were the same as for infantry, with red horsehair plumes in the shakos, red piping and turnbacks. The trim on the jackets was yellow, as were buttons and epaulettes, though silver buttons were also used. Brass cannon, crossed, made up the shako badge.

Short Model 1834 two-edged thrusting swords with all-brass hilts were issued to foot artillerymen. These were carried in black leather scabbards worn on white buff leather belts buckled with two-piece brass buckles. Horse artillerymen wore long, curved sabres from their belts, made with a single brass guard and a leather-wrapped grip. Their scabbards were shiny iron, and their belts were whitened buff. This man's waistbelt is not regulation but taken from a contemporary Huddy & Duval print.

2. PRIVATE, COMPANY A, 2ND US ARTILLERY

At the war's beginning only four companies, one from each artillery regiment, were equipped as light or horse artillerymen. In these companies everyone, from commander to cannoneer, rode–giving them great mobility and striking power. The companies were Company K, 1st Artillery (Taylor's); Company A, 2nd Artillery (Duncan's); Company C, 3rd Artillery (Ringgold's), and Company D, 4th Artillery (Washington's).

On 3 March 1847 one additional company per regiment was authorized to become light but only three such companies managed to get so equipped: Company I, 1st Artillery (Magruder's); Company E, 3rd Artillery (Bragg's), and Company G, 4th Artillery (Drum's).

Duncan's light battery is today Battery A, 3rd Armored Field Artillery Battalion, 2nd Armored Division.

3. CORPORAL, 2ND US DRAGOON REGIMENT

The dragoon dress uniform was different from that of the other corps. They also often wore gold earrings, and their hair was usually rakishly long. Dragoons carried either the Model 1847 musketoon (little more than a cut-down musket) or the 1843 Hall carbine, along with one or sometimes two pistols.

1. PRIVATE, 3RD US INFANTRY REGIMENT

Rank was indicated by the shako plume and number of buttonholes on the cuffs. Privates and corporals wore two white worsted tape buttonholes on each cuff, while sergeants had three and sergeants major four. Officers had silver lace buttonholes on their cuffs, with two for a lieutenant, three for a captain and four for a field officer. Collars were also trimmed with silver lace.

The 3rd Infantry was formed shortly after the War of American Independence. Its nickname was given by General Scott when, in Mexico City, he saluted it as the army's 'Old Guard'. This man wears the standard winter dress uniform.

2. SERGEANT, 6TH US INFANTRY REGIMENT

For fatigue a short, tailless sky-blue wool jacket, made with a single row of 15 white metal buttons, was worn. The standing collar was trimmed the same as dress coats. The jacket had shoulder tabs on each shoulder trimmed with white tape. The tight sleeves ended in a slit cuff with two buttons on each one. A similar jacket, of white cotton and quite plain, was worn in hot climates with plain white cotton trousers. Chevrons were worn on fatigue uniforms, though not on dress. The 6th Infantry Regiment was formed in 1812 and since the end of World War 2 has been stationed in Germany.

3. CAPTAIN, 4TH US INFANTRY REGIMENT

The fatigue uniform was designed for comfort. On the march officers carried red or dingy brown blankets, rolled up horse-collar fashion, across their bodies. Many infantry officers bought horses and rode. Officers wore their dress trousers for fatigue, as did the men. The officers' coats, however, were dark blue frock coats, single breasted for company officers and double breasted for field officers. With both uniforms, officers wore their crimson silk sashes, tied on the left, around their waists.

1

2

3

1. PRIVATE, 7TH NEW YORK REGIMENT

Originally raised as both the 1st New York and the California Battalion, men of the 7th were artisans who were to be discharged in California where they would settle. They and the Mormon Battalion were California's basic garrison and were probably the two best disciplined volunteer units in the Army.

2. TEXAS RANGER

Private Samuel Chamberlain of the 1st Dragoon Regiment described them in 'buckskin shirts, black with grease and blood; some wore red shirts, their trousers thrust into their high boots; all were armed with Revolvers and huge Bowie Knives'. Colonel Hays, who commanded a regiment of them, wore, wrote Captain J. R. Kenly of the Baltimore-Washington Volunteers, 'a round jacket, Mexican hat, and no badge or rank other than a silk sash tied round his waist after the fashion of the Mexicans...'

3. PRIVATE, COMPANY A, 2ND ILLINOIS

Typical of the different uniforms chosen by volunteers is this one, although hats other than the forage cap were also worn. Volunteers were to supply their own uniforms, horses and horse equipment, with the US government supplying arms. States were paid to procure uniforms and many individual companies designed their own. 'We were uninformed as every company selected,' recalled Chamberlain, originally a member of the 2nd Illinois, 'and strange grotesque costumes now filled the Camp. Ours, Co. A, 2nd Regiment, made choice of jacket and pants of blue mixed Kentucky jeans with yellow stripes across the chest like a Dragoon Bugler. By permission I had mine made with dark blue cloth, with only my Sergeant's chevrons, and it was quite a neat affair.'

Drinking was a real problem for the US Army in this war, and often led to fighting. On 7 September 1846 five companies of the 1st Georgia broke into a fight in which a newspaper reported ' ... firearms and bayonets and swords were very freely used'. The whole 4th Illinois was needed to quell it, in the process having two of their men killed and four more wounded, with two officers bayoneted.

1. US MAJOR GENERAL, FULL DRESS

The US Army's Commander-in-Chief had light yellow plumes in his fore-and-aft hat and three stars in each epaulette. In the field, generals dressed much as they pleased, and General Zachary Taylor was known by his brown linen dusters and floppy blue coats.

2. SERGEANT, US COMPANY OF SAPPERS, MINERS AND PONTONIERS

The only enlisted engineers in the US Army, the unit was called the 'Pick and Shovel Brigade' by the rest of the troops, but it was foremost in the fights in General Scott's campaign.

The unit had infantry-type shakos, with a brass castle badge. Their spherical pompons were black worsted, three inches in diameter. Their coats were dark blue with black collars and cuffs. Each collar had a single yellow tape false buttonhole but no other trim. Cuffs had yellow trimmed buttonholes, according to rank. Sergeants had two yellow silk epaulettes, 'corresponding on pattern with those of a Captain'. Corporals had two worsted epaulettes 'of the pattern of subalterns', and privates had fringeless epaulettes. The coat's turnbacks were dark blue and it had a 'small pocket covered by a flap on the right side for carrying percussion caps'. Buttons were brass.

3. FIELD OFFICER, US CORPS OF ENGINEERS

In this war, U. S. Grant wrote, 'the officers of the engineer corps won special distinction.' The most educated officers went into the corps.

All men, however, were prone to disease—with six men dying of disease to every one killed in action. Total American strength reached 115,906 all ranks, of which 103.8 men per thousand died of disease. Of the 42,374 regulars, 4,900 died of disease or accident, with another 4,149 being discharged due to disability, while only 930 were killed in combat. Of the 60,913 volunteers, 6,400 died of disease or accident, another 9,200 were discharged due to disability and only 600 were killed in action.

US CAVALRY ON THE PLAINS,

The sudden geographic growth of the US following the treaty of peace with Mexico brought a wealth of new problems to the small army. Hostile native Americans owned and lived in most of the newly acquired areas and American settlers would have to be protected from them just as much as the 200,000 Native Americans would need protection. This problem became greater when gold was discovered at Sutter's Mill, California in 1849. Now there was a virtual stampede across the Western plains, deserts and mountains.

Foot troops, infantry and foot artillery would be hard pressed to police the vast areas found in the West. This was especially true because, at least in the plains areas, the Native Americans were all well mounted.

The US Army did not have much cavalry with which to oppose them. After typical peacetime reductions in 1848, which included disbanding the 3rd Regiment of Dragoons, it was left with the Regiment of Mounted Riflemen and two regiments of dragoons. The Mounted Riflemen were sent to safeguard the Oregon Trail on the Pacific coast, which was to have been where they were stationed before being diverted to Mexico. The 1st Dragoons was divided into company-sized units which were posted in California, New Mexico, Kansas and Minnesota. The 2nd Dragoons was also divided, with companies in California, Texas and New Mexico.

Recognizing the potential danger, Congress authorized each company on the frontier to be enlarged to 74 privates; this would give the Army a total of 13,821 officers and men. But building an army to meet the needs would be hard and slow, for few Americans wanted to give up civilian life in favor of the miserable life as a soldier in a hut on the plains. Most recruits were European immigrants without jobs and even they were not quick to join up. In fact, even by June 1853 the Army had only 6,918 officers and men on the frontier.

They were lucky. No serious problems between settlers and natives occured until a Sioux party went on the warpath in 1855 on the Platte River. A 2nd Dragoons party sent after them was massacred, so another cavalry force, along with infantry and artillery, was sent out in revenge. The two sides met at the first pitched battle of what would be called the Indian Wars—and the badly defeated Sioux signed a peace treaty in March 1856.

It was obvious, even to those with tight fists around the public purse, that more mounted troops would be needed on the plains, and on 3 March 1855 two new mounted regiments, the 1st and 2nd US Cavalry Regiments, were authorized. These were to form a separate combat arm from both the Mounted Rifles and Dragoons, and were to be equipped initially with experimental arms and equipment. The result was that the new regiments found themselves armed with a

The brass crossed sabre insignia has been used by the US Cavalry from 1850 to the present day. Officers' versions of this cap badge were embroidered. The blades were made narrower than the example shown here after 1872. [*Philip Katcher*]

Troopers' saddlery and field equipment of about 1873: Model 1872 equipment on the 1872 modification of the 1859 McClellan saddle. (1) Blanket roll, tent half, overcoat, with spare clothing rolled inside, and lariat and picket pin strapped on top. (2) Brush and shoe pouch. (3) Forage sack, with oats or corn. (4) Saddlebags, with personal belongings, spare ammunition, etc. (5) Canteen and mug—some troopers carried cooking kettles, coffee pots, skillets and other camping gear. [*Christa Hook*]

1850–1890

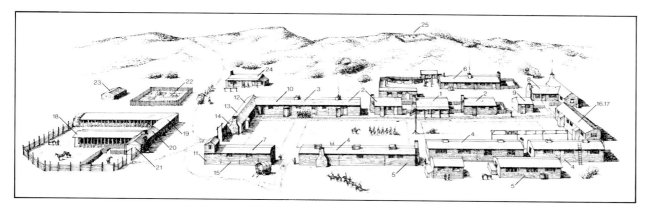

A typical larger fort layout of the period after the Civil War. (1) CO's quarters. (2) Officers' quarters. (3) Officers' kitchen and mess. (4) Company barracks. (5) Enlisted men's kitchen and mess hall. (6) 'Suds Row' – quarters for laundresses, and married enlisted men. (7) Adjutant's office. (8) Hospital. (9) Guard house. (10) Wainwright's workshop. (11) Storerooms. (12) Magazine. (13) Harness maker's workshop. (14) Bakery. (15) Commissary. (16, 17) Quartermaster's store and office. (18) Stables, corral. (19) Granary. (20) Saddler's workshop. (21) Smithy. (22) Vegetable garden. (23) Icehouse. (24) Sutler's store. (25) Cemetery. [*Christa Hook, after Glen Dines*]

bewildering array of weapons including muzzle-loading Springfield carbines, breech-loading Maynard and Perry carbines, 0.36 caliber Colt revolvers and Prussian-style sabres as used by the dragoons. The dragoons retained their breech-loading Hall carbines, single-shot muzzle-loading pistols, and sabres.

Such a variety of mounted organizations, complete with different styles of weapons and equipment, was both costly and inefficient. Therefore, on 3 August 1861, all mounted Army regiments were designated cavalry, with the 1st and 2nd Dragoons becoming the 1st and 2nd Cavalry, the Mounted Rifles becoming the 3rd Cavalry, and the new cavalry regiments the 4th and 5th Cavalry Regiments. A 3rd cavalry regiment, created on 5 May 1861, became the 6th Cavalry.

Soon the Civil War saw much of the Regular Army withdrawn from the West to aid in putting down the Southern rebellion and, true to the American military tradition, volunteer cavalry units were formed in the Western states and territories to maintain order. These, made up of better educated and motivated citizens than the regular units, were often more effective in policing the plains than the regulars had been.

While this was generally the rule, a massacre of peaceful Cheyennes at Sand Creek, Colorado, on 29 November 1864 by the poorly led 3rd Colorado Cavalry showed how stupid the cruel whites could be in the West, even under Army regulations.

When the Civil War ended in 1865 regular cavalrymen returned to the plains – but they returned to natives made angrier by years of mistreatment by white settlers. It was obvious that six cavalry regiments were not enough to both garrison the defeated South and maintain peace in the West, and on 28 July 1866 four new cavalry regiments, the 7th through the 10th, were authorized. The 9th and 10th Cavalry Regiments were unique in that they were manned with black enlisted men, although officers were white.

Blacks had been a part of America's fighting forces since 1755, but they had not been allowed to fight officially since the end of the Revolution. Manpower shortages in the Civil War caused the Army to create regiments of US Colored Troops, and these units would thereafter always be a part of the American military until all units were integrated during the Korean War.

The cavalry was not always successful against Native Americans. Few people today have not heard of how George Armstrong Custer, a poor but previously lucky soldier, led most of the 7th Cavalry to complete destruction on 25 June 1876 at Little Big Horn.

On the whole, however, the Cavalry had the upper hand throughout the West and complete white supremacy was an almost inevitable conclusion. In 1889, as a last gasp, a Nevada Paiute shaman started the Ghost Dance movement which foresaw a return of all dead native warriors and the removal of whites from the plains. The Army suppressed the ritual dancers and on 29 December 1890 the last band of defiant Ghost Dancing Sioux were surrounded at Wounded Knee Creek, where most of them were killed in a one-sided fight. The Indian Wars were over.

LEFT: Field equipment of about 1878; note the carbine loop on rear girth strap, common to most periods. The 1874 sideline and halter chain are now carried on the forage sack at the cantle. A haversack containing rations – hardtack, bacon, coffee, etc – is carried slung over one of the 1874 saddlebags. [*Christa Hook*]

1. SERGEANT, 2ND DRAGOONS, 1850

The sergeant's jacket is of 1833 pattern, with his chevrons worn points up, as made regulation in 1847. (In 1851, new regulations would reverse these chevrons.) Essentially, this is the same uniform as worn in the Mexican-American War, and would be worn officially until 1851. Officers were authorized a similar jacket in 1839, but piped with gold lace on the collar only; in addition, they had two diagonally inset pockets on the breasts, with a small pocket flap edged in yellow and fastened shut with one brass button. The Regiment of Mounted Riflemen wore the same jackets, trimmed with green, and wore dark blue trousers with black stripes edged in yellow cord.

2. PRIVATE, 2ND DRAGOONS, 1850

The Army made an effort to provide clothing suitable for the summer heat of the Plains during the years 1833–1851. The result was this two-piece white cotton suit, made to the same pattern as the wool dress uniform. This outfit was common, and apparently popular, on the frontier. In October 1850 Col. George A. McCall inspected the garrison at the Presideo de San Elizario, New Mexico, and reported that there was 'no woollen clothing on hand' there.

3. CAPTAIN, 1ST DRAGOONS, 1850

The 1839 dress regulations authorized frock coats for dragoon officers, these being slightly modified in 1847 when field grade officers were authorized double-breasted frocks, while company grade officers kept their single row of buttons. Officers were also authorized jackets, both in dark blue wool and white cotton duck or linen. The captain is in fact wearing private's trousers; regulations called for two yellow stripes on each leg—a rule that should also apply to the sergeant.

As described in 1833, rank was indicated by epaulettes. The regimental number and rank badge were to be embroidered on the strap, the number in the crescent and the badge on the strap. Rank badges included a silver eagle for colonel, an oak leaf for both lieutenant colonel and major, two gold bars for a captain and one for a first lieutenant, and a plain strap for a second lieutenant. Until 1851 the lieutenant colonel's leaf was gold and the major's silver; thereafter, the colors were reversed.

1. SERGEANT, 2ND DRAGOONS, 1854

Despite its appearance, there had been much dissatisfaction with the uniform authorized in 1847, with the result that a new set of very different regulations appeared in June 1851.

A cloth shako was now ordered for all ranks—something that most officers disliked—and frock coats were now to be worn by all ranks. The shoulders of these coats were originally to be topped with 'worsted bullion epaulettes', but these were replaced by all-brass shoulder scales in January 1854. All enlisted dragoons wore the same orange trim on their coats except musicians, whose coat fronts were covered with a large orange facing. The same coat was to be worn all year round—the summer uniform had been abandoned.

Other changes made in 1851 lasted throughout the period under discussion. One was the wearing of chevrons points down; another was the adoption for all ranks of a sword belt plate which bore the design of an eagle and clouds in brass within a silver wreath.

2. CORPORAL, 2ND DRAGOONS, 1854

A number of modifications were made to the mounted man's uniform in 1854. First of all, the wide band on the shako was replaced by a narrow welt of the facing color above a dark blue band. The reason was, apparently, that dye differences led to uneven fading and a poor appearance on parade. An even more striking change, as far as dragoons and mounted riflemen were concerned, was the reintroduction of the uniform jacket for all mounted men. Brass epaulettes, or shoulder scales, were still to be worn with the new jacket, but were often boxed and left behind when troops went into the field. Other frequently observed campaign items included civilian chaps or leggings and civilian knives carried on the sword belt.

3. CAPTAIN, 1ST DRAGOONS, 1858

Even with revised dress regulations issued in 1857 there was no provision for comfortable field dress. Consequently, it appears that both officers and men improvised when serving on the Plains. Their most common form of improvised dress was borrowed from clothing worn by American fighting men as early as the Seven Years War—the hunting shirt.

This officer has made his dress a bit more military by wearing the crossed sabre insignia authorized for dragoons in 1850.

1. SERGEANT MAJOR, 2ND COLORADO VOLUNTEER CAVALRY REGIMENT, 1864

When the first cavalry regiments were authorized in 1855 they were given the mounted man's uniform jacket trimmed in bright yellow. One innovative uniform item which they received was the black felt hat, authorized in August 1855. Originally it had yellow cords draped around its crown, dipping under a brass company letter in front. This version of the 'Jeff Davis' or 'Hardee' hat, as they were popularly known, was issued only from 1856 until about 1859, when the insignia design was changed to include brass crossed sabres, regimental number and company letter in front; and thereafter only one hat cord was to be worn. Often only the branch-of-service badge was actually worn on the hat front; sometimes no insignia at all were worn.

The 2nd Colorado Volunteer Cavalry were armed with the Merrill carbine, one of dozens of types of privately manufactured carbines which the Army bought between 1861 and 1865. It used a paper cartridge with a .54 caliber bullet; other carbines came in .52 caliber.

2. CORPORAL, 1ST BATTALION, CALIFORNIA VOLUNTEER CAVALRY, 1863

Finally admitting that there was a need for a fatigue uniform, the Army authorized in 1858 a dark blue, plain 'sack' coat and a blue cloth forage cap with a leather peak.

The 1st California Cavalry were armed with the New Model 1859 Sharps carbine. This was probably the best-known carbine of this period, some 50,000 being produced. It was .52 caliber, and used special linen cartridges. A .44 or .36 Colt six-shot revolver is also carried, along with the Model 1861 light cavalry sabre.

3. SECOND LIEUTENANT, 7TH IOWA VOLUNTEER CAVALRY, 1864

The 1861 dress regulations allowed mounted officers to wear 'for stable duty, a plain dark blue cloth jacket, with one or two rows of buttons down the front, according to rank; stand-up collar, sloped in front as that of the uniform coat; shoulder straps according to rank, but no other ornament.' This, rather than the uncomfortable frock coat, became the standard cavalry officer's field dress. This officer is armed with the ornate version of the 1861 light cavalry sabre which was regulation for officers. His sabre knot is gold, while other ranks had black leather.

1. CAPTAIN, 9TH TEXAS VOLUNTEER CAVALRY, 1864

Although Confederate Army regulations called for all officers to wear double-breasted frock coats, most mounted officers preferred the single-breasted shell jacket. His ranking is worn on the collar; the system was simple, with one, two or three gold bars for second lieutenant, first lieutenant and captain, and one, two or three gold stars for major, lieutenant-colonel and colonel. The number of braid stripes in the gold 'Austrian knot' worn on each sleeve also indicated rank—one stripe for a lieutenant, two for a captain and three for a field grade officer. The same number of stripes was worn to indicate rank on the French-style képi.

This officer wears a mounted man's two-piece belt plate bearing the 'Lone Star' of Texas. His sword is a Southern-made copy of the US officer's light cavalry sabre. His revolver is a Texas-made Dance Brothers copy of a Colt Navy in 0.36 caliber. Although they were officially to be dyed black, his accoutrements are russet brown, reflecting the supply difficulties of the Confederate Army. The accoutrements were made in the Confederate arsenal in Baton Rouge, Louisiana.

2. PRIVATE, 9TH TEXAS VOLUNTEER CAVALRY, 1864

Enlisted men wore much the same uniform as did officers. Frontier-style clothing was also commonly worn. Arms varied, but rarely included sabres. This man has a Cook Brothers Confederate-made copy of the pattern 1857 Enfield carbine. He also carries two revolvers made in Texas by Dance Brothers.

The stiffened Western-style leather hat shown here is copied from one worn by a C. Bassett, 48th Texas; note the embossed badge.

3. SERGEANT, 4TH TEXAS VOLUNTEER CAVALRY, 1864

Frontiersmen did not walk, they rode horses; so when it came to raising troops, Texas raised 106 cavalry units and only 41 units of infantry. However, many of these 'cavalry' units were in fact never mounted, although they clung to the yellow color and other distinctions of the cavalry. The 4th Cavalry was one such regiment. Luckily, a photograph of the regiment's Company D, taken in the spring of 1864, still exists, and shows a rather well-clad unit.

1. FIRST LIEUTENANT, 10TH CAVALRY, 1872

According to the 1872 dress regulations: 'On the frontier and campaign, officers may wear the soldier's overcoat, with the insignia of rank on the sleeve.' This insignia took the form of a circle of the branch-of-service color edged with gold embroidery, with the rank badge in its center. This is essentially the overcoat described for the first time in the 1851 dress regulations, although that coat was to have a stand-up collar, which was changed to a stand-and-fall collar in the 1861 regulations.

2. COLONEL, 1ST CAVALRY, 1872

In 1871 the Secretary of War authorized the wearing of white duck trousers and straw hats by officers and men stationed, at first, in Texas, and later everywhere south of Washington, DC, during specific summer months. This colonel also wears the enlisted man's fatigue blouse with shoulder straps of rank. Although not regulation, officers adopted these blouses widely, sometimes wearing metal rank badges on their collars instead of regulation shoulder straps.

3. SADDLER SERGEANT, 1ST CAVALRY, 1873

The uniform changed radically in 1872 with the appearance of yet another set of dress regulations. This saddler sergeant—a newly created grade whose chevrons were authorized 25 June 1873—wears the new, rather Prussian-looking dress uniform. With minor changes, this was worn until the end of the Plains Wars. The coat was modified in 1888 by making the collar solid yellow, eliminating the belt support loops, and simplifying the design on the back of the coat. The regimental numbers were ordered removed from the collar in 1884. In 1887 a more substantial change was made to this uniform, with the facing color changing from lemon yellow to a much darker, almost orange yellow; this decision was made when it was found that the lighter shade bleached almost white in the glaring Western sun.

The half-chevrons worn on the forearm indicate five years' service each; the red one indicates service during a war—in practise, the Civil War. This NCO wears the only medal awarded in the US Army at this period: the Medal of Honor. During the Indian Wars period 416 awards were made to soldiers—none of them to a rank above major.

1. QUARTERMASTER SERGEANT, 5TH CAVALRY, 1876

Only two years after its introduction the unfortunate 1872 blouse was replaced by a more traditional design, though still piped in branch-of-service color. This style was worn throughout the remainder of the Plains Wars, although the colored piping was removed by orders issued on 6 June 1883. The sergeant's cap is the 1872 style, which replaced the 1858 forage cap. The cap badge shown was changed in 1877, when the regimental number was added above the crossed sabres. A July 1876 description indicates that 5th Cavalry field dress included broad-brimmed hats and navy blue shirts.

The accoutrements worn here were first issued in 1874. The belt plate first appeared with the Model 1872 waist belt; thereafter, the 'eagle and wreath' plate was worn only by officers. The pouch, resembling the old 'cap box', was now used for pistol ammunition. Carbine ammunition was carried in the 1874 Hazen sliding cartridge loops on the back or side of the belt—a double-banked strip of 12 loops, making 24 in all, with belt attachment slides at each end and in the center.

2. LIEUTENANT COLONEL, 5TH CAVALRY, 1875

General Orders of 27 July 1872 described this new undress coat for officers. It was worn until orders of November 1876 removed the elaborate braid and the slashes at the hips. Of plain blue, rather like the fatigue blouse of 1858, the new coat was worn until the end of the period as the standard officer's undress uniform.

The pillbox cap was never a regulation item, but it was widely worn from about 1864 and throughout the 1870s. This was the most common of several styles; note that the badges were actually of brass, stamped to look like embroidered bullion.

3. FIRST SERGEANT, 1ST CAVALRY, 1873

The 1872 regulations brought the enlisted men a new style of pleated fatigue blouse, with branch-of-service colored piping. It was not a success, and the soldiers disliked it heartily.

On the other hand, his weapon was a great success. This is the single-shot, breech-loading Model 1873 carbine, also known as the '45/70' or 'Trapdoor Springfield'. With slight modifications over the years, this hard-hitting weapon was used for the rest of the Plains Indian Wars.

1. PRIVATE, 6TH CAVALRY, 1877

The great heat of the Plains in summer caused much thought to be given to providing cooler fatigue uniforms. In 1877 these flannel shirts were issued as field dress in a trial basis. From 1874 the Army had issued a similar gray-flannel shirt which differed in that it lacked a pocket and had a small, laydown collar. Before that date both gray flannel and white cotton shirts had been issued. Civilian shirts of all colors and designs were also worn–but shirts had rarely been seen worn as a field dress without either a coat or jacket.

This trooper's hat is of the type adopted in 1875 to replace the 1872 pattern. The final novelty is his cartridge belt, made with loops of woven web material.

2. SERGEANT, 4TH CAVALRY, 1890

The final attempt to solve the problem of summer dress was this cotton duck uniform; it came in bleached white for non-commissioned officers, unbleached for privates. The helmets were copies of the British Army's foreign service headgear, obtained through the help of the British Minister in Washington in 1875. These were made regulation dress in 'hot climates' in 1880. They were, however, totally unsuccessful, unpopular with the troops and officers and rarely worn in the field.

3. SERGEANT, 6TH CAVALRY, 1885

The concept of 'shirtsleeve order' as hot weather fatigue dress proved successful, but there was some dissatisfaction with the gray color. On 16 February 1881 the Army ordered a new blue shirt, trimmed with branch-of-service color, for fatigue dress. The sergeant's grade is not indicated by chevrons on the shirt–Hollywood's Indian War cavalry to the contrary–but rather by the one-inch stripe down each leg of his 1879-pattern trousers. The particular pattern of trousers is indicated by the lack of waistband. He wears the 1885 pattern woven webbing looped for carbine ammunition.

On 26 November 1883 this 1881-style shirt was ordered replaced by one of generally the same appearance but without the colored piping, and made 'pull-over' style, with only three buttons down the front placket. Moreover, while some 1881 shirts had pockets and others did not, the 1883 shirt always had two pockets, without flaps but with buttons.

1. Chief Trumpeter, 8th Cavalry, 1883

Cold was as great a problem as heat on the Plains. This chief trumpeter, marked by the chevrons specified under regulations of 25 June 1873, wears the coat which had been regulation issue, with only minor changes of detail, since before the Civil War. This particular model was adopted in February 1880 and is identified by the yellow-lined cape: capes before this date had been unlined. Chevrons had earlier been worn above the elbows, but, because they were difficult to see when the cape was thrown forward or buttoned up, on 6 June 1883 they were ordered moved to the forearm with the points a half inch above the cuffs. These coats, while sufficient for keeping a man warm back East, where not much use on the winter Plains, where temperatures of 60° below 0°F were not unknown.

2. Captain, 3rd Cavalry, 1885

This, basically the officer's overcoat throughout the period, was first made regulation in 1851. With this specific model, the pattern of 1884, it became truly double-breasted; the closure of earlier models was on the center of the body. Rank was indicated by the number of braids in the knot on the sleeve, a second lieutenant having a plain sleeve: a first lieutenant, one braid; a captain, two; a major, three; a lieutenant colonel, four; and a colonel, five.

The guidon in the background is the pattern carried from 1885 until the dismounting of the last horsed cavalry unit during World War 2.

3. Private, 3rd Cavalry, 1885

Continuing the search for good cold weather gear, the Clothing Bureau was issuing buffalo coats and muskrat caps and gauntlets in large numbers by 1881. These were quite expensive, however, and in 1883 the Bureau began experimenting with sheepskin. As early as 1876 canvas overcoats were being lined with blanket fabric by the Quartermaster's Philadelphia Depot, and these cheaper coats became widely issued by 1883. This private wears one, together with a muskrat cap of the style first issued in 1879. His 1884 gauntlets were at first made of goatskin; this was not successful, and later versions were made of calfskin. Canvas hoods and mittens, lined with blanket fabric, were also authorized in 1884.

THE CIVIL WAR, 1861–1865

A typical volunteer camp of an unknown unit from the North or South. Old men, women and children are visiting, the tents show no wear, and the men are all neatly clad in dark blue forage caps, gray uniform or shell jackets with shoulder straps, and gray trousers. Such a scene could have taken place near almost every town in America in early 1861. [*David Scheinmann*]

In November 1860 Abraham Lincoln was elected President of the United States. The South, which had up until then largely controled the federal government, feared Lincoln's election would mean a decline in the power of the states to regulate themselves. They reckoned that slavery, on which Southern society had been built, would be ended.

Rather than see that happen, South Carolina declared in December that it was no longer a part of the United States. Other Southern states followed their example, and the newly seceded states formed their own nation, the Confederate States of America. But neither side was prepared for war; neither side actually expected it. One politician went so far as to offer to wipe up all the blood spilled in any war with his pocket handkerchief.

Yet Lincoln's resolve to abide by his oath to protect the US constitution was strong, and he had US posts in the South reinforced rather than abandoned. On 12 April 1861 South Carolina troops fired on one such post, Fort Sumter, in Charleston Harbor. The action electrified both sides and thousands of men rushed to join local units to defend either the Union or their native states.

At first Southern hopes were high. The Eastern Union Army was totally unable to get past General Robert E. Lee's Army of Northern Virginia and capture the Confederate capital of Richmond, Virginia, while progress in the West was slow. But the North refused to give up the fight.

In fact the cruel war would drag on for four long years – a relentlessly slow grinding down of Southern troops, matériel and resolve. The North would go through dozens of generals before finding their winning combination of Grant/Sherman/Sheridan. The South was lucky enough in the Eastern Theater to find a Lee/Jackson combination, but it never found winners for the Western Theater. And it was the eventual losses in the West that led to defeat in the Spring of 1865.

This final defeat was far from obvious to either side in 1861. The Regular US Army, as of January 1861, included only 16,367 officers and men – hardly enough to subdue a land almost 1,500 miles across filled with men and women determined to be separated from their old country. It would take some two million men in the Union service to overcome the million or so men the South put under arms.

Many Regular US Army officers were of Southern birth and resigned their commissions to return to their homes when the war broke out, most of them taking up arms for the Confederacy. Enlisted men could not resign, but most probably would not have done so anyhow; a sizeable percentage were of foreign birth, mostly Irish and German, while most of the others had found their homes in the Army.

So both sides had once again to draw on the plethora of local volunteer and militia units which dotted America's landscape in 1861. These had continued to thrive during the first half of the 19th century. For the most part they were not under state control and were therefore free to set their own standards for membership, drill, weapons, equipment and even uniforms.

For the first time in US history, conscription was instigated to fill up the opposing armies to their required strengths. The Confederacy was the first to use conscription when it prohibited men who had been in volunteer units in 1861 from going home after their volunteered year's service was finished. Instead, Southern armies in the field were reorganized, with men given a chance to switch units and vote for new officers. Thereafter, Southern men without exemptions were forced to serve in Confederate military units. Exemptions were nevertheless many, including those for being a newspaper editor, minister or plantation overseer in charge of a set number of slaves.

The Northern draft came later, going into effect just after the dreadful casualties of Gettysburg and Vicksburg in July 1863. The Northern government, too, had exemptions, and both sides allowed a draftee to pay a tax to avoid service. There was, however, widespread resistance to conscription on both sides.

Volunteers still made up the bulk of both armies.

Northern volunteers tended to be better disciplined than Southerners. Public schools were widespread in the North and while most men on both sides were farmers there were more urban dwellers, who had learned to live and work well together, in Northern units than Southern ones. The result was that Northerners understood the value of discipline, and accepted it, better than their foes. Southerners compensated for this lack of discipline through dash and élan and were noted as ferocious fighters – but bad stragglers.

Most volunteers joined army units but, given the scope of the war, with fighting along rivers and on shores, naval units on both sides saw land action. An entire Naval Brigade formed part of the Army of Northern Virginia when it surrendered at Appomattox in April 1865. US Navy officers and sailors fought on land at Fort Fisher, North Carolina, in 1865 and in the First Manassas Campaign of 1861, as well as along many Southern rivers.

The Colt 'Navy' .36 caliber revolver, the most popular officer's weapon of the period. [*Philip Katcher*]

The North adopted a policy of raising new units for the field as needed. Northern governors liked this policy, since it enabled them to pass out more and more commissions among state voters, but it meant that Northern units were generally smaller than equivalent Southern ones and the North had to deal with new, untrained regiments taking the field throughout the war. The South, instead, used its conscripts to fill already raised units, a better policy that put combat-trained men alongside raw recruits.

Starke's Brigade of Louisiana troops, out of ammunition, holds off Federal troops with stones at Second Manassas, 1862. The South failed in its bid for independence, a victim of its own lack of true national purpose (maintaining slavery was not a good enough goal in itself), overwhelming Northern numbers and resources, inner political squabbling and some poor generalship, especially in the West. [*Battles & Leaders of the Civil War*]

THE UNION ARMY, 1861–1865

The US Army at the start of the Civil War was a small organization spread out mostly in company-sized units across the vast country, and consisting of only 16,367 officers and men (1 January 1861). The top brass decided that rather than split its regular units up to stiffen the enlarged army that would be needed to subdue the South, the Regular Army would be maintained as a cohesive unit—a sort of 'Old Guard'. For the rest, volunteers would form the basic armed force needed to return the South to the Union.

A call went out after Fort Sumter was fired on in April and the country responded with a fervor. By 1 July some 169,480 volunteers had been mustered into Federal service and by 1 January 1862, following the first major defeat at Bull Run, Virginia, on 21 July 1861, 507,333 volunteers were present for duty.

Many of these men came together in pre-existing volunteer companies, but most joined wholly new units raised for the war. These volunteer units often patterned themselves after French heroes of the Crimean and Italian Wars, wearing copies of zouave attire and using copies of zouave drill manuals.

The Army's Quartermaster and Ordnance Departments were hard pressed to clothe and equip all these volunteers. Old flintlocks were hurriedly converted into weapons that used percussion caps, and agents hunted all over Europe buying what were often the dregs of European armies' ordnance due to be scrapped. Otherwise, the Army simplified the single-shot, muzzle-loading rifled musket adopted in 1855 with a simple sight and the removal of the patented automatic percussion cap feeding system. The .58 caliber M1861 rifled musket that resulted remained the standard Federal longarm throughout the Civil War. British-made copies of the .577 caliber P1853 and P1858 Enfield rifled muskets were bought in such large numbers that they were the second standard Federal longarm. Many volunteers, however, acquired breech-loading, magazine-fed longarms, vastly superior to issue weapons in terms of firepower, on their own.

While the Army searched for matériel, new officers trained their raw recruits. Infantrymen learned a new system of tactics written by William Hardee, who joined the Confederacy's army, which had been adopted as the Army's standard on 29 March 1855. Hardee's tactics were replaced as standard on 11 August 1862 by a system written by Brigadier General Silas Casey. Cavalrymen learned Philip St George Cooke's tactics, adopted on 1 November 1861. The artillery manual, which replaced the 1845 tactics, had been adopted on 6 March 1860.

Other technical branches of service also had to cope with a demand that was greater than any they had known. The Corps of Engineers was enlarged to a full battalion of four companies. The one company that made up the Corps of Topographical Engineers was merged into the Corps on 31 March 1863. In addition four volunteer engineer regiments, two in the West and two in the East, served during the war.

Roughing it in the field in 1862 is this group from the 22nd New York State Militia. The 22nd, known as the Union Grays, saw active service for three months in 1861 and for a month in 1862. Note the red and blue képis with white trim. [*Library of Congress*]

Two US Army cavalry carbines. The top picture shows a Smith carbine carried by Sgt. Franklin I. Thomas, Company A, 12th Illinois Cavalry—the catch in front of the trigger allowed it to be 'broken' for reloading like a shotgun. The second photograph illustrates a Sharps carried by Sgt. Cannaday of the 2nd Pennsylvania Cavalry. [*Chris Nelson*]

The Medical Department was greatly enlarged to handle a record number of sick and wounded; between the war's start and end, the Surgeon General reported that the Army's hospitals treated no less than 6,049,648 cases. At the outbreak of fighting there were only 30 surgeons and 84 assistant surgeons in the Army, and civilian doctors, called Contract Surgeons, were often hired as needed. Volunteer regiments brought their own surgeons, while a corps of medical cadets, medical students aged between 18 and 23, was enlisted to serve as dressers in general hospitals and ambulance attendants in the field. The Hospital Corps, civilians dressed in uniform who helped in the hospitals, was created on 5 June 1862. Congress authorized the Army Ambulance Corps on 11 March 1864.

The Department was aided, sometimes unwillingly, by two civilian organizations, the Sanitary Commission and the Christian Commission. Both helped in hospitals, providing healthy meals from their own kitchens, writing letters, providing sick soldiers with small items to make them comfortable. A Union Commission, based in the West, helped resettle war refugees. Other technical units were also needed. Congress created the Signal Corps on 3 March 1863, and by 1 November 1864 the Corps mustered 168 officers and 1,350 enlisted men. To free able-bodied men for field service Congress authorized the Invalid Corps, later Veteran Reserve Corps, on 28 April 1863. It was to serve as provost guards, help in hospitals and guard prisons. Officers and men were to be good soldiers certified by surgeons as no longer fit for field service, and on 1 October 1864 the VRC consisted of 764 officers and 28,738 enlisted men. It was demobilized on 21 March 1865.

Modern technology prompted the creation of the Military Telegraph Service, a group of around 1,000 civilians under the Army's control, and by 1863 the service processed some 3,000 telegraphs a day. Civilians under the Army's control also staffed the US Military Railroads; at one time the organization's 24,964 men operated 419 locomotives and 6,330 cars on 2,105 miles of track.

In such a large army some system of identifying men by organizations was needed. The Army of the Potomac, which served on the Eastern Front, therefore adopted a system of cloth or metal badges worn on the cap or jacket breast. Each army corps had a unique badge, such as a trefoil for the II Corps. Members of the corps' three divisions wore red, white or blue corps badges respectively.

This practice spread throughout the Federal army. The same style badges were readopted during the Spanish American War and again in 1918, and they survive today as embroidered patches worn in sleeves that indicate the wearer's organization.

By 1865 the Federal army had triumphed and was largely demobilized, but several new regular units had been permanently added to the Army, as well as elements such as the Signal Corps. During the Civil War the Army learned for the first time how to handle a very large body of men—lessons it would need in the future.

This information sheet shows an improved system of leather accoutrements patented in December 1863 by William D. Mann. The Army bought 37,000 sets of infantry equipment and 12,020 sets of the cavalry version. These were mostly used for testing during the Civil War, however, and never adopted by the Army as a whole. [*Philip Katcher*]

1. FIRST LIEUTENANT, INFANTRY, 1861
In the field many officers continued wearing the frock coat, but with shoulder straps instead of epaulettes. This man wears the regulation officer's sword belt and a pre-war style cap box with a shield-type flap in front.

2. COLONEL, INFANTRY, 1861
This colonel wears the field grade officer's full dress, with dress hat, frock coat, and the 1861 dark trousers. His regimental number appears on each epaulette, on a circle of sky blue, the infantry branch-of-service color. His sword is the foot officer's sword.

3. SERGEANT MAJOR, INFANTRY, 1861
This sergeant major wears the enlisted man's version of the regulation full dress uniform, with a non-commissioned officer's sword, and staff non-commissioned officer's brass shoulder scales. Note also the national color of the 13th Illinois Infantry Regiment, which would be captured by Confederate troops and kept in Richmond, Virginia. Found there when that city fell in 1865, it was the first US color to fly over the city since Virginia left the Union in 1861. It is generally representative of all US infantry regimental national colors, although those carried by troops of some states differed slightly—those carried by Pennsylvania infantry units, for example, had the state seal painted or embroidered in the canton with the stars surrounding it (Inscription: '13th ILL.').

1. FIRST (ORDERLY) SERGEANT, INFANTRY, 1863

Many soldiers, given their choice, wore the dress frock coat in the field instead of the blouse. It is seen here from the rear, with its tell-tale buttons on the waistline. This sergeant holds the regimental, or second, color of the 60th Ohio Volunteer Infantry Regiment, which matches the regulation regimental color quite closely. The 60th served in the IX Corps in the 1864 campaign of the Army of the Potomac, from the Wilderness to the capture of Petersburg (Lower riband: '60TH REG'T O.V.I.').

2. SECOND LIEUTENANT, INFANTRY, 1863

In the field, officers dressed little better than their men. This lieutenant has a privately-made copy of the issue fatigue blouse. His slouch hat bears the badge of the 1st Division, V Corps. The haversack, privately bought, is of leather, with a removable unpainted canvas bag for food inside. His leather waterbottle has a pewter spout and copper rivets and is lined with tinfoil: it was patented in 1862, and is a surprisingly common relic.

3. PRIVATE, INFANTRY, 1863

This is the man who fought all the battles, who took most of the losses, and bore the brunt of fighting: a soldier of the infantry, the branch which the US Army calls the 'Queen of Battles'. This is how he generally looked in the field. He is little burdened with parade ground fancies, or much embellished with insignia. He does, however, wear the issue knapsack, while many of his friends would by now have lost or thrown theirs away.

1. CAPTAIN, CAVALRY, 1863

The short, plain jacket was prefered by mounted officers to the frock coat for field use. It was worn with one or two rows of buttons by company grade or field grade officers respectively. This figure also displays the low, stylish 'McClellan' or 'Chasseur' style cap so popular with officers. Typical of many officers in the field, he wears plain issue enlisted man's trousers.

2. LIEUTENANT COLONEL, CAVALRY, 1863

Mounted officers wore the regulation frock coat, as does this lieutenant colonel. Branch-of-service color formed the background for the shoulder straps, here in cavalry yellow. His cap has the pointed, narrow peak popular with many officers. He is armed with a cavalry officer's sabre embellished with a metallic gold thread officer's sabre knot—an item more generally carried by cavalry officers than by those in other branches of service. Note here the rear cut of the officer's frock coat.

3. SERGEANT, CAVALRY, 1863

Many cavalrymen preferred to wear the dress jacket, without shoulder scales, in the field. This NCO's fatigue cap has a branch-of-service badge, not generally worn by infantrymen but common in the cavalry. On his belt he carries—reading around from the right front hip—his cap box, holster, pistol cartridge box and carbine cartridge box.

This cavalry sergeant holds a guidon of the type used from 1863. The earlier type was of the same dimensions, but halved red over white. The letters 'US' and the troop letter appeared on the top half in white, and the regimental number on the bottom half, in red.

1. PRIVATE, 1ST DIVISION, IV CORPS, 1864

This private wears his regulation corps badge on his cap top. He has the issue gray flannel shirt and wears his trousers, as was most common, without braces. He holds a tin coffee boiler's cup, a piece of campaigning kit considered vital by every man: from the standpoint of morale, coffee was probably the most important single ration issue item.

2. COMPANY QUARTERMASTER SERGEANT, CAVALRY, 1864

Although it was not regulation until 1866, the single 'tie' over the chevrons of the company quartermaster sergeant appears in many photographs taken of soldiers as early as 1863. This one wears a popular cavalryman's item, the plain blue 'roundabout' or 'shell' jacket, with veteran's service stripes above his cuffs. His regimental number is worn on his cap top. His carbine is a Spencer repeater, and he carries the associated Blakeslee Quickloader cartridge box; this had a sling, and a loop low down for securing it to the sabre belt, and held ten tubular seven-round Spencer magazines. The Army bought 32,000 of them between 1862 and June 1866.

3. MUSICIAN, CAVALRY, 1864

All musicians were marked by the stripes and frame of branch-of-service color braid worn on their chests. This man holds an issue bugle with a branch-of-service color cord and tassels; riflemen often used green cords and tassels, while artillerymen had red. He has both a regimental number and a company letter on his cap top.

1. CAPTAIN, LIGHT ARTILLERY, 1864
Although not regulation, the black slouch hat was one of the most popular forms of headgear among both officers and men, especially those of the mounted branches. The short mounted man's jacket worn by light artillery officers featured the 'Russian' shoulder knot with the insignia of rank at the outer end. Company grade officers used this relatively simple shoulder knot, with one, two, or three rows of braid according to rank. Field grade officers wore four rows of braid in a somewhat more elaborate but basically similar design.

2. CORPORAL, LIGHT ARTILLERY, 1864
The full dress of the light artillery included this dress shako which was, in practise, very little worn. This corporal is a veteran, as indicated by the service stripe worn above each cuff. The artillery wore their stripes edged in sky blue when showing wartime service, as all other branches had the stripes edged in red. His sabre is actually a cavalry model rather than the unpopular and relatively rare light artillery sabre.

The guidon is that of the 19th Independent Battery, Ohio Veteran Volunteer Artillery, and is typical of light artillery guidons. The 19th served with Sherman from the Cumberland Gap to Atlanta, at the defense of Nashville, and finally at Durham Station, North Carolina. The unit received 29 battle honors by the end of the war, some of which have already been marked on this color.

3. REGIMENTAL QUARTERMASTER SERGEANT, HEAVY ARTILLERY, 1864
This regimental quartermaster sergeant wears the full dress uniform of the heavy artillery branch, including the rarely-seen M1833 foot artillery sword, a Romanesque fantasy inspired by the French M1831 'cabbage-cutter'. His shoulder scales are actually the sergeant's models rather than the riveted staff pattern he should wear, indicating recent promotion.

1. PRIVATE, LIGHT ARTILLERY, 1865
This soldier, armed with a light artillery sabre, wears the mounted man's overcoat, with its two rows of buttons and longer cape. He has a government-made brown leather gunner's haversack. This was used to carry ammunition from the limber chest to the piece when in action, thus protecting the flannel bags of powder from sparks.

2. MAJOR, HEAVY ARTILLERY, 1865
The officer's overcoat was dark blue, with black silk braids on the cuff indicating rank: this major's rank is shown by the three rows of braid. He wears a lower-type dress hat known as a 'Burnside' or 'Kossuth' hat, which was quite popular among officers of the period.

3. MUSICIAN, 3RD DIVISION, II CORPS, 1865
The foot soldier's overcoat, as worn by this drummer, was a popular piece of uniform. He wears a corps badge on his cap in divisional color. His drum is of the regulation design. The basic eagle and ribband design, similar to that which appeared on regimental colors, was the same for all branches of service, but the field for artillery was red instead of the infantry's blue. The drum is slung on an issue white web sling. Orders in the field were often still passed by drum, and drum calls also regulated the soldier's daily timetable in camp.

BRIGADE "A" SUTLER

1

2

3

1. PRIVATE, INFANTRY, 1862
The Army imported 10,000 of the French Army's Chasseur uniforms and issued them to a number of infantry units. Many of them had to be let out in the seams, as the Americans who wore them tended to be bigger than the French for whom they had been made. This man wears the issue '*bonnet de police*'; a shako was also issued for dress occasions.

2. PRIVATE, 35TH NEW JERSEY INFANTRY, 1864
The Zouave uniform, as seen from the back, shows the cartridge box protruding from under the jacket: many units wore the boxes on their waist belts, but the 35th wore theirs on shoulder belts worn under the jackets. The 35th also originally wore dark blue képis trimmed with yellow, these being replaced with fezes in 1864. The regiment was initially armed with P1853 Enfield rifled muskets, although these were later replaced with Springfields. This man already wears the Springfield bayonet scabbard. The regiment served in Sherman's XXII Corps in Georgia and the Carolinas.

3. PRIVATE, 5TH NEW YORK INFANTRY, 1863
The Zouave uniform worn by the 5th New York was probably the example most closely resembling that of the actual French Zouaves. A state belt plate was worn, although the cartridge box plate was the issue US item. The 5th took quite a beating at the hands of the Texas Brigade, both in the Peninsular Campaign and at Second Bull Run, never regaining its old fame after the latter battle.

1. PRIVATE, 3RD DIVISION, XIII CORPS, 1864

Some Western regiments adopted parts of Zouave dress, but usually nothing as elaborate as that worn by Eastern units. This simplified 'semi-Zouave' jacket was peculiar to men of the 3rd Division, XIII Corps, such as the 34th Indiana Infantry. It is typical of jackets worn by men from Ohio, Illinois, Indiana and other Western states.

2. PRIVATE, 155TH PENNSYLVANIA INFANTRY, 1864

Zouave uniforms were issued to this unit as a mark of its abilities at drill several years after the unit was first raised. The regiment wore its 1st Division, V Corps badges on their jacket fronts, making a part of the decoration. The soldier is armed with an M1863 Springfield rifled musket.

3. CAPTAIN, 155TH PENNSYLVANIA INFANTRY, 1864

Zouave officers did not wear the same uniforms as their men. In many units they were only distinguished by colorful képis and, perhaps, gaiters. In the 155th, however, there were several variations of Zouave officer dress, of which the one illustrated here was the most common.

1. FIRST SERGEANT, 50TH NEW YORK ENGINEERS, 1863

Engineers were proud of their special qualifications and showed off whenever possible the Corps' castle cap badge. This first sergeant's corps is marked, too, by the yellow stripe down each leg and his yellow chevrons. The color behind him was flown over the headquarters of the Chief of Engineers of the Army of the Potomac.

2. SERGEANT, 1ST US SHARPSHOOTERS, 1863

This typical Sharpshooter in the field is taken from photographs and original items of two sergeants. The buttons on an otherwise issue blouse are black thermoplastic or gutta percha, while the green chevrons and the stripes down the leg indicate the unit. The green cap, with its 1st Division, III Corps badge, was worn by a sergeant in Company H, 1st Sharpshooters; he also wore the chevrons with the corps badge. He has retained the Prussian Army knapsack issued to both Sharpshooter regiments.

3. SECOND LIEUTENANT, US MARINE CORPS, 1863

The short jackets was popular for field wear among Marine officers. His cap is decorated up the sides and on the top with dark braid, and has the officer's Marine Corps badge in front. His shoulder knots are plain, and his sword is the Corps' version of the Army officer's pattern.

1. HOSPITAL STEWARD, US ARMY, 1863
This hospital steward has one of the medical knapsacks issued after 1862: one of the steward's jobs was to carry it in the field, so the surgeon could have medical supplies immediately to hand. Behind him floats the yellow and green flag that indicated a hospital: smaller yellow flags marked the way to the hospital.

2. AMBULANCE CORPSMAN, US XVIII CORPS, 1863
The XVIII Corps was unique in having its ambulance corpsmen marked with red half-chevrons and cap badges instead of the standard green medical corps color used in the Armies of the Potomac and the Cumberland.

3. ASSISTANT SURGEON, 3RD DIVISION, US XVIII CORPS, 1863
The corps badge on top of this assistant surgeon's cap identifies his corps by its shape and his division by its color—blue for the third division. He wears the Old English letters 'MS' on his shoulder straps—against regulations, but commonly seen. His straps should have borne nothing but his rank bars. His green sash and the all-metal sword peculiar to this and the Pay Department branch further indicate his medical status. Behind him is a 'rocker' ambulance, which could carry four wounded men with water casks, cans of beef stock, bread, cooking and mess gear, and bed sacks.

65

1

2

3

1. SERGEANT MAJOR, 9TH US VETERAN REGIMENT RESERVE CORPS, 1864

The 9th Regt. Veteran Reserve Corps was one of the defending units at Fort Stevens, pictured here. It made several charges there, driving back Confederate skirmishers and holding up their advance until regular troops from Petersburg could arrive to save the city. The 9th, from photographs, had the tops of their forage caps marked with company letters, regimental numbers, and infantry horns; most VRC units had plain forage caps. The regimental color of the 9th is displayed here, similar in design to the regulation US Army infantry regimental color.

2. ORDNANCE SERGEANT, US ARMY, 1864

This ordnance sergeant wears the foot soldier's full dress uniform. The two half-chevrons on each forearm indicate ten years' service, with the blue edging indicating service in war. Only true ordnance sergeants could wear the star-above-three-chevrons insignia in the US Army, and these chevrons were always supposed to be red. He is armed with the M1840 non-commissioned officer's sword. He is standing inside Fort Stevens, one of the defenses of Washington, where President Abraham Lincoln came under fire during the Confederate raid on the city in early 1864.

3. PRIVATE US SIGNAL CORPS, 1864

This Signal Corps private holds a US Army signal pistol, used to send messages at night. He has around his waist the special cartridge box designed to hold the signal cartridges. Signals at night were also passed with torches that burned turpentine, and during the day with flags.

1. LIEUTENANT GENERAL ULYSSES S. GRANT, 1864

Grant was possibly the best all-round soldier the US Army has ever produced. He had an unerring grasp of what was needed to defeat the enemy, and an ability to do it with the men given him. His strategic abilities were somewhat better than his tactical abilities, but both were head and shoulders above his compatriots in either army. He was not, however, a dressy individual: his first campaigning service was under the successful but badly dressed Maj. Gen. Zachary Taylor in Mexico in 1846, and he saw then that clothes do not make the soldier!

Grant was described by one of his staff officers, Horace Porter, in what he wore during the Wilderness Campaign: 'General Grant was dressed in a uniform coat and waistcoat, the coat being unbuttoned. On his hands were a pair of yellowish-brown thread gloves. He wore a pair of plain top-boots, reaching to his knees, and was equipped with a regulation sword, spurs, and sash. On his head was a slouch hat of black felt with a plain gold cord around it.' This is essentially the costume illustrated here, minus the boots and sword, which he does not wear in any photographs taken at this period.

Behind Grant floats the headquarters flag of the Army of the Potomac, adopted by its commander, Maj. Gen. George G. Meade, in 1864. The earlier style had been a simple US national flag. When Grant saw this showy design in 'solferino' purple for the first time during the Wilderness Campaign, he exclaimed: 'What's this? Is Imperial Caesar anywhere about here?'

2. MAJOR-GENERAL GEORGE G. MEADE, 1864

Meade was photographed during the 1864 campaigns in a broad-brimmed hat and a double-breasted version of the sack coat. This was typical of the informal wear of general officers in the field.

3. MAJOR, US TOPOGRAPHICAL ENGINEERS, 1864

Mounted staff officers often wore waist-length jackets, single-breasted for company grade officers and double-breasted for field grade officers. He wears the St Andrew's Cross badge of the VI Corps on his coat front. His sword is the staff officer's pattern, heavier than the foot officer's sword although similar in design.

1. PRIVATE, 2ND NEW HAMPSHIRE VOLUNTEER INFANTRY REGIMENT, 1861

Two novel items are worn by this private of the 2nd New Hampshire: the 'Whipple' hat and 'camp shoes'. The Whipple hat was widely issued to troops from New Hampshire, New York, and Massachusetts. It is often incorrectly shown in modern drawings based on vague period engravings as a type of pith helmet, but it was actually made of blue felt with a leather peak and chinstrap. These caps were worn at least until mid-1862 and were highly popular, when captured, among Confederates, who called them 'Excelsior' hats (after New York's motto). The camp shoes were made of white canvas, with leather ties, toes and heels.

The 2nd was in the III Corps at Gettysburg, posted in the Peach Orchard behind the 3rd Maine on 2 July. The 3rd Maine withdrew and, to defend their position, the 2nd charged the attacking Southern line and drove them back. In turn, however, they were forced back under heavy fire, losing 193 of all ranks during the day.

2. PRIVATE, 2ND RHODE ISLAND INFANTRY REGIMENT, 1861

Rhode Island's state uniform was loose and comfortable: basically a blue hunting shirt–a garment with a long military tradition in America. A type of Mexican *serape* was also worn over the shirt in cooler weather. The regiment had switched to the regulation uniform when, as part of the VI Corps at Spotsylvania in 1864, they were in the center of the brigade sent to hold part of the captured lines. Four times they were assaulted, and on the last occasion the Confederates even managed to plant a flag on their works; but four times they held.

3. SERGEANT, 3RD MAINE VOLUNTEER INFANTRY REGIMENT, 1861

The 3rd Maine received state-produced gray uniforms, as well as distinctive tin drum-type canteens and state insignia belt plates. These uniforms were of poor material though, so were replaced when the regiment reached the front with US Army regulation dress; The belt plates and canteens were retained. The 3rd had its roughest day on 2 July 1863 at Gettysburg, where they were first sent as a skirmish line in support of the US Sharpshooters in front of the II Corps; and were then ordered to rejoin the III Corps in the Peach Orchard, where they suffered repeated attacks.

1. PRIVATE, COMPANY D, 7TH MICHIGAN VOLUNTEER INFANTRY REGIMENT, 1861

Although Michigan ordered blue uniforms from the first day it began to get supplies for its volunteers, a number of prewar or home-made uniforms appeared when the troops first mustered. This outfit was initially worn by the Monroe Light Guard, which became Co. D of the 7th Infantry; it did not last long in service, however. The state uniforms were of similar designs, but all dark blue. When the Union Army was held up by snipers inside houses in Fredericksburg, and artillery failed to dislodge them, the 7th jumped into pontoons along with troops from the 19th and 20th Massachusetts Regiments, and crossed the river, to drive the Conferderates out of the town. This allowed the engineers to get on with the job of assembling the pontoon bridges so that the rest of the Army could cross to the disastrous Battle of Fredericksburg.

2. PRIVATE, 10TH INDIANA VOLUNTEER INFANTRY REGIMENT, 1861

All Indiana's first six regiments wore a version of this basic uniform, some in gray and some in blue. Made of light-weight satinet, these uniforms wore out rapidly and were later replaced with regulation US Army dress. At the Battle of Logan's Cross Roads in January 1862, which saved Kentucky for the Union, the 10th were attacked and fell back, but rallied and moved to the front again to cover an exposed flank. Running out of ammunition and refilling their cartridge boxes while still under fire, they then charged and broke the Confederate line, which was never rallied again for the rest of the battle.

3. FIRST SERGEANT, 8TH WISCONSIN VOLUNTEER INFANTRY REGIMENT, 1861

The 8th Wisconsin was the last of the state's regiments to receive gray uniforms. The 8th, which served in Western campaigns including that against Vicksburg in 1863, was best known for its mascot, 'Old Abe', an American eagle that was noted for flying low over its ranks in battle, giving a mournful cry. This first sergeant is armed with a P1858 Enfield rifled musket from England.

1. PRIVATE, 22ND NEW YORK STATE MILITIA REGIMENT, 1863

New York's state militia was not the same as her volunteer regiments at the front—something that can be confusing since the same numbers were used by pairs of quite distinct regiments. Most state militia units wore uniforms that they designed for themselves and were not in state-wide use. The 22nd, a New York City regiment, prefered gray uniforms; the state insignia was worn on the cap box and buttons, while the company letter appeared on the cap front and belt plate. The regiment was made part of the New York National Guard in September 1861. It served at Harper's Ferry, Virginia, in June 1862, at which time it returned its gray uniforms and donned blue fatigue blouses, because the gray ones were too similar to Confederate ones. They were armed with P1856 Enfield rifles.

2. PRIVATE, 33RD NEW YORK VOLUNTEER INFANTRY REGIMENT, 1862

The 33rd was one of the many New York infantry units that received the state uniform jacket. They also wore the state belt plates. This was the typical uniform of the majority of New York's infantrymen. The 33rd was the last regiment in the rearguard when the Union army changed bases during the Peninsular Campaign. On 28 June 1862, when so serving, it was attacked by the 7th and 8th Georgia Regiments. The 33rd checked the attack, capturing 50 prisoners, including both Georgia colonels, and finding another 100 Southerners wounded or dead in front of their position.

3. FIRST LIEUTENANT, 69TH NEW YORK STATE MILITIA REGIMENT, 1862

The 69th Volunteer Infantry and 69th State Militia Regiments were closely associated—both were Irish units from New York City—with 500 officers and men from the State Militia Regiment volunteering for service in the Volunteer Infantry Regiment when it was organized. This figure is based closely on a photograph of the State Militia's First Lieutenant E. K. Butler, which shows him to have carried a silver flask as a canteen. His belt plate is the state sword belt plate. The color in the background was carried by the 69th Volunteer Infantry until late 1862. The Volunteer Infantry Regiment was part of the famous 'Irish Brigade' of the Army of the Potomac, who smashed into the Confederate line in the Sunken Lane at Antietam in September 1862 despite terrible losses.

1. PRIVATE, 1ST INFANTRY REGIMENT, RESERVE BRIGADE OF PHILADELPHIA, 1863

Pennsylvania's Reserve Brigade, organized in April 1861, continued to wear gray uniforms long after all the other Federal volunteers at the front switched to blue. When the regiment saw field duty, however, in the southern invasions of 1862 and 1863, and came under artillery fire at Carlisle, Pennsylvania, they wore dark blue fatigue blouses. Their belt plates were unique, with the state coat of arms over the letter 'RB'.

2. CORPORAL, 33RD PENNSYLVANIA VOLUNTEER INFANTRY, 1862

The state's first generally issued uniform was this simple gray affair, worn at least until mid-1862. This corporal holds the regimental color, like the US flag but with the state coat of arms in the canton along with the stars. Each of the state's regiments received one of these colors, which differed only in very minor points. The flag shown is in fact typical of all Pennsylvania regiments but not an exact copy of the actual 33rd PVI color. At Second Bull Run the 33rd charged down the slope of Henry House Hill, taking up a defensive line on the Sudley Springs Road, and driving every Confederate from their front. The Union Army's defeat could well have been much worse had it not been made.

3. SERGEANT, 1ST REGIMENT OF CONNECTICUT MILITIA, 1863

Companies A and B of Connecticut's infantry regiments were rifle companies, trimming their uniforms with green. This uniform was authorized by state regulations before the war and closely followed that of the US Army's 1858 regulations, replacing national insignia with state insignia. His canteen is a unique combination of canteen and ration carrier, issued to several 1861 Connecticut volunteer regiments: the top part holds water while the hollow bottom part is designed for rations. The 1st, which served only three months in 1861, were at 1st Bull Run where, after crossing the stream following Sherman's Brigade, they marched down Young's Branch and were pretty well out of the fighting for the rest of the day.

1. **COMPANY QUARTERMASTER SERGEANT, 30TH OHIO VOLUNTEER INFANTRY REGIMENT, 1864**

Ohio's troops, typical of many Westerners, were often issued short jackets instead of fatigue blouses or frock coats. This man wears a half-chevron indicating veteran volunteer status. His cross belt plate bears the state insignia, and he also wears the state belt plate. At the Battle of South Mountain the 30th charged into the 23rd North Carolina Infantry, who were positioned behind a stone wall. They drive the North Carolinians off and took the position.

2. **PIONEER, 17TH ILLINOIS VOLUNTEER INFANTRY REGIMENT, 1863**

The pioneer's grade is indicated by the crossed axe insignia worn on both sleeves. This regiment, when photographed near Vicksburg, Mississippi, in 1863, wore state-issue jackets and broad-brimmed hats. At the Battle of Shiloh, 'left unsupported and alone ... the 17th Illinois ... retired in good order ... and reformed under my direction', reported Union Gen. McClernand. This calm behavior, not typical of many of the units first hit by the Southern assault, helped to save the day, and the campaign in the West, for the Union.

3. **REGIMENT QUARTERMASTER SERGEANT, 3RD NEW JERSEY CAVALRY REGIMENT, 1864**

When the 3rd New Jersey Cavalry was raised in January–March 1864, the state decided to name them the '1st US Hussars' and to give them a fancier than usual cavalry uniform as a spur to recruitment. The state paid for the additions to the regulation cavalry uniform. The cap was the issue forage cap with the peak removed and worn sideways (although the crossed sabres insignia on top of the cap was worn facing the original front). Extra braid was added to the jackets. Called the 'Butterflies' by other troops when they first appeared, the regiment went on to establish a credible record as a good cavalry unit. Their most notable action was their charge to capture the entire 8th South Carolina Infantry Regiment, but they also made a successful charge at Winchester, Virginia, routed Southern cavalry at Tom's Brook, Virginia, and were at the Battle of Five Forks.

1. LIEUTENANT, CHICAGO LIGHT GUARD
Formed in the 1850s, the unit was in the state's 60th Militia Regiment in 1855. Its officers and men did not see active service as a formed unit, however, many ending up in other volunteer units during the war. The unit passed out of existence thereafter.

2. PRIVATE, GUTHRIE GRAYS BATTALION
Formed in 1854, the Guthrie Grays formed part of Neff's Independent Detachment of Infantry (Cincinnati Rifles), which served during the threat of a Southern raid into Cincinnati, Ohio for 15 days in July 1862. The Grays also sent a number of their members into the 6th Ohio Volunteer Infantry Regiment in May 1861. The uniform worn here was adopted in 1854.

3. SERGEANT, STOCKTON BLUES
The Blues were formed in 1856 in Stockton, California and many unit members joined the unit's commander in the 3rd California Infantry Regiment in Utah during the Civil War. The Blues wore M1851 US Army shakos which had white bands around the bottom for enlisted men and were all dark blue for officers. The single-breasted frock coats were plain dark blue, with gold epaulettes for officers.

1. LIEUTENANT, 3RD REGIMENT (HUSSARS), NEW YORK STATE MILITIA

Formed in New York City in 1847, the unit was noted as being drawn from poorer Germans whose mounts were also used to pull hacks and delivery wagons. As a unit it did not see Civil War service, although one troop was called to active duty for a short time during the war. The unit was disbanded in 1880 for lack of members. The 1850 dress uniform is illustrated here.

2. PRIVATE, 7TH REGIMENT, NEW YORK STATE MILITIA

A New York city regiment formed in 1806, the 7th was so designated in 1847. It was possibly the most famous volunteer unit of the 1860s, filled by members of New York's finest families, and was the first New York regiment to reach Washington after President Lincoln's call for troops in April 1861. The regiment was called into service several more times during the war, and was one of the units which put down the 1863 draft riots in New York City. Some 606 of its members became officers in other active Army units. The dress uniform is shown.

3. SERGEANT, NEW YORK CITY GUARD

Formed as the Pulawski Cadets in 1833, the unit was reorganized as the New York City Guard in 1840. It served in the Civil War as Company C, 9th Regiment, New York State Militia, although the entire regiment assumed the designation of City Guard. When in regimental formations during the war the unit wore regulation New York State uniform. In 1868 unit members formed the Old Guard, which is noted for its annual ball and still wears the white coatee, blue trousers, and bearskin shako.

1 [Right]. SERGEANT, AMERICAN GUARD

Organized in New York City as the American Rifles in 1850, this unit was intended to be made up of nothing but native-born Americans as a protest against the tidal wave of immigrants who had arrived in the city in the first half of the 19th century. It was designated the 71st Regiment, New York State Militia, in 1852. During the Civil War the unit served at First Bull Run before being mustered out of service; many of its members then served in the 124th New York Volunteer Infantry Regiment. The unit is still in existence as a member of the New York National Guard.

Dark blue was selected as the uniform color, as opposed to the gray which was more commonly used by volunteers, since it was spoken of as the 'national color' in US Army regulations. In much the same way the frock coat was selected by its largely mechanic-class members in preference to the coatee, since the newer fashioned coat reflected the revolutionary changes in society. This dress uniform was worn until 1941.

2. PRIVATE, WASHINGTON GRAYS

Organized as two separate battalions in New York City in 1808, the unit passed through several designations before being named the 8th Regiment, New York State Militia, in 1847. Volunteering for service on the outbreak of war in 1861, the unit had many losses at Bull Run and was mustered out of Federal service when its three months of service ended after the battle.

The dress uniform is shown here; there was also an undress uniform consisting of short gray jackets and French-type képis trimmed with black.

3. SERGEANT, 79TH REGIMENT, NEW YORK STATE MILITIA

Scotsmen living in New York City in 1859 founded this unit to reflect their native heritage. They ordered their uniforms from Scotland and requested, and received, the designation of 79th to establish a link to the traditions of the Cameron Highlanders, Britain's 79th Regiment of Foot. Volunteering for three months' service in 1861, the unit saw action at First Bull Run.

New York's adjutant-general refused the use of the kilts for the unit, but photos and surviving relics of the unit prove that they were indeed worn. In the field however, trews in Cameron of Erracht—the same tartan as the kilts—were worn by both officers and men. At Bull Run they wore only their distinctive bonnets and tunics, the trews having been replaced by regulation sky blue trousers.

A recently discovered original uniform in the Atlanta Historical Society differ significantly from this illustration. The collar is dark blue with red piping and a red gorget patch ending in a brass button. The whole jacket front is piped red, and the epaulettes are edged in thin brass around red worsted with an oval of the regimental number circled by thistles in the crescent. A silver thistle, not the state badge, is worn on the glengarry cockade. Hose is olive green and red diced, while the belt is white web with a rectangular brass beltplate with a silver number 79 in the center. Gaiters are plain white duck with white bone buttons.

1. CAPTAIN, NATIONAL LANCERS

Formed in Boston in 1836, the National Lancers formed Company A, 1st Battalion, Massachusetts Volunteer Militia Cavalry. Many of its members joined the 1st Massachusetts Volunteer Cavalry Regiment, which was formed in September 1861, and served both in Florida and South Carolina and with the Army of the Potomac during the Civil War.

This full dress uniform was worn until 1869. The unit was armed with M1840 cavalry sabres and M1842 single-shot, muzzle-loading pistols.

2. CORPORAL, FIRST COMPANY, GOVERNOR'S FOOT GUARD

Connecticut was novel among the states in that it maintained four Guard units which were not considered part of the state's active militia. They were largely of some antiquity, the First Company, from Hartford, having been established in 1771. The Guards, under their old names, still exist.

The First Company had a drill uniform as well as this dress uniform: it consisted of a scarlet peaked cap, a short red jacket with black velvet collar and cuffs and silver buttons, and white trousers. They were originally armed, as shown here, with M1842 smooth-bore muskets, but received M1855 rifled muskets in 1862.

3. PRIVATE, PUTNAM PHALANX

The Putnam Phalanx was organized in Connecticut in 1858 as a military organization outside the regular state militia system. It was chartered by the Connecticut General Assembly in 1877, but even then was not made part of the state's National Guard.

The Phalanx styled themselves after George Washington's Continental Army of the War of American Independence, using a drill written by that army's Inspector General, Baron von Steuben, and music of that period. Their dress was also a copy of that worn by the Continental Army. This form of dress became quite popular throughout the United States during the period just before the Civil War, and was worn by units from the Atlantic to the Pacific.

1. PRIVATE, CADWALADER GRAYS

The Cadwalader Grays were a company associated with the Artillery Corps, Washington Grays, which traced its origins in Philadelphia, Pennsylvania to 1777. The entire regiment was converted to infantry and redesignated Companies A and F of the 17th Pennsylvania Volunteer Infantry Regiment for three months' service in 1861. This was the first Pennsylvania unit to reach Washington in April 1861. After being mustered out, many of its members remained in the field with the 119th Pennsylvania Volunteer Infantry Regiment, while others remained at home but served with the Gray Reserves Infantry, Pennsylvania Militia. The unit exists today as the 103rd Engineer Battalion, Pennsylvania National Guard.

2. PRIVATE, NATIONAL RIFLES

The National Rifles was a company organized in Washington City, District of Columbia, in 1859. A large number of its original members, including its captain, were pro-Southern in sympathy in 1861, and the unit had drawn a large amount of extra equipment, including two mountain howitzers and a supply of sabres and revolvers, with the idea of defending Maryland against Northern troops coming to relieve Washington City. When the War Department discovered this, the commander's commission was declared invalid (he had not sworn the required oath); the pro-Southern members left to be replaced by more trustworthy men. (Many of the pro-Southern sympathizers served thereafter in Company F, 1st Virginia Infantry Regiment.) The National Rifles was mustered into duty on the Union side as the Right Company, 3rd Battalion, DC Volunteers during several emergencies, including the raid on Washington in 1864. The unit was disbanded in November 1864.

3. CORPORAL, FIRST CITY ZOUAVES

Organized in Pennsylvania's capital city, Harrisburg, in the spring of 1861, the unit volunteered for active service in May 1862. It was then designated Company A, 127th Pennsylvania Infantry and it served as such until May 1863. Several years after the war ended the company was renamed the City Grays, abandoning their zouave dress. As such, it remains a part of the 112th Infantry, Pennsylvania National Guard.

THE CONFEDERATE ARMY,

The Iredell Blues were photographed in Statesville, North Carolina (where they were founded in 1842) apparently in mid-1860. The unit saw Confederate service first as part of the 52nd Regiment, North Carolina State Troops, and soon thereafter as Companies A and C, 4th North Carolina Infantry. This company includes four officers, one in an undress plain dark blue frock coat, 34 enlisted men at 'present arms', and four bandsmen, two with fifes and two with drums. The six men on the left have carbine-like weapons with shortened forestocks. Coatees are dark blue with white plastrons, standing collars, and slash cuffs, worn with white trousers in summer; winter trousers were dark blue with a white stripe. [*North Carolina Division of Archives and History*]

It appears that the 13 Southern states left the Union in a fit of anger, without any realization of their actual situation if it came to war. A study published in 1857 showed that free states outproduced slave states in virtually every important agricultural product category. And there were 17,855 miles of railroads in free states, compared to 6,859 in slave states. In 1852 there were 1,381,842 militiamen in free states, compared to 792,876 in slave states – despite a military tradition in the South that was largely lacking in the North. In 1850 there were 493,026 illiterate white native adults in slave states, compared to only 248,725 in free states – a factor that would make a big difference in being able to field soldiers who could read and understand manuals.

In other words, the Confederacy would have to create a nation with the cards heavily stacked against them. That they survived for almost four years is a testimony to innovation and courage.

There were, however, some things in the South's favor. Many trained, professional military officers resigned from the US Army to join that of the Confederacy. Even the Confederacy's president, Jefferson Davis, had graduated from the US Military Academy, seen service in the Mexican War as colonel of the Mississippi Rifles, and been Secretary of War in the US government before the war. The Confederacy was a huge plot of land, with millions of acres to conquer and thousands of miles of coastline to blockade.

The new Confederate government quickly set about creating Army, Navy and Marine Corps. Since most of its officers had seen Federal service, the Southern military forces closely resembled those of the Union. Armories, many of them using machinery captured from the US arsenal at Harper's Ferry, Virginia, were set up and soon began turning out copies of the M1861 rifled musket and M1855 rifle. Contracts in London brought in so many P1853 Enfield copies that the British weapon became the standard Confederate infantry longarm, and a vast amount of other British military equipment was also imported.

As in the North, volunteers poured into the South's armies. They enlisted for a year's service but, when that was up, the Confederate Congress drafted them all into an army recruited for the war's duration. Congress also set up a Bureau of Conscription in an attempt to keep all its ranks filled.

The Confederacy managed to put around a million men under arms, though the exact number is not known due to the destruction of government archives at the war's end. In 1861 the Confederate Army was a close copy of the 1861 Federal Army, but as time went on the Confederates began to implement different organizations and practices to fit their unique needs.

In late 1863 their Congress authorized two regiments of engineers. Before that, there had only been a handful of engineering officers in the Army's ranks. Men detached to a Pioneer Corps did necessary entrenchment digging and bridge building work. The 1st Regiment and two companies of the 2nd Regiment served with the Army of Northern Virginia, while the rest of the 2nd Regiment served elsewhere, with several companies in the Trans-Mississippi Department.

A Signal Corps was authorized in May 1862 at 61 officers and men under a major's command. It not only passed messages by flags and torches, but also served as the South's secret service. A two-company Independent Signal Corps served in Virginia, while a Marine Signal Corps that worked on blockade running ships was drawn from both Army organizations. In all, some 1,500 Signal Corpsmen served the Confederacy. The Signal Corps was also responsible for the civilians who worked the South's telegraphs. However, the South had great difficulty obtaining telegraph wire and was never able to field anything like as extensive a field telegraph system as the Federal Army.

The Medical Department used the US Army's prewar system of a commissioned surgeon and an enlisted hospital steward assigned to each regiment; these were also massed into hospitals as needed. The Army of Northern Virginia also set up an Infirmary Corps with two men from each regiment assigned to it. They were marked by red cap badges which allowed them to pass freely from the line of battle to rear hospitals during battle carrying wounded soldiers.

On 17 February 1864 Congress authorized an Invalid Corps. Its officers and men were to be passed as no longer fit for active duty by surgeons, and were used as guards and hospital attendants.

1861–1865

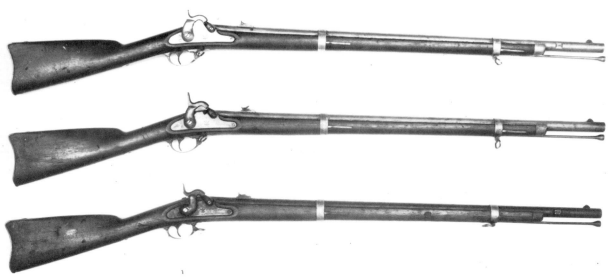

On 3 March 1865 Congress ordered that the Army's provost marshals had to be disabled men fit only for light duty or reservists as well. Confederate provost marshals acted as military policemen, magistrates and gaolers–something very necessary in a land where at one time or another as many as a third of the armed forces were deserters or stragglers.

Through brilliant generalship and great ésprit de corps, the Army of Northern Virginia was able to fend off every Federal attempt to take the South's capital and major industrial city of Richmond, Virginia, for almost four years. The poorer led and motivated Western

Confederate forces, however, muddled through defeats and steadily missed chances. At the end, the Virginia successes could not compensate for the Western losses, especially when coupled with a blockade of the South's ports.

The Mississippi River came under complete Federal control in July 1863, cutting off the far West from the rest of the Confederacy. In 1864 Atlanta fell, and a Federal army passed easily through Georgia to Savannah. The heart had gone out of the Southern war effort, and by the spring of 1865 a welcome peace had returned to the ravaged land.

ABOVE LEFT: The three models of Fayetteville Armory rifles, the earliest at the top and latest at the bottom. Like the Richmond weapons, these were made with dies captured from the Harper's Ferry Arsenal. [*Russ Pritchard/ Milwaukee Public Museum*]

ABOVE: Detail of the lockplate of the final Fayetteville rifle, showing the distinctive S-shaped hammer. These were among the finest Southern weapons made. [*Russ Pritchard*]

This drawing, done by a Confederate veteran and entitled 'On the Confederate line of battle "with fate against them"' gives a good indication of the ragged, non-uniform appearance and loose tactical formations of the Confederate infantry in action. [*Battles & Leaders of the Civil War*]

1. PRIVATE, INFANTRY, 1861

This man wears the popular overshirt as a jacket. He has a heavy Bowie knive, typically made with a 'D' guard; such knives were commonly brought from home, but many were lost or abandoned as useless weight after only a short time. His musket is a US M1835 flintlock—out of sheer necessity flintlocks remained common until late 1862, even though long absolete.

2. FIRST SERGEANT, LOUISIANA INFANTRY, 1861

Variations of the regulation frock coat were common in 1861. He also wears a white cotton 'havelock' over his cap; generally these were soon abandoned and used for coffee filters and gun patches. His sword is a Southern-made version of the US Army non-commissioned officer's pattern, and his beltplate is a 'Virginia-style' cast plate. He is armed with an M1841 percussion rifle, commonly called the 'Mississippi Rifle'; these were often rebored to Confederate regulation .577 caliber. Note the black trouser stripe.

3. PRIVATE, 4TH TEXAS INFANTRY REGIMENT, 1861

Based on an original photograph of a private in Company H, 4th Texas Infantry Regiment taken in 1861, this man wears a typical 'sack coat'. His waist belt and cartridge box sling are of painted canvas cloth, and he carries a Southern-made tin canteen. His haversack is of the type issued to the US Army during the Mexican–American War of 1846–48. His weapon is a US M1842 smoothbore percussion musket.

1. DRUMMER, INFANTRY, 1863

No special insignia was ordered to be worn by Confederate musicians, nor was there any regulation design for drums. Nevertheless, drums were important both for keeping the beat on the march and for passing on orders in the field and in camp. The white cotton web drum sling was apparently the most common type issued.

2. PRIVATE, INFANTRY, 1863

The typical Confederate infantryman in the field. His jacket is taken from an original made in North Carolina and issued to a Maryland soldier; it is lined in white cotton drill and has two pockets inside the fronts. He is armed with a Richmond Armory version of the M1861 Springfield, and his frame buckle is the 'wishbone' type. His cartridge box is also Richmond-made; its oval copper (CS) flap plate is hidden here.

3. ORDNANCE SERGEANT, 28TH NORTH CAROLINA INFANTRY REGIMENT, 1863

Photographs indicate that North Carolina ordnance sergeants, whose job was normally to pass out ammunition and to secure abandoned weapons from the battlefield, also carried regimental colors at times. (Usually an ordinary sergeant carried the color; on 17 February 1864 the Confederate Congress created the rank of 'ensign', who was to wear the insignia of a first lieutenant, and whose duty was to 'bear the colors of the regiment'. Each Confederate regiment carried only one color.)

This NCO carries a version of the Army of Northern Virginia battleflag, adopted in September 1861 as being easier to differentiate from the US national color on the battlefield. Different sizes were authorized for the different branches of service.

Regiments traditionally painted their battle honors on their color, a practice officially authorized from 23 July 1862. Here the outer lettering, in straight lines, is (clockwise from top) MANNASSAS/MECHANICSVILLE/HARPERS FERRY/FRAZIERS FARM; the smaller inner arcs read CEDAR RUN/HANOVER/OX HILL/COLD HARBOR. The actual 28th North Carolina Infantry color, incidentally, has white and not gold lettering, although gold was used on many other period Confederate colors.

The sergeant's cap is a version of the US Army M1839 forage cap; these caps were photographed still being worn by Confederate prisoners as late as 1864. His haversack is captured US Army issue.

1. CAPTAIN, CAVALRY, 1862

Mounted officers prefered short 'roundabout' jackets to regulation frock coats. The regulation Austrian knot of rank above the cuffs was often not worn. This captain is equipped with an English-made snake buckle and a cavalry officer's sabre made by Thomas Griswold & Co., New Orleans. The plumed slouch hat was a common affectation of Confederate cavalrymen.

Since most Southerners were used to riding in civilian life, using English saddles, the adopted regulation military saddle was the 'Jenifer' pattern, seen here. It used an English seat with a military pommel and cantle from which equipment could be suspended, and a surcingle passing through slots in the flaps. It was an easy ride but was found to wear on a horse's backbone and withers when the horse grew thinner and was replaced in the fall of 1863 by the US Army's McClellan saddle. The official saddle blanket was 'dark gray color, with a red border 3 inches wide, 3 inches from the edge. The letters C.S., 6 inches high, of orange color, in the center of the blanket.' In practice virtually any type of blanket was used. Other horse furniture, such as bridle and bit, was US Army style.

2. FIRST LIEUTENANT, ALABAMA CAVALRY, 1862

It was common even until mid-1862 for Confederate officers to use US Army instead of Confederate rank insignia, as worn by this figure based on a photograph of an Alabama cavalry officer. His beltplate is an Alabama issue model, while his sabre was made by L. Haiman & Bro., a Southern company. His cap pouch is English-made, his holster similar to the US Army issue type.

3. SERGEANT MAJOR, CAVALRY, 1862

Because of their feeling of being an élite force, it appears that cavalrymen tried to obtain yellow material for their facings even though it was uncommon for many other branches of service to wear facing colors. This sergeant major's carbine is a copy of the Enfield type made by Cook & Brother, and his Southern-made copy of the US cavalry sabres was made by C. Hammond.

1. PRIVATE, 2ND MARYLAND INFANTRY REGIMENT, 1863

Prewar Zouave-style uniforms worn by the Maryland Guard were apparently saved for dress occasions, such as this preparation for a parade in Richmond. The Guard itself served first in a Virginia outfit; then, when Maryland units were raised, they transferred to the 1st Maryland Battalion, most of whose members joined the 2nd Maryland Infantry Regiment when the 1st Battalion was disbanded in 1862. The 2nd Maryland successfully assaulted the Union works on Culp's Hill, near Gettysburg, on 2 July 1863, but were unsuccessful in an attack mounted on the 3rd in conjunction with Pickett's Charge. The regiment lost heavily at Gettysburg, but went on to be commended for its stand at Cold Harbor in 1864.

Two jackets of this style, worn by Maryland Confederates, survived the war and are today in the Museum of the Confederacy. The uniform is a good example of the Southern version of the French Zouave dress, though this man has had to get a replacement made which varies from the original style in several details. Other Confederate Zouave uniforms were similar in design, but details varied from unit to unit.

2. CORPORAL, PRESIDENT'S GUARD, 1863

The President's Guard was made up of soldiers no longer capable of the physical endeavors needed in the field. It was neatly uniformed.

3. BANDSMAN, 1863

This soldier's hat is taken from one in the Museum of the Confederacy, while his waistcoat is in a Mississippi collection. It has small US general service buttons down the woollen front, which has a coarse brown cloth backing, leather wear-strips on the bottom inside edge and muslin lining. Its back is brown polished cotton and it has a small belt on the back for size adjustment. The shirt shown here was an imported British Army item dated 1859; the original one was worn by the officer in the 1st Virginia Artillery. This soldier's trousers, taken from a pair worn by a Washington Artillery enlisted man in 1864, are medium-weight charcoal gray wool; the exterior stitching used black thread, while the interior stitching was in white. His band instrument is an over-the-shoulder 'B'-flat tenor saxhorn, the most popular brass instrument of the period.

1. LIEUTENANT COLONEL, ARTILLERY, 1862

Officers generally wore costumes closer to regulation dress than enlisted men, and caps were also less unusual among commissioned ranks. Note the gold trouser welt; and see opposite page (2) for jacket cuff button layout. This officer's sabre is a Southern-made copy of the US light artillery officer's model—although cavalry-type sabres were equally, if not more popular than the over-curved light artillery model. The regulation sash worn here would not last long in the field.

The cannon in the background is the 3in., 10-pdr. 'Parrot rifle' of which numbers were captured from the Union armies; this iron muzzle-loader was the most common rifled piece in Southern service.

The most popular of all Confederate ordnance was the bronze, smoothbore 12-pdr. 'Napoleon' (M1857 gun-howitzer). Despite the rifle's greater range and accuracy, the smoothbore fired faster (having fully fixed ammunition); and at normal battle ranges, especially in wooded country, it was at least as effective as the rifle. The 'Napoleon' was made in many Southern foundries.

2. PRIVATE, ARTILLERY, 1862

The jacket shown here is taken from one worn in 1864 by a private of the Washington Artillery of New Orleans; note the belt loops on the side, as well as the red trim. He has a US Army gunner's haversack slung over his shoulder. This was used to carry ammunition from the limber chests so that loose ammunition would not have to be carried exposed.

3. PRIVATE, ARTILLERY, 1862

For some reason, more photographs show artillery enlisted men in regulation double-breasted frock coats than men from any other branch of service. This figure, taken from a photograph of a corporal in the Hanover, Virginia, Artillery varies from the regulations only in that his trousers are gray with a red stripe down each leg. He wears a belt and primer pouch, in which are kept the friction primers used to fire the cannon. His képi is taken from one worn by a member of the Richmond Howitzers and now in the Museum of the Confederacy.

1. QUARTERMASTER SERGEANT, ARTILLERY, 1864

This quartermaster sergeant holds the 'guide flag' of the Palmetto Battery from South Carolina. His Southern-made sabre, produced by Hayden & Whilden, is a good copy of the US Army's light artillery sabre. His beltplate is an interesting variation on the standard type, lacking the laurel wreath on the female piece.

2. MAJOR, ARTILLERY, 1864

Standing near a 24-pdr. gun in a siege battery, this major wears a common variation of the regulation frock coat. His insignia is worn on the lay-down collar, cut in civilian style; note the red trouser stripe. He is holding a Southern-made foot artillery sword, the only weapon issued to foot artillerymen for their defense.

3. SECOND LIEUTENANT, ARTILLERY, 1864

This officer wears another common version of the mounted officer's jacket; it is single-breasted, and has the regulation Austrian knot on the sleeves. He also wears the regulation sash; light artillery officer's sabre, and 'chasseur'-pattern képi.

1. FIRST LIEUTENANT, 2ND REGIMENT SOUTH CAROLINA RIFLES, 1864

Although Confederate regulations do prescribe a button for riflemen, no other indication of regulation rifle dress is to be found. Nevertheless, rifle buttons were made, and rifle regiments such as this one were organized. Green (not as dark as British rifle green) was the branch-of-service color in the US Army and militia rifle units, and appears to have been worn by Confederate riflemen as well. Lt. Joseph M. Adams, whose photograph forms the basis for this figure, wore a single-breasted frock with green facings but without the Austrian knots. He is shown here with a Boyle & Gamble Southern-made copy of the US foot officer's sword, and a rare two-piece beltplate with fancy letters and the female piece lacking the usual wreath. Adams was wounded and captured in an unusual night attack made by his regiment against Union forces attempting to relieve Chattanooga on 29 October 1863, and he spent the rest of the war as a prisoner.

2. PRIVATE, INFANTRY, 1864

This view shows how the infantryman's accoutrements hang from the rear. His cartridge box was produced by the Houston, Texas, Ordnance Department in 1864, while his canteen is taken from a wooden one carried by an Alabama soldier. His weapon is the Fayetteville Armory rifle, and his haversack is a Southern-made white cotton model.

3. SERGEANT, 4TH KENTUCKY INFANTRY REGIMENT, 1864

The Western Confederate armies did not generally use the St Andrew's cross battle-flag of the Army of Northern Virginia, in their ranks a variety of styles was observed. In Hardee's Division, later Cleburne's Division, the most common color carried was a variation of this blue and white 'Hardee' flag, which was adopted in mid-1861. The color was usually smaller than those of the Army of Northern Virginia: that of the 1st Arkansas Infantry was 31ins. by 38ins. Battle honors were usually placed on the edge of the flag. This dark blue flag is edged top, bottom and down the 'fly' in white.

This sergeant's regiment is noted for its heavy losses in a single battle; the place was Shiloh, where the 4th Kentucky lost 30 killed and 138 wounded.

1. PRIVATE, INFANTRY, 1865

Some Southern-made overcoats were issued but they were rare. This figure is taken from a painting by a Confederate veteran. The fur cap and boots were probably obtained from home, as such items do not appear to have been issued to infantrymen. The soldier's buckle is the 'Georgia' frame type, and he has received a British Army cap pouch and cartridge box with his Enfield rifled musket.

2. PRIVATE, INFANTRY, 1865

This soldier illustrates to what extent captured US Army uniforms, accoutrements and weapons were used. If his comrades did not know him, they might well mistake him for a 'blue belly'. His gray cap gives him away, as does the beltplate made by heating a US beltplate until the front fell off and only the frame was left. Otherwise, his cartridge box, cap box, waist belt, haversack, canteen, and M1861 Colt contract rifle musket are all US Army issue items captured and widely used by the Confederates.

3. COLONEL, 4TH GEORGIA INFANTRY REGIMENT, 1865

Colonel Robert A. Smith of the 44th Georgia was photographed in a plain gray frock coat, with his rank insignia on his standing collar; yet this was not necessarily the regimental norm since other photographs of officers from the same unit show a variety of uniforms, most of them double-breasted. Regardless of dress, however, the 44th were one of the South's toughest regiments; they led the assault at Chancellorsville, driving the Union troops back over two miles and capturing several cannon in the process. They paid a price of 121 officers and men killed, wounded and missing in this action.

The cap badge shown here was taken from the US Army infantry officer's cap badge. Such badges were occasionally worn by Confederate officers, but on the whole were rarer than not. Note the sky-blue trouser stripes. His foot officer's sabre was made by Thomas Griswold & Co., New Orleans—one of the best Southern sword-makers.

1. GENERAL ROBERT E. LEE, 1863

Raised by postwar legend almost to the status of a god. Lee was an outstanding and inspiring leader. His tactical sense was usually sound, although his errors—like Gettysburg—were too often fatal. His strategic sense was apparently not as great; nor was he able to bring himself to discipline his generals as they should have been disciplined. Nevertheless, he became the very symbol of the Confederacy.

Lee's first dress described by a private of the 1st Tennessee Infantry Regiment in West Virginia in 1861: 'He was dressed in blue cottonade ... he had no sword or pistol, or anything to show his rank. The only thing that I remember he had was an opera-glass hung over his shoulder by a strap.' Lee described his own outfit to Mrs. W. H. F. Lee on 22 June 1862: 'My coat is of gray, of the regulation style and pattern, and my pants of dark blue, as is also prescribed, partly hid by my long boots. I have the same handsome hat which surmounts my gray head ...'

In November 1862 he requested a waistcoat 'of blue, black or gray cassimere or cloth, rolling collar & army buttons. He mentioned wearing an old blue overcoat in February 1863, and a gray sack coat in May 1863. On 13 June 1863 he wrote home that he found his 'old blue flannel pants yielding to the wear & tear of the road. I have another blue pair in my trunk of summer cloth, which I wish you would send me. They are plain without cords on the seams.' He requested a pair of similar plain blue trousers in May 1864, and check shirts in November 1864.

In the early war years he wore a standing collar, as seen here; after 1863 he began wearing a laydown collar. According to a veteran of the Washington Artillery, Lee 'always wore during the campaigns a gray sack coat with side pockets like the costume of a business man in the cities.' At Appomattox, however, this veteran 'noted particularly his dress. He was in full uniform, with a handsome embroidered belt and dress sword, tall hat and buff gauntlets.' Photographs generally show this uniform worn with gray trousers that matched his coat.

2. LIEUTENANT GENERAL A. P. HILL, 1863

A. P. Hill, original commander of the Army of Northern Virginia's Light Division, was one of Lee's better generals. He was photographed in a regulation Confederate general's uniform, complete with forage cap. All general officers, regardless of specific rank, wore this basic uniform. The horse furniture in the background was used by 'Stonewall' Jackson.

3 [Left]. SURGEON, CONFEDERATE STATES ARMY, 1863

The regulation Confederate officer's dress is worn by this surgeon, with the addition of a non-regulation but common 'MS' within a wreath on the cap front. His sword is a cavalry officer's sabre made by L. Bissonnet, Mobile, Alabama—a copy of the US Model 1840 cavalry officer's sabre, there was no special sword required for Confederate medical officers.

1. LIEUTENANT COLONEL, 2ND ENGINEER'S, CONFEDERATE STATES, 1864

The sack coat, as worn by this officer, was typical field wear for many staff officers, and even on occasion of General Lee. He wears a two-piece Virginia belt plate and a foot officer's sword. The flag behind him designated the headquarters of the Chief Engineer of the Army of Northern Virginia.

2. LIEUTENANT, CONFEDERATE STATES NAVY, 1864

This lieutenant, taken from a photograph of Lt. Arthur Sinclair, wears regulation Confederate Navy dress. His sword is a regulation weapon made by the London firm of Firmin & Sons. Regulations called for a gold band on CS Navy officer's caps. This man has abnormally been unable to obtain this material in the hard-pressed South, though according to photographic evidence many of his mates did.

3. SERGEANT, 1ST ENGINEERS, CONFEDERATE STATES ARMY, 1864

Confederate engineers played a vital part in the fighting during the Appomattox Campaign, bridging rivers in front of the army, burning down bridges behind them and fighting off the advancing troops as they moved on. The white tape this sergeant has used for chevrons is an alternative to the regulation buff required for staff officers. In keeping with the dual mission of the engineers, he has both an Enfield rifled musket and a shovel.

1. SEAMAN, CONFEDERATE STATES NAVY, 1865

This seaman, serving with the defending forces at Drewry's Bluff, outside Richmond, Virginia carries the British-made equipment issued to the Confederate Navy. His cutlass was made by R. Mole in England and was imported by Courtney & Tennant, Charleston, South Carolina: it is a copy of a Royal Navy cutlass. He also carries a British naval pattern rifle.

2. SERGEANT, CONFEDERATE STATES MARINE CORPS, 1865

This sergeant wears the typical dress uniform of the Confederate Marines, with British-made leather accoutrements and a Southern-made haversack and tin water-bottle. His weapon is an 1853 pattern Enfield. Marines serving in the defenses of Drewry's Bluff were also noted wearing waist-length jackets. A recently discovered photograph confirms this dress and kit closely save that the belt and cap box are black rather than brown.

3. SECOND LIEUTENANT, CONFEDERATE STATES MARINE CORPS, 1865

Dark blue facings distinguished the Confederate Marines from Army officers: otherwise, this lieutenant could pass for an infantry officer. His sword is a Southern-made copy of the US Army foot officer's sword. He wears a rare Confederate Navy beltplate, made in England. His handgun is the Le Mat revolver, a number of which were bought for the Navy.

1. CAPTAIN, SOUTH CAROLINA, 1861

The dark blue uniform worn by this staff captain is described by British correspondent William H. Russell on 17 April 1861 as 'blue military caps, with "palmetto" trees embroidered thereon, blue frock-coats, with upright collars, and shoulder-straps edged with lace, and marked with two silver bars, to designate their ranks of captain; gilt buttons with the palmetto in relief: blue trowsers, with a gold-lace cord, and brass spurs–no straps.'

2. CORPORAL, ALABAMA VOLUNTEER CORPS, 1861

The state uniform, with minor variations from unit to unit, was worn at least into 1863. The corporal is armed with an M1842 smoothbore 0.69-caliber musket; the bayonet scabbard is the M1840 model which was designed for this musket.

3. PRIVATE, 11TH MISSISSIPPI INFANTRY REGIMENT, 1861

Photographs indicate that the 11th Mississippi, as well as a large number of other state infantry regiments, wore the basic state uniform, at least in 1861. This private's belt plate bears the state insignia. Hat brims were folded up according to individual or unit taste on one or both sides, and sometimes even to form tricornes. The 11th, then part of Hood's Division, defended the part of the Southern line near the Dunker Church at the Battle of Antietam. Charged again and again, they lost 104 killed or wounded in the action, including all their field officers, but they held their line.

1. ORDNANCE SERGEANT, 3RD NORTH CAROLINA STATE TROOPS, 1863

This ordnance sergeant holds the regimental color, a dangerous privilege that seems often to have fallen to those who wore the insignia of ordnance sergeants in North Carolina units. He wears the regulation state uniform, with the prewar state belt plate. His canteen is made of two pieces of shaped wood nailed together. The 3rd was in the lead in the famous flank march made by 'Stonewall' Jackson at Chancellorsville.

2. PRIVATE, 7TH FLORIDA VOLUNTEER INFANTRY REGIMENT, 1863

Florida did issue some uniforms to its troops including this 7th Infantry private. The jacket and trousers were lightweight, made with cotton rather than wool. His canteen is a copper copy of the US Army tin canteen. The 7th, in Finley's Brigade of Bate's Division of the Army of the Tennessee, served in the defense of Atlanta.

3. SERGEANT MAJOR, 4TH GEORGIA INFANTRY REGIMENT, 1863

This sergeant major wears a common variation of the regulation chevrons for this grade. He also wears a belt plate with the state insignia; and his wooden canteen is taken from one carried by a member of Company G of this regiment. The 4th was one of the regiments that fought the delaying action at South Mountain, thus preventing the Union Army from destroying the Army of Northern Virginia piecemeal.

1. CAPTAIN, LYNCHBURG HOME GUARD

Formed just before the Civil War, the Lynchburg Home Guard became Company G, 11th Virginia Infantry Regiment in the Confederate service. When it entered active service Virginia issued the unit 120 yards of white webbing for belts, '20 sets plates' (probably including a cross belt and a waist belt plate), and 20 muskets that had been converted from flintlock to percussion. The rest of the 11th were dressed differently, with the Lynchburg Rifle Grays and Preston Guards wearing gray uniforms, while the Southern Guards wore black jackets and gray trousers with a black stripe down each leg.

2. PRIVATE, RICHMOND GRAYS

Virginia's Richmond Grays were formed in 1844 and assigned to the state's 1st Regiment in 1851. One of the city's best drilled companies, they were designated Company G, 12th Virginia Infantry Regiment in April 1861.

The dress uniform illustrated was adopted in 1861. The unit also had a fatigue uniform, adopted in 1859, which consisted of a gray jacket, with gray trousers for winter and white for summer. Knapsacks were varnished black, with white lettering on the back.

3. CORPORAL, CITY GUARD

Formed in Petersburg, Virginia in 1852 as the City Light Infantry Guard, this unit was attached to Virginia's 39th State Militia Regiment. In early 1861 the unit was designated Company A, 12th Virginia Infantry Regiment, under which designation it served throughout the war.

The unit's dress uniform is shown. The cross belt plate is a stock type sold by military equipment makers to many different units called 'City Guards' throughout the country. The unit also had a fatigue jacket of dark blue with white trimming on cuffs and collar, as on the dress coats, but also on shoulder straps. The star, the significance of which is unknown, was not worn on the fatigue uniform.

1. PRIVATE, GUILDFORD GRAYS

Formed in Greensboro, North Carolina in early 1860s, the Grays were ordered to occupy the US Army's Fort Macon near Beauford, North Carolina in April 1861. There they were reinforced by other volunteer units, which together formed the 27th North Carolina Infantry Regiment. The Grays became the 27th's Company B, surrendering at Appomattox in 1865.

Officers wore the same uniform as their men, save that their coats were double-breasted rather than single-breasted as shown here. The Gray's flag is now in the Confederate Museum at Richmond, and features the arms of North Carolina on one side and a wreath with an inscription of the Edgeworth Female Seminary on the other, all on a blue silk field, edged with yellow fringe. It was mounted on an ebony staff with a silver-plated battleaxe finial and a gold and blue tassel.

2. FIRST LIEUTENANT, CLINCH RIFLES

The Clinch Rifles were formed in Augusta, Georgia in 1852, being named after General Duncan L. Clinch who had served in the Seminole Wars. In 1861 the unit became Company A of the 5th Georgia Infantry Regiment—a regiment that lost over half its men at the Battle of Chickamauga. It was armed, in 1861, with M1841 rifles with sword bayonets.

The uniform was described in a letter from the unit commander to the governor of Georgia dated 10 February 1860: 'Our Dress uniform is a dress coat of dark green broad cloth, with gilt Rifle buttons, and trimmed with gold lace and cord; pants of the same material as the coat, one or two shades darker, with a gold cord on the outside seams; cap of dark green with the letters "C.R." surrounded with a gold wreath, light green pompon; wings of brass, army style. Our fatigue dress consists of a dark green cloth jacket, trimmed with gold lace, green cap, and black pants.'

3. PRIVATE, WASHINGTON LIGHT INFANTRY

Raised in 1807 in Charleston, South Carolina, most of this unit's members saw Civil War service in either Hampton's Legion or the 25th South Carolina Infantry Regiment.

Rank identification was unusual on these dress uniforms. Commissioned officers wore not only US Army regulation epaulettes but also gold chevrons, points up, above each elbow.

1. PRIVATE, MONTGOMERY TRUE BLUES

The Montgomery (Alabama) True Blues were also known as the Montgomery Light Artillery and the Montgomery Light Artillery Blues. Originally converted into infantry in 1861 as Company G, 3rd Alabama Infantry, they were later reconverted into artillery, serving as Andrews' Battery, Alabama Artillery. The stock pattern dress shako badge, featuring a flaming bomb over crossed cannon, indicated the unit's artillery background.

2. PRIVATE, BATTALION OF WASHINGTON LIGHT INFANTRY

The socially élite Washington Light Artillery of New Orleans, Louisiana had its beginnings as a volunteer company formed there in 1838 and first saw service as an artillery battery in Texas in 1845. The first four batteries of the battalions were sent to fight in Virginia in 1861; the fifth battery was mustered into Confederate service in March 1862 and served in the West. The unit badge worn on the soldier's breast appears in a number of photographs of members of the first four battalions, but its significance is not known.

3. SERGEANT, TOM GREEN RIFLES

Formed in the Texas capital, Austin, in 1858 as the Quitman Rifles, the unit took the name Tom Green Rifles before it began its trip to Virginia in 1861 to become Company B, 4th Texas Infantry, in the Army of Northern Virginia. This uniform dated from 1861, and came in four different shades of gray, being cut out by a local tailor from available cloth stocks and sewn together by the ladies of Austin before the unit left for Texas. The choice of headgear was left to the individual volunteer; most prefered broad-brimmed hats, which some decorated with tin stars obtained at a local photographer's establishment. The unusual flag, presented to the 4th Texas when it was organized in Virginia, was carried until after the Battle of Antietam, and was returned to Texas in October 1862 bearing 65 bullet and three shell fragment holes.

On 28 July 1867 Congress authorized an army of 54,302 officers and men, a vast drop from the 1,034,064 wearing the Federal uniform on 1 May 1865. This number was reduced to 45,000 in 1869 and again to 27,442 in 1876, with the latter representing the Army's authorized strength until the Spanish-American War in 1898.

The Army that remained had three functions. It had to police the Western Plains, defend the nation's borders and garrison a defeated South. In 1867 about a third of the Army was in Southern posts, but by 1870 local Southern civil authorities were largely in control of their own states. The last regular troops in Southern garrisons were withdrawn in April 1877, leaving only militia to guard against the emerging terrorism of the Klu Klux Klan.

The militia itself had come a long way from 1861, when the volunteer and militia systems were virtually the same as they had been in 1755. New York had taken the lead during the Civil War in turning its local volunteer militia into the New York National Guard in April 1862, and ten years on this consisted of 37 regiments and six battalions of infantry, one regiment, one battalion, and nine troops of cavalry, and 12 artillery batteries. New breech-loading Remington rifles were now being issued to the National Guardsmen.

Other states followed suit. 'In the elimination of the independent, separate company, and establishing the regimental unit as the basis of organization, in her assimilation of her brigades and division to the army requirements, and in her early inspection of her National Guard, it may fairly be claimed for Pennsylvania that from the beginning she was in the lead of her sister States,' wrote James Latta, the Adjutant General of Pennsylvania in 1873. The National Guard Association was organized in St Louis, Missouri, in 1879, and by 1890 a well-organized National Guard had replaced the hodgepodge of militia and volunteer units that had been the mainstay of national defence.

At the same time the Regular Army was evolving as technology progressed. One Civil War general, Emory Upton, devised a new system of tactics which were adopted in August 1867 to replace Casey's tactics. The new system allowed a commander to form line quickly in any direction, whereas before units often lost invaluable time in getting from column into line and then facing the proper way.

In 1865 the Ordnance Department introduced a method of converting M1861 rifled muskets into breech-loaders that used brass cartridges. A stop-gap method, a new M1866 single-shot breech-loader, was then adopted, and it was this weapon, which looked like the M1861 rifled musket, that became the standard infantry longarm throughout the rest of the period. Slight changes were evident in the M1868, M1870, M1873, M1879, M1884 and M1889 versions of the M1866.

Technology was especially advanced in the Signal Corps. In 1867 the civilian telegraph organization was disbanded and control of telegraphs went to the Signal Corps, who quickly developed a field telegraph train that used batteries, sounders and insulated wire.

The Signal Corps also used the telegraph in its role running the nation's first modern weather service. The idea was to provide warnings of storms approaching the Great Lakes and coasts, and data sent by stations was gathered in Washington. The service continued under Signal Corps control until it was placed under US Department of Agriculture authority in 1890. Within a couple of years of the invention of the telephone, Signal Corpsmen had also adopted this new technology, and by the end of the era most army posts were equipped with telephones.

The Medical Department's Army Medical Library was opened in 1868, around the same time as the Army Medical Museum. Both drew greatly on medical experience gained during the Civil War.

The Army was also active in establishing further training for its officers and men during the period. The Artillery School at Fort Monroe, closed since 1860, was reopened in 1868, and a Signal School of Instruction was started the same year. The School of Application for Infantry and Cavalry was opened at Fort Leavenworth, Kansas, in 1881. This evolved eventually into the General Service and Staff College. Finally, the Engineer School of Application began in 1885.

In 1866 the first non-engineer had been appointed Superintendent of the US Military Academy. No longer

Lieutenant Colonel George Custer's column of troops in the Black Hills expedition, Dakota Territory, 1874. Two 12-lb Napoleon cannon are in the foreground, while cavalry rides along the flanks, left and right. The near officer on the left appears to be wrapped in a blanket or waterproof. [*Office of the Chief of Engineers*]

1866–1890

Officers in 1872 dress uniforms at Fort Walla Walla, Washington Territory, in 1874. From left, the seated are an infantry and two mounted officers. Standing, from left, they are an infantry private, an infantry company officer, a mounted officer, a field-grade infantry officer, two company-grade mounted officers, a surgeon, and another company-grade mounted officer. Note the surgeon's chapeau and unique sword. [*US Signal Corps*]

would the school's main concern be producing engineers for a young republic; now it would concentrate on turning out good officers for all branches of service.

With so many excellent young officers, both Academy graduates and others who has seen service during the Civil War, often at high ranks with volunteer units, the Army's lack of a retirement scheme clogged the system. Good officers, weary of remaining a company grade officer for 20 years or more, quit the service at alarming rates. In 1870, therefore, Congress provided that an officer could retire after 30 years voluntarily, or mandatorily at the President's discretion, and retirement became compulsory at the age of 64 in 1882. A system of examinations for promotions for all officers lower than the rank of major was introduced in 1890, guaranteeing at least a minimal level of competence.

Actual fighting during this period was largely limited to the Western frontier. The Army's campaigns included ones in Kansas, Colorado and the Indian Territory (1866–1869); the Modoc War in Oregon (1872–1873); one against the Apaches (1873); in Kansas, Colorado, Texas, the Indian Territory and New Mexico (1874–1875); against the Cheyennes and Sioux in the Dakotas (1876–1877); one against the Nez Perce in Utah (1877); the Bannock War (1878); one against the Cheyennes (1878–1879); the White River Campaign against the Utes (1879); and Wounded Knee (1890).

Besides the frontier fights, the Army aided the National Guard during riots caused by railroad strikes in Pennsylvania and Maryland in 1877.

Sioux Chief Big Foot lies dead on the field of Wounded Knee after the last major battle of the Plains Indian Wars, in 1890. [*US Signal Corps*]

1. SERGEANT MAJOR, US CAVALRY, 1866
The familiar laced shell-jacket bears chevrons of rank on both sleeves, and the trousers, yellow-striped for non-commissioned officers, are tucked into the boots. The carbine cartridge box is carried on a broad leather cross-belt.

2. CORPORAL, US CAVALRY, 1866
The shell-jacket seen from the front: it was popular, and often worn in place of a fatigue blouse, minus its full dress brass epaulettes. The company letter appears above the branch badge on the crown of the cap. Note the cap pouch for the percussion weapons, worn on the right front of belt; 'butcher knife', a private item carried by most soldiers; and a snap-hook attachment on cross-belt for the carbine.

3. CAPTAIN, US CAVALRY, 1866
The officer wears his frock coat over a checked shirt, quite common on the Plains. In the background is a trooper wearing the caped sky-blue overcoat and a black slouch hat.

4. SERGEANT, US INFANTRY, 1866
This NCO wears absolutely regulation uniform, down to the sash and sword of his rank and the backbreaking so-called 1864 contract knapsack.

1. FIRST SERGEANT, US ARTILLERY, 1875
Following an old and still-practised Army custom, this light artillery NCO hands out cigars to celebrate his promotion. Service chevrons were authorized on dress coats only at this period, but this NCO is apparently proud enough of his Civil War service to wear his on the sleeve of his 1874 piped fatigue blouse–the kind of deviation from regulation dress frequently observed. Authorization of this practise in 1882 indicates that it was already established; in 1888 authorization was reversed again.

2. FIRST LIEUTENANT, US CAVALRY, 1875
Great latitude was observed in the manner of campaign headgear, and the straw hat was popular in both climates. The fancy braided shirt, a personal purchase, is also typical of the officers of the period. Note the locally-made canvas leggings, the field-glasses in a slung case, and the 'butcher knife' in a sheath decorated with brass rivets.

3. QUARTERMASTER SERGEANT, US INFANTRY, 1875
The pleated 1872 fatigue blouse was suppressed in 1874–officially–but continued in use long afterwards. The non-regulation gray slouch hat was more popular than black items. Bullet loops have been sewn to an old leather NCO's belt; such belts were widely used, being more capacious and much easier of access than the regulation pouch.

1. OFFICERS AND MEN, 7TH US CAVALRY, 1876

These figures display the far-from-uniform appearance of the Indian-fighting cavalry in the field. The corporal [1] has tied his blouse to his saddle and rides in an old issue gray flannel pullover shirt. His belt has large loops for carbine ammunition, and a small extra length of belting attached with loops for pistol ammunition while his trousers are worn over his boots. Note the saddle fixtures, including rope and picket-pin, and the slung canteen which has been re-covered with old blanket cloth.

The second lieutenant [2] wears a fringed buckskin jacket, of the kind popularized by the 7th's famous commander, George A. Custer. Note the field-glasses, the issue holster worn butt-forward on the right hand side of a privately acquired looped belt, the shoulder straps attached to shoulders of the jacket, and the fancy shirt. The odd-looking hat is the 1872 issue campaign slouch, a disastrous piece of design which rapidly lost its shape under field conditions. It was provided with hooks and eyes along the edges of the brim so that it could be worn as illustrated, resembling a 'chapeau-bras', a small three-cornered silk hat which could be carried under the arm and worn by gentlemen at court or in full dress in the 18th century.

The trooper [3] wears the same hat flapped down, and a fatigue blouse made from an old 1861 dress frock-coat cut down—note the nine buttons. The trousers are heavily reinforced on the inside leg, as was normal for mounted troops. The carbine is the .45/70 issue weapon, still carried clipped to a cross-belt. Note that bandanas were personal items, and were of many different shades and patterns.

1. OFFICERS IN WINTER FIELD DRESS, 1870s–1880s
Officers provided themselves with a wide variety of fur and hide garments against the cold during the Indian Wars.

2. TROOPER, 10TH US CAVALRY, 1870s–1880s
A 'buffalo soldier' of the Negro 10th Cavalry, wearing the issue buffalo-hide winter coat over an old piped 1874 blouse and a privately acquired neckerchief.

3. BRIGADIER GENERAL GEORGE CROOK, 1870s–1880s
The Army's best Indian-fighting general had an individual taste in clothing for field duty. Here he wears his modified sky-blue cavalryman's overcoat, lined red and with a collar made from the pelt of a wolf he shot. In hot weather Crook often wore a weird-looking sun-helmet and a canvas jacket; since he frequently rode a mule and armed himself with a shotgun, he made a striking picture.

4. SERGEANT, NORTH-WEST MOUNTED POLICE, 1870s
The 'Mounties' enforced the Queen's peace north of the Canadian border during the period of the Indian Wars, with notable success. This NCO wears the 1873 uniform, apart from the corduroy trousers, more comfortable and hard-wearing for field dress than issue blues. Note the unusual cut of the front of the red tunic.

APACHE SCOUTS AND CAVALRY OFFICER, 1880s

The US Army made great use of Indian auxiliaries, and one of the major reasons for the defeat of the tribes was the willingness of warriors to fight alongside the white man against other clans and tribes. Scouts usually wore a mixture of Army and native dress; Army jackets were common, but Army trousers virtually unknown. The scout in the background [1] has obtained a recruit's lined fatigue blouse (only recruits received lined blouses) and has reversed it for camouflage in the bleached landscape of the South-West. The senior scout [2] wears the chevrons of a sergeant major in cavalry yellow, and the red head-cloth common among Apaches serving with the Army. The renegade prisoners [3] wears typical native dress; the officer [4] wears a fancy shirt with a plastron front, Indian leggings and a straw hat.

THE US ARMY, 1890–1920

The wool OD overseas cap with a blackened collar disc insignia. The caps have a vaguely Serbian look, although they were copied from a French model. [*Philip Katcher*]

In 1890 the US Army was still a small, introverted force whose mission was to protect Americans from harm, largely from hostile native Americans. Its infantry was armed with single-shot weapons that looked much like the weapons that the infantry of 1755 had used, and the cavalry still considered the sword a primary arm.

The army as a whole was spread in company-sized posts across the country, mostly in the West, with few units as large as a battalion being posted together. No general staff or even commander-in-chief position were authorized, and schools for training for higher commands were non-existent. In all, by 1895, the Army had 2,154 officers and 25,341 enlisted men on its rolls.

Thirty years later the US Army was a modern force, spread across the globe from Hawaii to occupied Germany and from the Philippines to Puerto Rico, and had fought five major campaigns overseas. Formal full divisions has been created, starting with a 'maneuver division' which had been assembled near San Antonio in March 1911. A commander-in-chief now actually commanded the Army and he had a professional general staff at his disposal. Officers were groomed for high command at several professional schools including the National War College (Fort McNair, Washington, DC, founded in November 1903), and the Command and General Staff College (Fort Leavenworth, Kansas). On 21 January 1903, too, the Congress began regulating the National Guard, calling for Federal inspections of the Guard and assigning regular officers for Guard training. In 1920 the Army's muster rolls listed 18,999 officers and 185,293 enlisted men.

By then weapons included airplanes, machine-guns and even a magazine-fed rifle, the M1903, that could be fitted with a semi-automatic firing mechanism (the Pedersen device). Personal equipment had been rationalized into a single system which could be adopted to fit

These cavalrymen appear to be part of an 1898 victory parade. They wear khaki uniforms on which the yellow has, typically, photographed black. [*Philip Katcher*]

individuals' needs with the M1910 equipment. Blue uniforms had been retired except for dress purposes, with khaki and olive drab uniforms becoming the standard field wear.

Nobody in 1890s could have predicted all of or even many of these changes; nor were they evident in the early years of this era. America's first war of the period, after all, did not take place far away from her shores. Indeed, before the Civil War many Southern congressmen called for an American annexation of Cuba as a new slave state, and America had long looked on her Southern neighbors as places for possible expansion.

So it was, when the battleship USS *Maine* was accidently blown up in Havana's harbor in 1898, that Americans all over the country demanded war against the unpopular Spanish regime in the island republic. The campaign in Cuba was short and victorious, with most volunteers never leaving their basic training camps before the war was over. What had not been expected was America's capture of much of the old Spanish Empire, including Puerto Rico and the Philippine Islands.

The Filipinos expected the Americans to give them their freedom, as had been done with Cuba, after the Spanish left, but when the Americans decided to retain control of the islands for use as a naval refueling station, the people continued fighting for their independence.

The war became a long, bleeding guerilla affair. But the American public and the Army seemed willing to pay whatever it cost in lives and treasure to retain the Philippines. Though the war was declared over on 4 July 1902, in fact it lasted until World War 2.

While many National Guardsmen still used single-shot breech-loaders, the regulars in Cuba and the

Philippines were equipped with a magazine-fed rifle, the Krag Jorgensen. This Danish weapon was first issued in 1892 and M1896 and M1898 models with slight changes followed.

Basic changes also came to the Army's handgun. The M1896 .36 caliber revolver had been in use, but it was said to produce too slight an impact to stop Filippino natives and a new Colt .45 revolver was ordered in large numbers, beginning in 1902. However, this weapon was rapidly replaced by the massive M1911 Colt .45 caliber automatic – a pistol that remained in the Army's inventory for more than 75 years.

Once Americans were fighting in the Philippines, it became an easy matter for them to join the other Western Powers in China when the Boxers began killing Westerners there in 1899. A small, Regular Army force participated in the taking of Beijing and the saving of embassy personnel there.

In 1916 a Mexican force under Pancho Villa, sometimes national leader and sometimes bandit, raided Columbus, New Mexico, and killed civilians and soldiers alike until the Army unit there drove them out. Brigadier General John Pershing was given a force made up of Regular Army and National Guard units to drive into Mexico, with the Mexican government's lukewarm cooperation, and capture Villa.

The campaign failed in that objective, but it gave the Army a great deal of experience at all levels as they fought the campaign with one eye over their shoulder towards Europe, where the greatest conflict since the Thirty Years War had broken out in 1914.

Troops in Mexico were armed with the M1903 rifle, a six-shot, 0.30 caliber gun based on the Mauser. An excellent design, this tough weapon saw service for 50 years, at first as the basic infantry arm and then as used by rear echelon troops and sharpshooters in World War 2. Color guards often still carry M1903 rifles today.

Because the Spanish-American War was so brief, most of the thousands of National Guard units that had been called up saw no service beyond training camps. In much

LEFT: Washington Volunteers under fire in Taonig, Philippines, in 1899. Note how conveniently the white smoke of their 45/70 Springfields locates them for the enemy. One, half sitting, wears braces. [*Philip Katcher*]

This interesting scene at the summer camp of the 9th Pennsylvania National Guard Regiment shows how seriously the men took their annual training. A company quartermaster sergeant, dressed, is at the left. The man on the right wears issue underwear. [*Philip Katcher*]

RIGHT: A French-made Renault light tank, with a crew of two and very slow speed, was the mainstay of American armor. George S. Patton, Jr. made his reputation as an armor commander during World War 1. [*Philip Katcher*]

the same way regular troops, were, in the main, the troops that fought the Philippine War for Independence, aided in putting down the Boxer Rebellion and hunted Pancho Villa.

But far more than the small Regular Army would be needed if America were to become involved in the great war in Europe. Initially, public opinion was against involvement, and 'he kept us out of war' was President Woodrow Wilson's successful election campaign slogan in 1916. But hardly had he been reelected when the German Navy sunk the *Lusitania*, a ship filled with Americans, while the German foreign office was discovered offering Mexico a great deal of American territory for going to war against the US. The United States went to war against Germany in 1916.

Even though the Army at the war's end numbered 3,685,458 officers and men, the American war effort on the field was tiny compared to that of Britain, France, Italy, Russia and the other Allies. In terms of boosting morale, however, fresh American troops and large amounts of matériel such as American grain made a significant contribution in defeating the Central Powers.

The war ended on 11 November 1918 when the American First Army was driving deep through German lines. General-of-the-Armies Pershing, still tanned from Mexico, was against stopping the fighting, wanting to take the war into Germany to show the people some of the destruction they had visited on Belgium and France. He was overruled, but lived long enough to see the horror that was World War 2 to some extent justify his position.

These troops man a captured German machine gun, with three German hand grenades next to their two-man foxhole. [*Philip Katcher*]

The 20th century brought a great number of changes to the US Army, some caused by new technology, some by new organizational needs. Heavier and heavier guns were devised for engaging warships from seacoast fortifications, for example. On 2 February 1901 a Coast Artillery Corps was formed as a separate organization from the Army's field artillery.

The Medical Department evolved more than most Army corps or departments. The Army Nurse Corps was created in 1901, the Army Dental Corps was authorized 3 March 1911, the Medical (Officers) Reserve Corps was set up in 1908, and a Veterinary Corps was initiated on 2 June 1916. The Sanitary Corps was organized from 30 June 1917 and this was reorganized as the Medical Administrative Corps three years later.

A War College Board was authorized on 27 November 1901 to study the problems of reserves and the idea of creating a general staff. The General Staff Corps, in charge of determining basic Army policy, was formed on 14 February 1903. Such an organization was a major step forward in putting the Army's affairs and forward planning on a professional basis. In addition, the Militia Bureau, in charge of all National Guard matters, was set up in 1916.

Tanks came into use and on 26 March 1918 the US Tank Corps was formed. This was to include a headquarters, three tank centers for training, two army tank headquarters and ten tank brigades. By 11 November 1918, the day the war ended, the Tank Corps included 1,090 officers and 14,780 enlisted men.

Since the Americans entered the War in Europe so late, they decided to use Allied tanks instead of attempting to design and manufacture their own. In September 1916 they chose the Renault FT-17 light tank and the British Mark V heavy tank. American factories were geared up to make these types, but only a handful were actually produced before the end of the war.

To fill the gap the Army gave a contract to Henry Ford to produce light tanks based on civilian Ford trucks and cars and propelled by two Model 'T' car engines, one for each tread. Each was armed with a single machine gun

and had a two-man crew. Other versions were fitted with 75 mm howitzers or carried cargo. Again, only a few were built before the war ended, but at least Americans gained experience in converting civilian motor plants into tank manufacturers.

The Chemical Warfare Service was authorized on 28 June 1918 to handle gas warfare, both devising toxic gases and their delivery systems and producing protective masks and clothing. It became a permanent branch of the Regular Army as the Chemical Corps on 1 July 1920. A Finance Department was created on 1 July 1920 to handle all Army money, including payrolls. Before that each Army corps or department had its own.

The Army had come a long way in 30 years. Thereafter it would stagnate, deprived of necessary funds by a tight-wad Congress who refused to see any need for a large standing Army, until world conflict once again changed the political and diplomatic climate.

Company E, 31st Infantry Regiment, marches down a street in Vladivostok, Russia, during the Allied 1918 occupation. Some of the men in the front ranks wear the M1918 BAR ammunition bearer's bandoleer. [*US Army*]

1. FIRST LIEUTENANT, CORPS OF ENGINEERS, 1893
The 1892 pattern dress coat worn here was changed in 1895 by eliminating the braid on the sleeves and across the chest. This lieutenant wears canvas and leather 'garrison shoes', which were worn for comfort on post. His sword is the 1860 staff officer's sword, the standard foot officer's edged weapon.

2. ORDNANCE SERGEANT, 1893
This Ordnance sergeant has six gold half-chevrons on each sleeve of his jacket, indicating extremely long service prior to his appointment. Ordnance sergeants were responsible for the maintenance and repair of all the weaponry on the post.

3. SERGEANT, 24TH INFANTRY REGIMENT, 1893
The 24th Infantry, which consisted of black enlisted men and white officers, had been founded in 1869. In 1893 the Regiment had been split into its companies and scattered all over New Mexico and Arizona, guarding Apaches on their reservations and settlers from Indian outbreaks. This soldier is armed with a single-shot Springfield and, indeed, looks very similar to soldiers who served in the Civil War 30 years before.

1. COMMISSARY SERGEANT, 71ST NEW YORK VOLUNTEER INFANTRY, 1898

The 71st was one of the few volunteer regiments to see action during the Spanish-American War. Before going to Cuba, however, they exchanged the awkward Merriam Patent Knapsacks shown here for the more comfortable blanket roll. The pack was designed with straps to cross the hips and supporting braces to take the weight off the shoulders and free the chest from constriction. The pack was divided into two compartments for clothing and rations, but despite its unique design features, it was universally hated and rarely used.

2. FIRST LIEUTENANT, 1ST MASSACHUSETTS ARTILLERY, 1898

The 1st Massachusetts did not see action in Cuba, though its officers did acquire the new khaki coats first issued during the Spanish-American War. Most officers wore similar uniforms with branch of service colors. The U.S.V. on the collar stands for United States Volunteers.

3. PRIVATE, INFANTRY, 1898

Virtually all infantrymen in the Cuban and Philippine Campaigns looked the same in their dark blue wool shirts, light blue trousers, and brownish hat and gaiters. Although better for hot climates, khaki uniforms were not generally available until after active campaigning. The weapon this soldier holds is the standard M1898 .30 caliber Krag-Jörgensen rifle.

1. MAJOR, MILITARY SECRETARY'S DEPARTMENT, 1905

This major wears the cap introduced in 1905, the coat introduced in 1895 and the sword introduced in 1903. The Military Secretary's Department was created from the Adjutant General's Department in 1904 and lasted until it was again named the Adjutant General's Department in 1907. The shield on this major's collar indicates his Department membership.

2. LIEUTENANT COLONEL, SIGNAL CORPS, 1905

The 1902 dress regulations specified khaki unforms for all occasions except 'dress'. This officer wears the coat authorized in 1903, which lacked any branch of service colors. His collar badge was first worn in 1863, when the Signal Corps was organized.

3. SQUADRON SERGEANT MAJOR, 1ST CAVALRY, 1905

The 1st Cavalry was formed in 1833 as the US Regiment of Dragoons. During the period 1890–1920, it received battle honors for Santiago (1898) and Luzon, Philippines (1901–02). The sergeant's sabre is the M1860 light cavalry sabre.

1. CAPTAIN, QUARTERMASTER GENERAL'S DEPARTMENT, 1915

The various branches of service colors were shown on the officer's full dress uniform on the hat, sword-belt and coat collar. Another row of cuff lace was added for each rank higher. The auguillette was only authorized for officers of the General Staff Corps and permanent and detailed officers of the Adjutant General's and Inspector General's Departments, aides-de-camp, regimental adjutants, artillery district adjutants, engineer battalion adjutants and military attachés, such as this officer.

2. COLOR SERGEANT, INFANTRY, SOUTH CAROLINA NATIONAL GUARD, 1915

All enlisted men wore basically the same dress uniforms, with branch of service colored trim. State National Guardsmen were marked by their state initials on their coat collars. By this time, the chevron situation had grown quite confusing with many corps, such as the Medical and Signal Corps, using special chevrons with unique markings. However, standard grades, such as color sergeant, wore the same chevrons throughout the US Army.

3. BRIGADIER GENERAL, 1915

All mounted officers wore breeches and boots for full dress. The sash marked the rank among general officers; major generals wore their sashes across the body from the right shoulder to the left side and not extended around the waist. The sword is the standard M1903 officer's sabre, carried by all US Army officers.

1. BATTERY QUARTERMASTER SERGEANT, 1ST BATTALION, 4TH REGIMENT OF FIELD ARTILLERY (MOUNTAIN), 1916

The 4th Regiment Field Artillery was organized in 1907 and its 1st Battalion was on the Mexican border when Pancho Villa raided Columbus, New Mexico in March 1916. It was then sent into Mexico to capture Villa, whose *Villistas* had killed civilians, looted and burned before being driven off by the 13th Cavalry. This sergeant is armed with a Colt automatic pistol and an M1903 Springfield rifle. The hat cord indicates the branch of service.

2. FIRST LIEUTENANT, 1916

When wearing the shirt as the outer garment, as was the practise in the campaign against Pancho Villa, the officer's branch of service could not be told. Indeed, the second lieutenant, who did not have a rank badge but wore plain officer's dress, would wear no insignia at all save his gold and black hat cord that would mark him as an officer.

3. COLONEL, INSPECTOR GENERAL'S DEPARTMENT, 1916

The all-white uniform was worn as a dress uniform in hot climates. The duties of officers of the Inspector General's Department, as defined in 1865, were to inspect 'all matters pertaining to the military art of having interest in a military point of view'. They made sure that company funds were not misused, that the men were treated fairly and that all public property was accounted for.

1. FIRST SERGEANT, 88TH INFANTRY DIVISION, 1918

The 88th Division came from Illinois, Iowa, Minnesota and North Dakota. This sergeant has armed himself with the short-bladed trench knife with its ribbed guard which was intended for use in hand-to-hand combat. He is armed with both an automatic pistol and an M1903 Springfield.

2. MECHANIC, 79TH INFANTRY DIVISION, 1918

While we have shown shoulder insignia on all World War 1 figures, this was generally not authorized until the war was almost over and, in fact, the vast majority of units never wore such insignia until after the hostilities. Yet it is worth noting that some unit insignia was worn that was not all like the insignia generally associated with the unit today. Different elements of many divisions wore different insignia from each other. For example, the best-known 79th patch includes a white Cross of Lorraine on a blue shield edged in white. However, this variation was also worn within the division in 1918. The 79th was recruited in Pennsylvania, Maryland and the District of Columbia.

3. CAPTAIN, ARTILLERY, 83RD INFANTRY DIVISION, 1918

The 83rd (Ohio) Division was recruited in Ohio and western Pennsylvania. All Army officers wore essentially the same uniform as did enlisted men, save for the worsted lace stripe on each cuff. The russet brown Sam Browne belt was adopted by officers of the American Expeditionary Force (AEF) in Europe to bring them into line with all other Allied officers.

1. CAPTAIN, 1918
The officer's overcoat came with an Austrian knot on the cuff that indicated rank. One more braid was added for each higher rank. These braids were made in black, dark brown and a khaki that matched the coat color, according to the individual officer's taste. The coat buttons were a hard, translucent plastic without design on their fronts.

2. REGIMENTAL SUPPLY SERGEANT, 371ST R.I.U.S. DE LA 157ME DIVISION 'GOYBET', 1918
This soldier is in one of four American regiments (369th–372nd) which served with the French Army. The men wore their American uniforms but were issued French weapons and accoutrements, such as the 'Berthier' M1916 rifle this sergeant holds. The metal canister holds his French gasmask. The men of the 371st were awarded their shoulder patch for service with a French colonial division at Verdun, where the regiment lost a third of its men in action. Enlisted men and many officers were coloured, hence their French commander nicknaming them 'my Black Watch'.

3. COMPANY SUPPLY SERGEANT, MILITARY POLICE COMPANY, SECOND ARMY HEADQUARTERS, 1918.
The US Army did not have any official military police unit especially trained for that duty until the AEF set up its own Military Police Force 15 October 1917. Most MPs wore black brassards with 'MP' in white outlined letters, though some wore red Roman letters 'MP'. Others wore red brassards with black letters. The sergeant is armed with a Colt New Service revolver; the pouch on his front hip contains six clips of three .45 caliber rounds each.

1. MILITARY AVIATOR, VII CORPS AERO SERVICE, 1918

On 27 October 1917 it was ordered that military aviators were to wear two silver wings with a shield and a star above the shield. Junior and reserve military aviators lacked the star and observers wore only one wing. At that time aviators were in the Signal Corps and wore that corps' collar insignia; the wings and propeller collar badge was adopted in June 1918. This man's silver wings on his right cuff indicated that he is a flying instructor, while the two chevrons indicate a year of overseas service. He also wears a watch bracelet, a leather strap holding a pocket watch on his wrist for convenience. This practise became widespread during World War 1 although it was uncommon before that.

2. FIRST LIEUTENANT, 310TH ENGINEERS, 1919

For some Americans the war was not over when the Armistice was signed. In August 1918 the 1st Battalion of the 310th Engineers, along with other troops, was sent to North Russia to aid troops fighting the Bolshevik government which had overthrown the Czar and their struggle continued until 1919. Their equipment was a mixture of British and American, but neither was totally effective against the Russian cold and improvizations were made. This officer's coat, based on one worn by a lieutenant in the regiment's Co. B, has the standard Austrian braid that indicates his rank. The 'polar bear' shoulder insignia was authorized on 11 June 1919. Most examples were silkscreened but some were cut from white flannel and sewn onto blue backgrounds.

3. COMPANY MESS SERGEANT, 339TH INFANTRY REGIMENT, 1919

The 339th, a Michigan National Guard Regiment, was in the Russian AEF in 1918–19. Some of its companies had plain white helmets, while others wore the elaborate and colorful camouflage patterns used on the Western Front. Both has the word 'RUSSIA' stencilled on their helmet tops when they returned to the United States in 1919. The 339th had a welcome home parade in Detroit on 4 July 1919, and wore special brassards for the occasion.

THE US ARMY IN WORLD

The years between 1918 and 1940, when war seemed possible if not likely, were barren ones for the US Army. It had been reduced in terms of both men and dollars to the point where it very little real preparation for a war the size of World War 2. There had been some technical development, such as on an 'automatic musket', but the results were slow getting into the troops' hands, and as late as 1939 only 1.2% of the Army's budget went to research and development.

After Hitler's invasion of Poland and the Japanese invasion of China, however, most responsible military and government officials foresaw that America would have to fight again sooner or later, and army troop level authorizations were raised. In 1940 the US Army had a total of 269,023 officers and men in its ranks; in 1945 it had 8,267,958. World War 2 would make a giant of the US Army.

Americans faced the prospect of war reluctantly, as they had in 1916. There were strong 'American First' elements in the country who felt that quarrels between European and Asian countries were none of their affair. But President Franklin Roosevelt, personally siding with the British against the Germans and aghast at Japanese attempts to steamroller over Asia, began a slow, steady build up of America's armed forces.

By 1943 Kendall Banning, an American journalist, would write in a book describing that era's Army: 'Today it is the largest and the most powerful Army this country has ever known. It is the best-equipped, the best-trained, the best-clad, the best-housed, the best-fed, and the best-paid Army in the world. It has attained this commanding position through rapid and sweeping changes and improvements in its organization, its war material, its training methods and its combat technique.'

Even given some of the doubtful claims of wartime hype, it is true that the World War 2 US Army was among the best the country ever fielded and in some ways the best in the world at the time. This was true partly, as Banning said, because of organization and materiel; but it was also true because of the fact that by then the country was almost wholly behind its men in uniform.

Indeed, after 7 December 1941, when Japanese forces struck the US Pacific Fleet at Pearl Harbor, Hawaii, no American could avoid the fight any longer. Once again the US was at war and all thoughts of 'America first' were lost in a national cry to 'Win The War'.

Jointly, the Allies decided to turn their attention to Germany first, then Japan. General-of-the-Army Dwight D. Eisenhower, an American, was given command of the new European Theater of Operations, leading the Allied troops into North Africa and Italy in 1942 and France in 1944. The Germans fought bravely and well, but were unable to withstand the combined might of America and Britain, especially when pressed ever harder on the Eastern Front by the Soviet Union. By 25 April 1945 US and Russian forces met on German soil near Torgau, and on 7 May 1945 Germany surrendered.

In the Asian theater Marines had landed on the Pacific island of Guadalcanal on 7 August 1942. There, later reinforced by US Army units, they stood off a number of Japanese attacks to hand the Empire of the Rising Sun its first defeat. It was only one in a string of defeats as American Marines and soldiers hopscotched from island to island in a drive towards the Japanese homeland. Marines landed on Saipan on 25 June 1944 and on Guam on 21 July, giving the Allies airports from which their bombers could reach Japan itself.

The finishing touch was provided, however, by the Army Air Force, which delivered the first atomic bombs in the world on Japanese targets, Hiroshima (6 August 1945) and Nagasaki (9 August) – bombs that had been developed under command of an Army general, Leslie Groves. Japan sued for peace on 10 August 1945.

The atomic bombs that finished off Japan and ushered a new era into the world were only one of the many

WAR 2, 1941–1945

technological advances the Army made during the period. At the other end of the scale the basic infantry longarm American soldiers and Marines carried was by far the best used by any army. This M1 rifle, a 0.30 caliber, semi-automatic, gas-operated, eight-round weapon that had been adopted in 1936, saw service in three wars – World War 2, Korea and Vietnam.

American tanks were not quite as superior as the M1. The M3, the first medium tank in general use, used a 75 mm gun in a sponson on one side, with a 37 mm gun in the turret. The weapon displayed a high profile, with its gun given only a limited sideways range.

The M3 was replaced by the M4, better known as the Sherman, which became the Army's standard battle tank. It also used a 75 mm gun, but in the upper turret. This gun was lightweight compared to German armament, but American armor often overcame German resistance through sheer volume rather than armor strength. A 76 mm gun later replaced the 75 mm gun, which was a slight improvement.

America's best known and loved vehicle, however, was not a weapon of war but the jeep. Originally called a 'peep', the jeep seated four men, including a driver, in something that only approached comfort. It had four-wheel drive so off-road driving in rough terrain was no real problem for it. Jeeps were used as command vehicles, weapons carriers, ambulances, ammunition

and cargo carriers – and virtually anything else men from a car-crazy country could come up with.

Army organization also changed to meet new needs. The last mounted cavalry command was dismounted in 1942, for example with armored troops receiving the old cavalry unit designations.

As the Army conquered territory, it found populations unable to govern themselves, in areas with destroyed infrastructures. Soldiers became governors. The Army had set up a School of Military Government at the

The paratrooper carried a massive personal load during the jump, since resupply was so uncertain. Two comrades help this paratrooper secure backpack harness and equipment before adding the chest reserve rig which can be seen at left foreground. Above the musette bag slung in front of his groin is a Thompson SMG with two box magazines taped along its length. The first-aid packet is taped to the front of the helmet net, where it can be ripped off instantly if needed. Note (left) national flag patch, and holster for the folding-stock M1A1 carbine; and (right) leather shoulder holster for a .45in. pistol. [*US Army*]

Troops on maneuvers in Australia in March 1943, displaying typical tropical field dress. Shirts are worn outside the trousers with rolled sleeves, and trousers are not always tucked into leggings. [*US Army*]

A wide assortment of gear is carried by these 29th Infantry Division troops near Brest, France, in 1944. [*US Army via Shelby Stanton*]

University of Virginia, Charlottesville, on 11 May 1942. And the Civil Affairs Division, which took over the school and troops it trained, was created on 1 March 1943.

The Medical Department continued to expand. A branch of Medical Department Dietitians was created in 1942 (though disbanded in 1943), and physical therapists were given their own branch within the Medical Department. The Pharmacy Corps was formed on 12 July 1943.

As the Army grew huge a higher number of bad elements came into its ranks. Many men convicted of minor crimes were given the choice of the Army or gaol. Other criminal elements were picked up by the draft, the mandatory conscription that was in effect. At the same time, police methods had improved to the point where police specialists were necessary to detect criminals.

In the past US field armies had raised their own local provost marshal departments, sometimes with assigned individuals and sometimes with whole units being assigned the duty. This type of hit-or-miss effort would not work in 1941, however, and in August 1941 the Provost Marshal's Office and a Corps of Military Police were set up.

Around the same time as the Military Police were created, the Army organized a Tank Destroyer Corps for anti-tank warfare, with a Tank Destroyer Center established at Fort Meade, Maryland, in February 1942. By the end of World War 2, however, it was seen that tanks were in fact the best anti-tank weapons, along with hand-held infantry-used rocket launchers, and so the Tank Destroyer Corps passed out of existence by the war's end.

In the past, too, the Quartermaster Department had been responsible for transporting men and equipment. But with all the overseas shipping involved in World War 2, the job simply became too big to be just one part of the Quartermaster Department. In March 1942 transportation responsibilities were given to a new Service of Supply branch, an arrangement altered on 31 July 1942 when the Transportation Corps was organized.

Since so many people were required in the defense effort for a war embracing two oceans and every

The front-line GI: heating up a snatched meal on a field cooker, this squad wear the M1941 field jacket and, over their OD wool trousers, the trousers of the grayish-green herringbone twill fatigue suit as improvised combat dress. Most men have the web chinstrap of the helmet fixed above the rear lip of the shell and a narrow leather chinstrap from the fiber liner fixed over the front lip. [*US Army*]

continent in the world, men alone would not be able to do all the jobs necessary. Women had seen service in World War 1 as telephone operators and, before that, as nurses, so it was no great leap for the Army to establish the Woman's Army Auxiliary Corps on 14 May 1942. The word 'auxiliary' was dropped on 1 July 1943 when the Corps became a component of the Regular Army. By the war's end, 8,000 WACs had served in Europe and 5,500 in the Southwest Pacific (most in postal units). The Army Air Force got most of the WACs in fact; a total of 40,000 of them.

In June 1940 the Army created a test platoon of infantry parachute troops. They proved successful enough for the Army to authorize the 1st Parachute Regiment on 16 September 1940. The 82nd Infantry Division, which had been activated 25 April 1942, was made wholly airborne. It was followed by the 101st Airborne Division (15 August 1942), the 11th Airborne Division (25 February 1943), the 13th Airborne Division (13 August 1943) and the 17th Airborne Division (15 April 1943). Each division included one glider infantry regiment as well as parachute troops.

The highly trained, all-volunteer airborne troops proved themselves to be among the best in the Army. Their defense of Bastogne during the Battle of the Bulge, when completely surrounded, was one of the Army's shining moments of the entire war.

Although Germany and Japan surrendered in 1945, genuine peace still seemed distant. American soldiers were not dying on battlefields, but a dedicated international Communist movement began trying to turn peoples and governments to its system. A Soviet Union

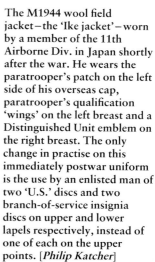

The M1944 wool field jacket – the 'Ike jacket' – worn by a member of the 11th Airborne Div. in Japan shortly after the war. He wears the paratrooper's patch on the left side of his overseas cap, paratrooper's qualification 'wings' on the left breast and a Distinguished Unit emblem on the right breast. The only change in practise on this immediately postwar uniform is the use by an enlisted man of two 'U.S.' discs and two branch-of-service insignia discs on upper and lower lapels respectively, instead of one of each on the upper points. [*Philip Katcher*]

which distrusted the West, comprised mostly of former allies, set up an array of Communist-run buffer states all along its borders and set the scene for four decades of 'Cold War'.

The result was that, while millions of American soldiers were demobilized, the draft continued to refill the Army's ranks, and the Army itself stayed on more of a wartime footing than it ever had after any of its previous wars. Wartime organizations, instead of being folded as many of them had been in the past, were this time continued.

Both one-piece (center) and two-piece camouflage-printed combat fatigues are worn in this photo of US infantry on Bougainville, winter 1943: these may be men of the 3rd Marine or the 37th Infantry divisions. Very light personal equipment is carried and trousers flap loose at the ankle; note also cotton clip bandoliers slung round the center soldier – the most popular and practical way to carry rifle ammunition. [*US Army*]

1. SECOND LIEUTENANT, 1941

The short overcoat for commissioned officers was first authorized in 1926. It could be worn only on military bases, and not for ceremonies or official duties; and if the troops were dressed in their long overcoats, the officers had to follow suit. However, the short overcoat could be worn in the field or when mounted, and it was ideal for riding—this officer's riding breeches and boots indicate service with a mounted branch, either cavalry or field artillery. The branch is not otherwise identified, since only rank insignia—here, the gold bar of second lieutenant—are worn on the coat.

2. TECHNICAL SERGEANT, 9TH INFANTRY, 2ND INFANTRY DIVISION, 1941

Obviously a World War 1 veteran, this man holds the second highest non-commissioned officer's pay grade, indicated by the chevrons on both upper sleeves. His embroidered left shoulder patch identifies the 2nd Infantry Division, while the gilt badges on each lower lapel identify the 9th Infantry Regiment, assigned to that formation. His upper lapel insignia carry 'U.S.' above '9' on his right, and the crossed-rifles infantry branch badge on his left. His ribbons include a Silver Star, awarded for bravery; a Purple Heart, for suffering a wound; and the rainbow ribbon of the World War 1 Victory Medal. Under them is pinned an Expert's Badge, the top shooting award, with clasps for pistol and rifle.

The 2nd Infantry Division was to land in Normandy on 7 June 1944; fighting their way across Europe, they reached the German-Czech border by VE-Day, their last action being the capture of Pilsen.

3. LIEUTENANT COLONEL, GENERAL STAFF, 1941

The officer's service uniform was of dark olive drab, although trousers of a light shade, known as 'pinks', could also be worn with this cap and coat. The russet-brown M1921 'Sam Browne' belt was worn until 1943, officially, although it was often abandoned before that date. On 26 November 1942 a belt of the same material as the coat, with a brass buckle, was authorized to be sewn to the waist of the coat, replacing the Sam Browne, which was forbidden from 7 June 1943.

This officer wears the insignia of the General Staff on his lower lapels. The silver oak leaves of this rank are worn on both shoulder straps.

1. PRIVATE FIRST CLASS, ORDNANCE CORPS, PACIFIC THEATER OF OPERATIONS, LATE 1941

The Army's khaki 'chino' shirt and trousers were designed originally to serve both as summer service dress and field uniform. In practice it saw service as a field uniform only in the Pacific Theater and in exercises in the US early in the war, being replaced by specialized combat uniforms.

2. MAJOR, 4TH ENGINEERS, 4TH INFANTRY DIVISION, 1941

The overseas cap, worn in France in 1917–18, was then abandoned until 22 August 1933, when it was revived for use by tank and mechanized cavalry units. Originally officers wore authorized piping in corps colors, while enlisted men wore unpiped caps; on 19 April 1940 all officers below general rank were ordered to wear intermixed black and gold campaign hat cords and overseas cap piping, and enlisted men wore corps-colored piping thereafter. Officers of the Corps of Engineers were unique in wearing special coat buttons—all others wore the standard button bearing the Arms of the United States.

3. MASTER SERGEANT, 59TH COAST ARTILLERY; UNITED STATES, 1941

The Coast Artillery Corps had the task of attacking enemy naval vessels with artillery and submarine mines, and enemy aircraft with A/A fire. The campaign hat was the standard field headgear in the United States except among armored and airborne troops, who wore the flat overseas cap.

4. COLONEL, 2ND CAVALRY REGIMENT, 2ND CAVALRY DIVISION, NORTH AFRICA, 1944

The 2nd Cavalry Division had been inactivated on 15 July 1942, but was re-activated on 25 February 1944, with all black enlisted men. It was sent to North Africa on 9 March 1944 and performed garrison duties until the end of the war.

The overseas cap also came in khaki cotton chino, edged in the same colors as the olive drab winter-weight wool cap. On 25 August 1942 officers were ordered to substitute, for the distinctive unit insignia previously worn, their rank insignia; enlisted men retained unit insignia. The ranking of a colonel was a silver eagle, always worn so as to face forward.

1. FIRST SERGEANT, 28TH INFANTRY DIVISION, 1942–43

The NCO on field exercises wears combat uniform which was to be typical of the European theater. The M1 steel helmet, first authorized in November 1941, was usually worn with the chinstrap hooked up over the rear lip out of the wearer's way. The 1941 pattern wool knit cap or 'beanie', authorized on 14 August 1942, could be worn under the helmet, with its rear flap folded down over the ears in cold weather. The olive drab field jacket, of (theoretically) water-repellant and wind-resistant cotton cloth, was first authorized on 10 November 1941.

Pennsylvania's National Guard, the 28th Inf. Div., was to land in France on 22 July 1944. It was badly mauled in the Hürtgen Forest that winter, and its last combat was the drive on the Ahr on 6 March 1945.

2. FIRST LIEUTENANT, 8TH INFANTRY DIVISION, 1942

The officer's overcoat was first authorized in 1926. The buttons were of bone. Ranking, here the single silver bar of first lieutenant, was worn on the shoulder straps, and the formation patch on the left upper sleeve. These trousers are of the light olive drab shade known as 'pinks'.

The 8th Inf. Div. was to land on Utah Beach, Normandy, on 4 July 1944. It went on to fight throughout the NW Europe campaign, its final battles coming with the destruction of German forces in the Ruhr Pocket in mid-April 1945.

3. CORPORAL, 1ST CAVALRY DIVISION, 1942

The coat worn here is the 1942 pattern mackinaw, first authorized on 26 November 1942; NCO chevrons and left shoulder formation patches were applied. The three-strap leather boots for mounted men replaced the laced type worn previously from mid-1940. The rifle is the recently-issued M1; as a mounted man this corporal also carries an automatic pistol, in the usual russet holster on the right hip, with two spare clips in the web pouch slipped over the rifle belt at front left.

The 1st Cav. Div. arrived in Australia on 11 July 1943 and first saw combat in the landing on Los Negros Island on 29 February 1944. The division formed part of the invasion force which landed on Leyte on 20 October 1944, and fought in the Philippines until active operations there ended, officially, on 1 July 1945.

1. SERGEANT, 45TH INFANTRY DIVISION, NORTH AFRICA, 1943

The one-piece herringbone twill overalls were authorized for field use on 5 April 1941. They were supposed to be worn over another uniform, like the khaki cotton chino shirt and trousers, but were usually worn by themselves, tucked into the web leggings. This NCO wears full marching equipment with pack, including the large gasmask case worn under the left arm by straps round the waist and over the right shoulder; in practise this item rarely survived for long once soldiers reached the combat zone. The rifle is the M1 Garand. The divisional patch is worn on the left shoulder and chevrons on both upper sleeves.

2. TECHNICIAN FOURTH GRADE, 51ST SIGNAL CORPS, FRANCE, 1944

Although photographers were found on the tables of organization of many types of unit, the Signal Corps was officially responsible for all the Army's photographic efforts. This photographer's overseas cap is therefore piped in Signal Corps orange and white, and he wears on it the distinctive insignia of his unit, the 51st Signal Corps. The overcoat was designed for both field and dress wear, but was not very popular in the field as it became heavy when wet and muddy. The shoulder patch is that of 3rd Army, activated in August 1944, and commanded by Lt. Gen. George S. Patton Jr. during its famous dash across France and forcing of the Rhine.

3. BRIGADIER GENERAL, SERVICE OF SUPPLY, 1942

The mission of the SOS was to provide services and supplies to meet the military requirements of all but the Army Air Forces, which had unique requirements. As a full general officer this brigadier general wears all-gold pipings on his overseas cap. A single silver star marks his rank, and is worn on the cap, the shoulders of his model A2 Army Air Force leather crew jacket (a desirable item, acquired through the unauthorized channels for which SOS personnel were famous), and both points of the OD wool shirt collar—general officers wore only rank and not corps badges on the collar. Over the shirt he wears the olive drab knitted wool jacket intended for wear under the 1941 field jacket. The Services of Supply patch is sewn to the left shoulder of the crew jacket.

1

2

3

PRIVATE, US CAVALRY, 1942

Strange as it may seem, mounted cavalry did not die quickly; even the sabre was not eliminated as an issued weapon until 1934, and it was not until 9 March 1942 that the office of the Chief of Cavalry was eliminated, with the 2nd Cavalry Division remaining mounted until March 1944. Even as late as November 1944 some serious consideration was being given to using mounted cavalry against the Japanese.

This trooper wears the cotton herringbone twill fatigue combat uniform, over an OD shirt and riding breeches and the boots seen in more detail on page 123, with the steel helmet. Practising the 'pistol charge', he holds his .45 caliber automatic, its butt secured by a lanyard passing diagonally around his body from right armpit to left shoulder; the doubling was held in the desired place by a russet leather slide. He wears the web rifle belt and braces, with the long bayonet scabbarded diagonally behind his shoulder, attached to the right hand brace. The saddle is the Model 1928 McClellan, basically the same as used before the Civil War of 1861–65, with Model 1940 wooden stirrups.

1. TECHNICIAN THIRD GRADE, TANK BATTALION, 102ND INFANTRY DIVISION, FRANCE, 1944

Armored units were attached to each US infantry division, and this figure represents a crewman from the division's Sherman tank battalion.

Specialized clothing for armored units began to appear in 1941 with the introduction of this waist-length, weatherproofed cotton tanker's jacket. With its blanket lining and knit wool cuffs, collar and waistband it was a comfortable and popular item, much sought-after by officers and men of other branches.

2. TECHNICIAN FIFTH GRADE, 94TH INFANTRY DIVISION, GERMANY, 1945

By the Geneva Convention medical personnel were non-combatants and should not have been targets. They wore regulation brassards and marked their helmets—usually with red crosses on white discs, but in some units with the crosses simply outlined in white. These precautions did not prevent many medics from being shot, however, and the Germans claimed that they were not sufficiently visible.

3. STAFF SERGEANT, 17TH AIRBORNE DIVISION, BELGIUM, 1944

Specialized equipment for airborne troops included the M1942 jump jacket and trousers, sometimes worn alone, sometimes over other combat clothing. This suit had extra-large pockets for equipment, and tie-tapes from the inside leg seams helped control these when they were swollen out with rations, ammunition and all the other necessities carried on a drop. The cloth used for this suit tended toward a khaki shade; subsequent reinforcement of knees and elbows with cloth from other sources sometimes gave a strongly contrasting 'patchwork' effect. The russet 'Corcoran' jump boots laced all the way up the ankle and lower calf, and no gaiters were needed.

The web pistol belt is worn here, in preference to the rifle belt; a more flexible mix of items could be attached to it, an important factor for paratroopers. This NCO is armed with the M1A1 folding-stock carbine; its double clip pouch is slipped over the belt at front left. A first-aid packet is worn at front right, a canteen at right rear, and an entrenching tool at left rear.

1. PRIVATE FIRST CLASS, ALAMO SCOUTS, US 6TH ARMY, PACIFIC THEATER, 1944

The Alamo Scouts were organized by 6th Army headquarters in late 1943 and trained to penetrate deep into Japanese-held territory. Their first action was a reconnaissance of Los Negros Island on 27–28 February 1944. They later formed part of a force which freed 516 Allied prisoners of war from Cabanatuan prison camp, 25 miles behind enemy lines on the Philippines.

Their dress was basically the same as that worn by all combat soldiers in the Pacific: two-piece herringbone twill utility fatigues. This soldier's weapon is the Thompson sub-machine gun.

2. PRIVATE 17TH ARMORED ENGINEER BATTALION, 2ND ARMORED DIVISION, NORMANDY, 1944

The US Army did much work in developing camouflaged uniforms, and an early type issued to some units in the Pacific in 1942 was of this pattern but made in one piece, supported by a system of internal braces. It was not a sucess, its one-piece design being highly unsuitable for men fighting in a climate where digestive disorders were frequent. This two-piece suit, which has a similar design in shades of brown and tan on the inside for use on beaches, lasted slightly longer; but the Marines complained that they made the wearer even more visible when he was moving, and they were withdrawn in favour of the plain olive drab fatigues.

During the fighting in the densely-wooded Normandy *bocage* country this engineer battalion was issued with the camouflage uniform shown here; it was as unpopular in the ETO as it had been in the Pacific, having the added disadvantage of similarity to the clothing worn by Waffen-SS troops in that Campaign. The personal equipment of this GI, shown loading his M1 Garand, is otherwise conventional.

3. SECOND LIEUTENANT, 81ST INFANTRY DIVISION, PACIFIC THEATER, 1944

The two-piece herringbone twill fatigues are worn with rolled sleeves, and trouser legs hanging loose over the boots. No insignia of any kind were worn in the field: Japanese snipers were rightly feared, and officers and NCOs were priority targets.

1. FIRST SERGEANT, 1ST SPECIAL SERVICE FORCE, ETO, 1944

The last SSF was an outfit unique in the US Army. Including both Canadians and Americans, it was organized for 'Project Plough', a plan to raid enemy plants in Norway or Italy in winter 1943, to keep the Germans on their toes and guessing about the actual target of the Allies' invasion. The 1st SSF participated in the airborne assault on Kiska, Alaska, and after transfering to the ETO they fought in the Naples–Foggia and Rome–Arno areas before taking part in the landings in the South of France. The unit was de-activated on 5 December 1944, Canadians returning to their own army and Americans going into other airborne and infantry units. This young NCO wears the typical airborne-trained soldier's uniform, including the proud distinction of tucking the dress trousers of the OD wool uniform into jump boots.

2. TECHNICIAN FIFTH GRADE, MILITARY POLICE, III CORPS, GERMANY, 1945

The Model 1943 field jacket and matching trousers were adopted in response to complaints about the poor quality of the M1941 jacket. Of wind-resistant and water-repellant cotton cloth, it was in an olive drab shade generally of a stronger green than the M1941 jacket. First issued in 1943 to troops of the 3rd Inf. Div. in Italy, it was increasingly available in NW Europe during the last year of the war, but it never entirely replaced the earlier items; both styles were seen together, sometimes mixed in the same man's kit, right up to VE-Day.

This military policeman is assigned to the MP company of III Corps, as shown by the triangular left shoulder patch representing a caltrop, an ancient anti-cavalry device. The brassard was regulation for all MPs, while the helmet was sometimes marked as illustrated, sometimes only with the letters 'MP', and sometimes left plain; in rear areas helmets were painted all white. High-visibility markings were important, since a primary duty was traffic direction near the front, often under fire.

3. CAPTAIN, 32ND ARMOR, 3RD ARMORED DIVISION, GERMANY, 1945

This battalion medical officer wears the M1944 wool field jacket—the 'Ike jacket'—first suggested by Gen. Eisenhower in May 1943 as a garment for both combat and dress use, like the British battledress. In practice the jacket was largely reserved for dress use.

US Army Rangers & LRRP

The 1st Rangers seen at Achnacarry Castle in July 1942. Left to right: Lt. Col. William Darby, 1st Rangers CO; Lt.Col. M. E. Vaughn, Commando Depot Commander; Brig. Gen. Lucian Truscott, the Army Chief of Staff's Ranger project officer; Maj. Max. Schneider, 1st Rangers XO (later 5th Rangers XO and CO). [*US Army*]

On 1 June 1942 the Army's Chief of Staff ordered yet another new organization to be set up, an 'American Commando' unit. Exploits of the British Commandos filled the papers and the Americans wanted to have the same type of offensive capability.

The title of commando was, however, too British and instead the Army chose to name their new unit after the ranging companies formed during the Seven Years War along the Western frontiers. On 19 June 1942 the 1st Ranger Battalion was activated in Northern Ireland, where it received British commando training.

A 2nd Ranger Battalion was formed and trained in the US in April 1943. The 3rd Ranger Battalion was drawn from volunteers and 1st Battalion members in North Africa; it was to be attached to the 3rd Infantry Division during the invasion of Sicily. The 4th Ranger Battalion

was organized in May 1943 in the same way as the 3rd, and attached to the 1st Infantry Division during the Sicilian invasion. The 5th Ranger Battalion was activated in September 1943 in Camp Forrest, Tennessee. The 6th Ranger Battalion was formed in New Guinea on 20 August 1944 from officers and men of the 98th Field Artillery Battalion.

The 1st, 3rd and 4th Battalions were badly battered in Italy and were disbanded there in 1944. Some of the men were assigned to the 1st Special Service Force, an élite mixed Canadian-American force. Others returned to the US to act as training personnel. The 2nd Battalion was disbanded in Czechoslovakia and the 5th Battalion in Austria in early June 1944. After seeing action in the Philippines, the 6th Battalion was disbanded in Kyoto, Japan, on 30 December 1945.

Generally, a Ranger battalion had about 538 officers and men in six line and one headquarters company. Each company had two rifle platoons with an additional mortar and a headquarters and service platoon. Two squads made up each rifle platoon.

Besides the official Ranger battalions, many infantry divisions raised their own squads of Rangers for reconnaissance and patroling. These units were not authorized to wear unique insignia, although many of them did, nor did they receive full Ranger training.

The Ranger concept died in the cost-cutting moves after World War 2, but the Korean War would again show the need for Ranger-trained soldiers. The Ranger Training Command was formed on 17 October 1951 and between 1950 and 1951, 14 independent Ranger Infantry Companies were organized. The companies were attached to divisions.

The 1st, 5th, 6th, 7th and 8th Ranger Infantry Companies were sent to Korea to be attached to divisions fighting there. They suffered fearful losses – so many that, considering a new branch, the Special Forces, could take over basic Ranger duties, the Army disbanded all Ranger companies in 1951. Instead, two highly classified companies, the 8240th and 8242nd Army

Ranger students paddle an inflatable Zodiac boat down the Yellow River – Camp Rudder, Eglin Air Force Base, Florida. [*US Army*]

UNITS, 1942–1990

Units, were given basic reconnaissance and raiding duties.

Special Ranger schooling for airborne volunteers was offered to individuals thereafter. In April 1957 a veteran of World War 2's 4th Ranger Battalion, James Altieri, visited the Ranger Training Command in Fort Benning, Georgia. He reported it was 'turning out 1,500 tough, spirited, resourceful Rangers every year'. He went on: 'Each Ranger, after receiving his training, goes back to his own outfit and helps infuse it with his spirit and know-how. The entire Army benefits. Eventually every unit in the Army will have a hard core of daring, spirited combat leaders, imbued with the same qualities of initiative and valor that [Colonel William] Darby [the first US Ranger commander] inspired in his original troopers.'

Starting in February 1969, independent Ranger Companies that had been formed mostly in Vietnam – except for Co. A, which was formed in Fort Benning, B (in Fort Carson, Colorado) and O (in Alaska) – were formed into battalions of the 75th Infantry Regiment (Ranger). The regiment was formally activated on 1 January 1969, with Congress authorizing a third Ranger battalion on 3 October 1984.

In 1977 the Army revealed that the 75th included two 600-men battalions, one stationed on each coast. According to Lieutenant Colonel Ed Vargo, when he commanded one of the battalions in 1978: 'We're light infantry. Basic light infantry. Take our weapons. We carry M16s. Grenade launchers. M60 machine guns. 60mm mortars and 90mm recoilless rifles. That's it. Nothing fancy. We've got men who are qualified in all sorts of foreign weapons, just like we've got men who are demolitions specialists. But what we carry and what we train with is basic Army issue.'

In addition to Rangers, the Army began developing Long Range Reconnaissance Patrol (LRRP) units around 1958 in Germany. The units would conduct passive, deep penetration to collect intelligence on the movements of enemy units. A number of LRRP units were formed thereafter, but they did not exist in every major combat unit.

The concept really took hold during the Vietnam War, however. After 1967 each field force and division there had a full LRRP company, with a headquarters and two patrol platoons of eight six-man patrols. They located and reported enemy forces, performed ambushes, recaptured prisoners of war and handled point security. All Vietnam LRRP companies were disbanded between 1969 and 1972. On 1 February 1969 all LRRP units were assigned to the 75th Infantry Regiment and the men redesignated Rangers. The LRRP concept was allowed to die.

It returned in 1984, however, as the Long Range Surveillance (LRS) unit; one LRS Company (LRSC) was

thereafter assigned to each corps and one LRS Detachment (LRSD) to each division. The Army also began an LRS training course, under Ranger supervision, in October 1986.

Arctic Rangers of Company O, 75th Infantry board a Lockheed C-130A at Elmendorf Air Force Base, Alaska, prior to conducting the first jump on to the Polar ice cap, 4 March 1971. They put on their parachutes during the flight. [*US Army*]

Ranger course students rappel down a 50-foot cliff as a Ranger Instructor watches at Camp Merrill, Georgia. [*US Army*]

VOLSTAD

1. **SERGEANT, ASSAULT SQUAD LEADER, 1ST RANGERS, ARZEW, ALGERIA, NOVEMBER 1942**

The Rangers generally wore the wool shirt and trousers, even after herringbone fatigues were introduced. Wool gave the fast-moving Rangers a measure of warmth during cold desert nights, thus eliminating the need for blankets. Black-on-OD rank insignia were generally worn by the 1st Rangers. White armbands on both arms and a printed US flag on the left shoulder were worn as a means of identification for both Allied forces and the Vichy French. The .45 caliber M1 Thompson submachine guns were pooled at battalion level and issued to individuals as required. Some Rangers managed to acquire M1928A1 pistols.

2. **STAFF SERGEANT, ASSAULT SECTION LEADER, 1ST RANGERS, SENED PASS, TUNISIA, NOVEMBER 1942**

During the various raids conducted by the 1st Rangers in North Africa, they generally wore wool knit skull caps or OD M1941 wool knit 'jeep' caps. The latter had a small stiff bill and knit ear flaps. He wears the very popular tankers' jacket.

3. **CORPORAL, PLATOON SPECIAL WEAPONS SECTION, 4TH RANGERS, ANZIO, ITALY, JANUARY 1944**

Rangers battalions were issued 20 2.36-inch M1 rocket launchers, 'bazookas', for tank- and bunker-busting. The 4th Rangers utilized burlap helmet covers during their operations in Italy. This Ranger wears the M1941 field jacket and special issue climbing boots with M1938 leggings cut down to five inches in height, a popular Ranger practice. His web equipment is standard issue.

4. **LIEUTENANT COLONEL WILLIAM DARBY, 1ST RANGERS, COMMANDO DEPOT, SCOTLAND, MAY 1942**

The 1st Rangers wore the one-piece herringbone twill work suit during their training and on many active operations in North Africa. The M1917A1 helmet was initially worn until replaced by the new M1 helmet in the autumn of 1942. Darby is outfitted with the M1928 haversack, the standard Army backpack throughout most of the war. Though armed with a .45 caliber M1911A1 automatic pistol, the colonel also carried a .30 caliber M1903A1 Springfield rifle, even after the unit was re-equipped with the M1 Garand that autumn.

1. **Technician 5, Automatic Rifleman, 2nd Rangers, Pointe du Hoc, France, June 1944**

The three assault companies carried only four .30 caliber M1918A2 Browning automatic rifles (BAR) apiece. Normal Ranger practise was to remove the bipod to reduce the weapon's weight. Twelve 20-round magazines were carried in the M1937 belt. The 2nd and 5th Rangers made general use of the herringbone summer fatigues, combined with the M1941 field jacket. Both battalions had an orange diamond and unit number painted on the backs of their helmets. Officers were further identified by a vertical, and NCOs by a horizontal white bar beneath it. On the beach lies one of the many rocket-propelled grapnels, launched from landing craft, which failed to reach the cliff top due to the added weight of wet ropes.

2. **Private First Class, Machine Gunner, 5th Rangers, Irsch-Zerf Road, Germany, February 1945**

By the winter of 1944–45 most infantry units had been issued the M1943 field jacket to replace the M1941. Its basic style is retained to this day in Army field jacket designs. Heavy field trousers were issued along with the jackets. He also wears M1944 shoepacs—cold/wet weather boots. The .30 caliber M1919A4 Browning light machine-gun was one of the mainstays of small unit firepower.

3. **Private First Class, Rifleman, 29th Rangers, Norway, 1943**

Having been trained by a 1st Rangers cadre, the 29th Rangers adopted many of its clothing practises. However, during its raid with the Commandos, British battle-dress was worn along with US paratrooper boots. The .30 caliber M1 rifle, tipped with an M1905 bayonet, was the most common weapon used by Ranger units. The pole charge, used to shove through pillbox firing ports, was fabricated by attaching two MkIIIA1 concussion grenades to a former tent pole. The insert depicts the unit's unofficial tab over the 29th Infantry Division patch.

1. CORPORAL, AUTOMATIC RIFLEMAN, 5307TH COMPOSITE UNIT, BURMA, 1944

This Marauder is also wearing the herringbone fatigues, but with a field hat, popular in this unit. Though the Marauders' mission required light loads carried under arduous tropical conditions, there were few suitable special equipment items available. Even the M1910 entrenching tool, replaced by the M1943 folding model, was issued. Concessions were granted, however, including the issue of canvas and rubber jungle boots and the M1922 BAR. Originally designed for cavalry use, it was shorter and a few pounds lighter than the more common M1918A2. Many of the troops carried scarves made of supply parachute fabric, which came in four of the colors designating combat teams—red, white, blue and green. The unoffical 'Merrill's Marauder' patch is shown, made by unit members just before the 5307th was disbanded; officially they wore the US Armed Forces, China-Burma-India patch.

2. PRIVATE FIRST CLASS, SNIPER, 6TH RANGERS, PANGATIAN PW CAMP, LUZON, JANUARY 1945

Each Ranger platoon HQ was assigned a sniper with an M1903A4 rifle, a specially selected M1903A1 with a 2.5 power M73B1 telescope added as well as other modifications. He is wearing the almost universal M1943 herringbone fatigues with an M1941 field cap. He is also wearing the new combat boots, which came into general issue in late 1944. On his side is an M3 combat knife.

3. 2ND LIEUTENANT, TEAM LEADER, ALAMO SCOUTS, PHILIPPINES, 1945

He wears the M1943 two-piece camouflage suit and the M1945 field cap, although the Scouts more often wore the olive green herringbone fatigues. He is armed with the .30 caliber M1A1 paratrooper carbine and an M1911A1 pistol. In order to disengage with the enemy, he is carrying an M15 white phosphorus (WP) and MkII fragmentation grenades. Pictured is the semi-official Alamo Scouts patch, always worn on the *right* shoulder, designed by PFC Harry Golden.

1. PRIVATE FIRST CLASS, RIFLEMAN, 4TH RANGER COMPANY, MUNSAN-NI, KOREA, MARCH 1951

The T-7A parachute, an improvement over the World War 2 T-5, was introduced in 1948; it utilized a 24-foot flat circular camouflage or white canopy. Beneath the reserve parachute is an M1945 combat pack to which is secured an extra belt of .30 caliber ammunition for his platoon's M1919A6 light machine gun. His uniform consists of the M1943 field jacket and trousers with an M1C parachutist's helmet.

2. PRIVATE FIRST CLASS, 10TH RANGER COMPANY, CAMP POLK, LOUISIANA, 1951

Only a few of the Korean War era Ranger companies actually wore the black beret, at the time unauthorized. The 1st to 8th Companies did not receive them, and of the later companies, only the 10th and 13th are known to have worn them—though others may have. Beret flashes, which owe their origin to Special Forces, were not used; instead a jumpwing background common to all companies was displayed.

3. CORPORAL, GRENADIER, 3RD RANGER COMPANY, KOREA, SUMMER 1951

A slightly improved version of the World War 2 herringbone fatigues was introduced in 1948. The OD-on-navy-blue chevron had recently been reintroduced, but many troops had continued throughout to wear them in the field rather than the small 'goldenlite' stripes. Web gear was essentially the same as that used in the previous war, but olive green equipment had replaced most khaki items. He has the M1943 folding entrenching tool and a more recent addition, the three-pocket hand grenade pouch. Armed with an M1 rifle with an M7A1 grenade launcher and M15 grenade sight, he is preparing to launch a standard MkIIA1 fragmentation hand grenade, fitted to an M1 grenade projection adapter. On the ground are M9A1 AT and M19 WP grenades.

4. SERGEANT, SQUAD LEADER, 2ND RANGER COMPANY, KOREA, JANUARY 1951

The M1943 field jacket and trousers were still in use, but soon to be replaced by the M1951. One postwar winter uniform improvement was the popular pile cap. Wearing light equipment and rubber overboots, this Ranger is standing guard in a rear area. The semi- and full-automatic M2 carbine, introduced in 1945, is now in wide use.

1. **SPECIALIST 4, SENIOR SCOUT OBSERVER, V CORPS LRRP COMPANY, WEST GERMANY, 1961**

Both V and VII Corps LRRP Company wore French-made maroon berets, but only with fatigues in the field and home garrison. Maroon was selected since most other NATO LRRP units wore it. They were banned in 1964 by Lt.Gen. Creighton W. Abrams. The fatigues were the cotton OB 107 introduced in the late 1950s. The V Corps LRRP Company used a special version of the Corps' patch, with the addition of a black border; by 1963 it had fallen out of use, and a white/blue airborne tab was adopted. His web gear is the M1956 load bearing equipment (LBE) used by the entire Army. It was supplemented by an M1951 mountain rucksack, necessary due to the large loads required by LRRP's independent and extended-duration missions. He is armed with a 7.62mm NATO M14 rifle.

2. **SPECIALIST 4, SENIOR RADIO OPERATOR; COMPANY F (LRP) 425TH INFANTRY, CAMP GRAYLING, MICHIGAN, 1968**

This radio operator is uniformed in the improved version of the OG 107 fatigues (buttoned sleeve cuffs were the principal innovation, but were still not supposed to be rolled up) and the ever-unpopular OG 106 hot weather 'baseball' field cap introduced in 1964. The jumpwing oval, formerly used by 1st Bn., 225th Inf., was used by F-425 until 1986. His radio is an AN/PRC-74B, an AM single-sideband set. He is keying an encrypted message into an AN/GRA-71 coder/burst transmission group's magnetic tape cartridge; the message could be burst-transmitted at 300 words per minute. M1956 LBE is used along with the lightweight, aluminumframed nylon rucksack. LRRP, SF and airborne units were the first in the National Guard to receive the 5.56mm M16A1 rifle.

3. **STAFF SERGEANT, PATROL LEADER, COMPANY (LRP), 58TH INFANTRY, WEST GERMANY, 1967**

Cross-country skiing has always been a part of training for LRRPs stationed in snow regions. Clothed in the M1951 field cap, jacket, and trousers, he wears only the overwhite trousers and not the parka. This provides a remarkable degree of camouflage in wooded areas, as the white trousers blend into the ground snow, and the olive green jacket with evergreen trees.

1. CAPTAIN, ARVN RANGER ADVISOR, RANGER TRAINING CENTER, DUC MY, VIETNAM, 1967

Ranger-qualified US advisors assigned to ARVN Ranger units wore ARVN Ranger insignia, and sometimes their uniforms. This advisor wears US-style fatigues made from ARVN Ranger/SF camouflage fabric, the ARVN Ranger qualification badge over his left pocket, and the ARVN Ranger patch beneath it.

2. SPECIALIST 4, SENIOR RADIO OPERATOR, COMPANY L (RANGER), 75TH INFANTRY, VIETNAM, 1969

Ranger companies of the 75th Infantry (and some of the earlier LRP units) wore the black beret on a generally limited and unofficial basis.

3. PRIVATE FIRST CLASS, SCOUT/OBSERVER, RANGER COMPANY, 75TH INFANTRY, VIETNAM, 1970

By this stage of the war there were numerous improvements in clothing, equipment and weaponry. There were still, of course, wide variations in dress and equipment depending on mission, weather, the latest 'discovery' (fad) of what worked, and individual tastes. Headbands, made from issue triangular bandages, were common, as was the use of sweat towels—'drive-on rags'. Cord was sometimes tied around legs to prevent trousers from snagging on brush—and because it looked 'salty'.

The Army, having determined that an issue camouflage uniform was impractical due to vegetation differences in Vietnam, reversed its decision and issued the camouflage jungle uniform in 1967.

4. SERGEANT, PATROL LEADER, INFANTRY LRP COMPANY (AIRBORNE), VIETNAM, 1968

This NCO could be a member of any one of the various provisional or established LRRP units. Tigerstripe uniforms were worn extensively along with olive green and camouflage jungle fatigues. In Vietnam the patrol leader normally carried one of the team's radios, an AN/PRC-25, or the improved -77. The senior radio operator would carry a second radio of the same model or, if extreme range was needed, an AN/PRC-74B—used in a voice mode. The radio was the team's 'key to life' as it was needed to report information, to direct artillery, air strikes, and helicopter gunships, and also to request medevac and emergency extractions.

VOLSTAD

1. SPECIALIST 4, SENIOR SCOUT/OBSERVER, LRS DETACHMENT, 7TH INFANTRY DIVISION (LIGHT), FT. ORD, CALIFORNIA, 1985
This member of the first LRSD officially activated wears the battledress uniform (BDU) with the maroon beret, worn by all LRS units. The beret flash shows the unit's relationship with its parent 1st Squadron, 10th Cavalry; it is possible that many of the divisional LRSDs may adopt this flash. He wears the ALICE LBE and the large LC-1 ALICE pack on an LC-2 frame. He is equipped with M19 7 × 50 binoculars and an M16A1 rifle.

2. 1ST LIEUTENANT, PATROL PLATOON LEADER, COMPANY A (RANGER), 75TH INFANTRY, FT. HOOD, TEXAS, 1972
This last of the Active Army Ranger/LRRP companies was attached to the 1st Cavalry Division. Ranger-qualified officers wore their tab above their badge of rank, while enlisted men wore the 75th Infantry crest rather than rank insignia. Non-Ranger qualified troops wore a gold/black air-borne tab in the same manner. The black beret was not made official until 20 December 1978.

3. SERGEANT, ASSISTANT PATROL LEADER, COMPANY G (RANGER), 143RD INFANTRY, ENGLAND, JULY 1986
This APL is clothed in olive green jungle fatigues. No longer authorized after September 1987, they are being replaced by a similar model printed with the woodlands pattern of the battledress uniform (G1). This unit is fortunate in that large numbers of personnel train with various NATO LRRPs (Danish, German, British and French). This is reflected by the British jumpwings (an on-going exchange program is conducted with the SAS) and the International LRRP School pocket patch. Unit insignia and badges are not normally worn on mission uniforms, however. His LBE is the ALICE (all-purpose light individual carrying equipment) with the addition of a STABO extraction harness. He also carries a survival kit: each man is required to construct one of these. Many unit members carry an Indian-made MkIII Gurkha *kukri* knife, an excellent tool for clearing brush and cutting roots when constructing an observation post. An M17A2 protective mask is carried on his left leg. His Alpinist II rucksack is a custom-modified commercial model, pur-
(continued on page 138)

1. SPECIALIST 4, SNIPER, 1ST BATTALION (RANGER), 75TH INFANTRY, EGYPT, 1984
Elements of the Ranger battalions take part in the annual 'Bright Star' deployment excercise in Egypt. This Ranger is uniformed in the desert camouflage version of the BDU, adopted in 1982. He is armed with the M21 sniper rifle, an accurized version of the M14, fitted with a 3-9 power adjustable ranging telescope. LBE consists of ALICE gear, but with the substitution of old MLBE M14 magazine pouches.

2. SERGEANT FIRST CLASS, HHC, 75TH RANGER REGIMENT, FT. BENNING, GEORGIA, 1986
HQ and HQ Co., 75th Rangers wear a beret flash similar to those worn by the three battalions. Its colors represent the designations of the six combat teams that made up Merrill's Marauders—red, white, blue, green, khaki, and orange. This same style flash was worn by the 1st and 2nd Bns. from 1974 to 1984, with no differentiation between battalions.

3. SPECIALIST 4, BUILDING CLEARING TEAM, 2ND BATTALION (RANGER), 75TH INFANTRY, FT. LEWIS, WASHINGTON, 1981
Tasked with securing transfer airfields for Delta Force's deep penetration raid and hostage rescue operations, the Ranger battalions organized several sub-units. This member of a BCT wears camouflage jungle fatigues and a wool watch cap. Black spray-painted tennis shoes complete his clothing. Special equipment includes AN/PVS-5 night vision goggles, 9mm MP5A3S noise-suppressed sub-machine gun, .45 caliber M1911A1 pistol in a civilian holster, and an assault vest in lieu of LBE.

4. PRIVATE FIRST CLASS, SQUAD AUTOMATIC WEAPON GUNNER, 3RD BATTALION, 75TH RANGER REGIMENT, FT. BENNING, GEORGIA, 1986
The 5.6mm M249E1 squad automatic weapon (SAW), issued too late for Grenada, is allocated two per squad. It uses a 200-round belt in an assault pack; standard 20- and 30-round M16A1 magazines may also be used. The extended cold weather clothing system (ECWCS) Gor-Tex all-weather suit is in the process of being issued to Ranger, LRS, SF, and light infantry units. Gor-Tex is a special water- and windproof fabric which 'breathes', thus permitting sweat vapor to escape.

'GUN JEEP', SECURITY TEAM, 2ND
BATTALION (RANGER), 75TH INFANTRY,
FT. LEWIS, WASHINGTON, 1981
An M151A2 ¼-ton utility truck – 'jeep' – was
used by security teams to move rapidly to
their roadblock sites or other objectives
when securing airfields. They could be
carried on C-141 and C-130 transports or
HH-53 and CH-47 helicopters. While
armed with two 7.62 mm M60 machine-
guns, other weapons were also carried:
90mm M67 recoilless rifle, 66mm M202A1
'Flash' four-barreled incendiary rocket
launcher, 66mm M72A2 light anti-tank
weapon (LAW), M18A1 'Claymore' anti-
personnel mines, and various grenades.
Barrier materials and warning signs (in the
native language) were also carried. Team
members were equipped with AN/PVS-5
night vision goggles, and some of their
weapons with AN1PVS-4 starlight 'scopes.

(continued from page 136)
chased by the unit, as they have almost
twice the load-carrying capability of the
large ALICE pack. Strapped on the 'ruck' is
a roll of chicken wire used for camouflag-
ing OP's. Each patrol has one 40mm M203
grenade launcher fitted to an M16A1 rifle.

4. PRIVATE FIRST CLASS, RADIO
OPERATOR, COMPANY O (ARCTIC
RANGER), 75TH INFANTRY; POLAR ICE
CAP, MARCH 1971
The Arctic Rangers jumped on to the Polar
ice cap in the winter of 1971 to conduct a
search and rescue exercise. At the exercise's
end, a mass re-enlistment ceremony was
held. Being held on the ice cap, the re-
enlistment was considered to have been
conducted in international 'waters': this
exempted the re-enlistment bonuses from
being taxed. (A regulation was issued
shortly afterwards, prohibiting re-
enlistments on the pack ice!) It was required
that a guard be posted to keep a polar bear
watch. Armed with a special issue .300
H&H Magnum Winchester Model 70 rifle,
this trooper is outfitted in the cold-dry
uniform. This ensemble takes the layering
principle to the extreme; long underwear,
wool shirt, field jacket and trousers with
liners, Arctic parka and trousers with
liners, insulated cap, fur-ruffed hood, and
wool mitten inserts with leather shells and
fur-ruffed Arctic mittens. He wears white
insulated Arctic boots, similar to the black
model but with additional insulation. His
sleeping bag consists of the M1949 inside
the down-filled Arctic outer shell.

1. STAFF SERGEANT, RANGER INSTRUCTOR, 3RD RANGER COMPANY, FT. BENNING, GEORGIA, 1986

The 'RI' holds powers of life and death over Ranger students, or so they quickly and sincerely come to believe. He can inflinct pain and award pleasure, i.e. food or sleep–true rarities. This RI is clothed in a typical running outfit. Usually, they wear olive green jungle fatigues or other appropriate seasonal clothing.

2. RANGER STUDENT, CAMP DARBY, FT. BENNING, GEORGIA, 1951–90

Reduced to the lowest common denominator, this Ranger student learns his place in his new world on the edge of Victory Pond. His rank may be anything from Spec. 4 to Captain; it makes no difference, as students wear no rank insignia, being refered to only as 'Ranger'. They wear only their name and US Army tapes–no unit insignia or special skill badges are permitted.

3. SERGEANT FIRST CLASS, RANGER INSTRUCTOR, 1ST RANGER COMPANY, CAMP RUDDER, EGLIN AIR FORCE BASE, FLORIDA, 1986

This Florida Phase RI wears a black beret with the Ranger Department flash and Infantry School crest. This flash was also worn by some other Ranger companies. The Ranger Department wears the Infantry School patch (similar to the crest) with a white/blue airborne tab.

4. SERGEANT, FIRE TEAM LEADER, 1ST BATTALION (RANGER), 75TH INFANTRY, HUNTER ARMY AIRFIELD, GEORGIA, 1984

This Grenada veteran wears the Army Green uniform. His participation in Operation 'Urgent Fury' is denoted by his Combat Infantryman's Badge, combat jump star on his jumpwings, and an Armed Forces Expeditionary Medal ribbon with an assault arrowhead device (indicating an airborne–as in his case–or amphibious assault). He wears the scroll on his right shoulder, denoting combat service with the unit. A rifle squad's two fire teams consist of four men each.

THE US MARINE CORPS,

Men of Company B, 1/5 Marines pause on a Naktong hillside for a radio check in August 1950. They wear a mixture of M1942 and M1944 utilities with leggings. The World War 2-vintage radios are (center) the SCR-536 'handie-talkie', and (right) the SCR-300 'walkie-talkie' – the nickname often wrongly used for the former set. [*USMC*]

Younger than the Army, the US Marine Corps is a land-fighting unit under US Navy control. Originally, Marines were to serve as ships' policemen and landing parties. Until World War 2 the Corps was fairly small, actually fighting in World War 1 as part of the Army's 2nd Infantry Division, and during much of its existence its need has been questioned by those politicians who see the Army serving all land-fighting requirements.

It was, however, by and large saved from extinction by its brave and well publicized actions in World War 2. It had gained a name during the campaign across the Pacific islands as especially tough and well trained, the kind of troops needed to keep the peace in any sudden hotspot. But, even so, the Corps' future lay in doubt after 1945 as Defense Secretaries began cutting their budgets, and Congress produced a number of plans to phase Marine operations into other services.

Despite this, the Marines led the way in considering the possibility of amphibious assaults by air, using helicopters as early as late 1946. And the Corps survived many political attacks.

Marines were sent to garrison both Japan and China in 1945, Congress then authorizing a peacetime Corps of 107,000 officers and men. In China they saw a number of skirmishes against the locals before the last Marines left in June 1949. While they patroled local roads, two major changes in the Corps were taking place. First, in June 1948, the integration of women into the Regular Marines was authorized; women Marines had served in both world wars, but only in reserve capacities. Then, in June 1949, it was ruled there would be 'no distinction' between black and white Marines—before that most black Marines served in labor units or as messboys.

On 25 June 1950, members of the North Korean People's Army crossed the 48th parallel and invaded South Korea. The Marines were sent in, landing at Inch'on after the Allies had been driven almost to the tip of the Korean peninsula. The landing was a complete success and the Marines joined the general advance North, almost reaching the Chinese border. There, they met a strong Chinese advance that almost trapped them at the Chosin Reservoir; how the 1st Marine Division cut their way out, in biting cold, carrying their dead and wounded, became one of the legends of the war.

The Allies were driven back, but held on virtually along the line where the war had started, and on 27 July 1953 an armistice was signed between the two sides.

On 28 June 1952, partly in response to the Corps' Korean War efforts, a law had been signed that made the Marines a permanent separate branch of service and placed its Commandant on the Joint Chiefs of Staff.

The next time Marines were to see serious action was in Labanon in July 1958, when two landing teams were sent to aid the Lebanese against a feared Syrian invasion. But the invasion did not take place and by 18 October the Marines had gone.

Marines saw another landing in April 1965 when they were sent to the Dominican Republic, ostensibly to protect US nationals from a Communist-inspired coup. Insiders said later that the troops were actually sent as a show of force to boost the government's chances of survival—though these seemed to be good even without US intervention. South American troops were also sent as an international 'peace force'. The rebels were soon disarmed and the last Marines were gone by 6 June.

The 9th Marine Expeditionary Brigade landed near

1945–1990

ONTOS M50A1 of the 1st Anti-Tank Battalion at Chu Lai in May 1966. Not a particularly successful vehicle, it came into its own during the Hue street fighting of Tet 1968, when its 106mm recoilless rifles proved devastating in direct support of infantry. The crewmen wear standard utilities and CVC (Combat Vehicle Crewman's) helmets. [*USMC*]

Da Nang, in Vietnam, on 8 March 1965, and this time the Marines would not leave so quickly. In Vietnam Marines were reinforced in the general military build up that followed and at its peak strength, in 1968, the Corps had 85,755 Marines there. The Corps as a whole reached a strength of 317,400 during the war. On 29 April 1975 the last Marines in Vietnam, 865 embassy guards, supervised the dramatic evacuation of US personnel.

Marines were busy on the other side of the world in July 1974 when they evacuated US nationals from Cyprus, then the scene of fighting between Greeks and Turks. Marines also evacuated US personnel from Cambodia in April 1975. And, the following month, Marines were sent to rescue the crew of the US container ship SS *Mayaguez*. The operation was done, but faulty intelligence cost more Marine lives than crewmen, who were actually already in the process of being released.

Marines were to return to Lebanon in June 1982, as an Israeli invasion toppled its political structure, leaving Muslim and Christian militiamen to instigate open civil war. The Marines were landed in an effort to get foreign troops, Israeli and Syrian, out of Lebanon, end the civil war and establish a permanent government – an almost impossible task for a military force given orders not to consider themselves as on a 'combat operation'. Continuous firing on Marines took place, ending with a suicide bombing of their quarters in Beirut on 23 October 1983. In all, 218 Marines died in that one bombing, and survivors were withdrawn in November.

The 22nd Marine Amphibious Unit, however, was more successful when they landed that year on the Caribbean island of Grenada. There, the US government felt, a Marxist government threatened the peace of the

Western Hemisphere. The Marine part in the invasion, a northern amphibious landing, went smoother than that of the Army and US Navy SEALS. As one Marine sergeant later reported: 'We haven't fired too many rounds at all. We've just gone from town to town, collecting weapons and prisoners.' In all, the Navy and Marines combined had seven men killed and another seven wounded. Finally, Marines saw limited action during the invasion of Panama in December 1989.

In 1990, the Corps' basic combat unit is the USMC battalion landing team (BLT), complete with armor, artillery, engineers, aviation, sealift and service support.

The ALICE (All-Purpose Lightweight Individual Carrying Equipment) web gear being worn over the PASGT by a 32nd MAU (Marine Aviation Unit) engineer. Note the 'Y' configuration of belt suspenders. The device in his trouser pocket is part of the Wurlitzer mine detector. [*USMC*]

1. CAPTAIN, BLUE DRESS 'B', 1970
The famous Marine Blue Dress uniform—the color has been traditional for most of the Marines' history. Other features recall past successes. The Mameluke sword, for example, commemorates one presented in 1805 by the Pasha of Tripoli to Marine Lt. O'Bannon for the capture of Derna. The red trouser stripe, worn only by officers and NCO's traditionally represents the bloody battle of Chapultepec in the Mexican War: it is $1\frac{1}{2}$ in. wide for company and field grade officers, and 2ins. wide for general officers. Majors and above also wear gold braid on hat visors. Since the end of World War 2 the only major change to this uniform has been a 1963 directive which changed the color of all Marine leather items (shoes, cap frames, gloves, etc.) from brown to black.

2. STAFF SERGEANT, BLUE DRESS 'B', 1957
One of the first postwar uniform changes was the 1946 reintroduction of the Blue Dress uniform for enlisted men. (Its wear, except for some special cases, had been suspended during World War 2.) The new uniform differed from its prewar predecessor in the addition of pockets to the jacket; formerly, this was a feature of the officer's uniform only. Otherwise the styling differs little from enlisted uniforms worn at the turn of the century. The $1\frac{1}{8}$ in red trouser stripe is worn by NCOs—corporals and above. The blue cloth belt is worn as walking-out dress; the white belt and full-dress buckle are usually prescribed for ceremonies. The hat is actually a frame, worn with different covers. The blue one shown was abolished in 1957 and only the white is now used. The service stripes below the chevrons represent the completion of two previous four-year enlistments.

3. LANCE CORPORAL, BLUE DRESS 'C', 1973
According to regulations, Blue Dress 'C' may be prescribed by local commands authorized to wear the Blue uniform. Usually 'Blue Charlie' is worn as a duty uniform in summer and is not authorized for wear off-base. When worn on State Department posts, the white web Military Police belt and buckle are used to 'dress up' the Embassy Guard's uniform. Other items of MP equipment may also be worn. Blue Dress 'D' is similar to 'C', but uses the quarter-length-sleeve khaki shirt without a tie.

1. FIRST LIEUTENANT, WHITE DRESS 'A', 1983

The White Dress uniform for Marine officers dates back to 1912 and is virtually unchanged since then. When worn with medals (the 'A' uniform, as here), no metal badges are worn. The hat's quatrefoil decoration is a traditional distinction for marine officers and appears on all their hat covers.

2. STAFF SERGEANT, BLUE-WHITE DRESS 'A', 1975

This is a dress uniform authorized for special events and ceremonies, for both officers and enlisted men. It is an 'organizational' uniform, i.e. not authorized for individual wear, created by wearing the blue tunic with white trousers and white hat cover. Swords for officers and NCOs may be prescribed, and enlisted ranks wear the white dress belt and buckle. (This staff sergeant has the NCO pattern; below the grade of corporal, the dress buckle is plain.) The Blue-White uniform is usually worn by unit drill teams and color guards, and these may, in turn, authorize special accessories. These might include a black Sam Browne belt for officers, white frogs and bayonet scabbards for enlisted men, and gold-plated (Hamilton Wash) buttons for all. Certain units with ceremonial duties in Washington have even been authorized to procure non-standard raincoats and overcoats so that the uniform may be worn during bad weather.

3. MUSICIAN, US MARINE BAND, 1983

The United States Marine Band has carried out ceremonial functions in Washington since 1800. The variety and importance of its duties are reflected in the dress regulations, which devote an entire section to this unit. Some of the uniforms prescribed, such as those of the director, assistant director and the band's drum major, are among the most colorful ever worn in the American military. Ordinary musicians, male and female, are also issued a variety of uniforms. The one illustrated in the summer full dress uniform with the red coat traditional for the Marine Band. The white trousers are summer issue, blue ones are worn in winter. No rank insignia are now worn with this uniform, although medals are permitted. Members of bands of other Marine commands wear the normal range of dress uniforms, with the addition of such honor guard equipment as may be prescribed by local authority.

1. **FIRST LIEUTENANT, WINTER SERVICE 'A', 1983**

This contemporary officer's uniform is virtually identical in style both to marine enlisted uniforms, and to the service dress of World War 2. The only changes for officers during this period were the dropping of the Sam Browne belt in 1942 and the change from brown accessories to black in 1963. However, during the postwar period, two other forms of service dress were worn. The green wool service jacket (2) was authorized from 1945–1968; and in 1957 a special version of the service coat was authorized for officers and staff NCOs. This had a bellows back, and was worn until the end of 1970.

2. **STAFF SERGEANT, WINTER SERVICE 'A', 1954**

This uniform had its origins in early 1943, when the veteran 1st Marine Division arrived in Australia for rest and re-equipment after Guadalcanal. Lacking any form of service uniform, the Marines were issued with Australian battledress. This proved extremely popular, and in 1944 it was decided to adopt it as a standard item for the Corps. (At the same time, in Europe, the US Army had adopted their own approximation similar 'Ike jacket', based upon British battledress.) The Marine jacket was virtually identical to the Australian model, except that eyelets were provided in the open lapels to attach the 'glove and anchor' insignia, and green plastic buttons replaced the original tan ones. Designated the Green Wool Service Jacket, it was first issued in quantity to returning World War 2 veterans. It was issued in addition to the normal service coat until the early 1960s, and was finally abolished in 1968.

3. **STAFF SERGEANT, WINTER SERVICE 'A' 1945**

'Marine Green' was adopted for the Corps' service uniform in 1912, and the introduction of an open collar in 1928 brought the uniform to virtually its present form. During World War 2, in an effort to conserve strategic metals, brown plastic was substituted for bronze in enlisted men's hat and collar devices. (Officers substituted sterling silver for lapel devices only.) The enlisted man's leather garrison belt was supplanted by a cloth type in 1943, but both types remained in use for the remainder of the war; indeed, the garrison belt was still issued as late as 1949 for some guard duties.

1. LIEUTENANT COLONEL, SUMMER SERVICE 'A', 1956

The first khaki summer uniforms were adopted by the Marine Corps at the time of the Spanish-American War. The officer's version changed little between 1928 and its abolition at the end of 1976. Only the abandonment of the Sam Browne belt in 1942, and the change in leather color in 1963, affected it. This officer's ribbons indicate participation in several World War 2 campaigns, postwar duties in Japan and North China, and service in Korea.

2. CORPORAL, SUMMER SERVICE 'B', 1961

Marines started wearing khaki for summer during the Spanish-American War, but the shirt and trouser combination as service dress dates only from 1938. As with many Marine uniforms, there were versions in different fabrics: in this case, tropical worsted and cotton. The khaki shirt and trousers were worn as standard enlisted summer uniform until the early 1970s, with virtually no changes in appearance. This was also authorized wear for officers (their Summer 'C') during that period. The 'globe and anchor' device was worn on enlisted men's shirt collars only between 1952 and 1961.

3. DRILL INSTRUCTOR, SUMMER SERVICE 'C', 1983

All the American armed forces introduced light-weight synthetic fabrics for their service uniforms in the early 1960s. A decade later this would bring about a radical change in the appearance of service dress. The woollen winter uniforms were replaced by lighter weight versions which could be worn all year round. Specialized summer dress also disappeared: in summer, troops would now wear a shirt and trousers version of the winter uniform. For the Marine Corps the change was less radical than for some of the other services, but it meant the end of the all-khaki uniform in 1976. This Marine drill instructor wears green polyester/rayon wash-and-wear trousers with the quarter-length-sleeve khaki shirt, introduced in 1960. The campaign hat, a symbol of the 'Old Corps' dropped in 1942, was reinstated in early 1961 for drill instructors and members of Marine shooting teams. The non-commissioned officer's sword is only worn for ceremonies, but the Senior DI of each recruit platoon will also wear the swordbelt alone as a symbol of his status. The other DIs wear the pistol belt during training.

1. TANK COMMANDER, KOREA, SUMMER 1950

This Marine officer wears the later, M1944 pattern utilities, also worn as summer combat dress in Korea. These had some odd features. The trousers had only three pockets: two side cargo pockets, and a single large horizontal 'seat' pocket at the rear, each closed by a flap and two visible buttons. In addition to its single breast pocket, the jacket had two flat map pockets concealed beneath the front. As with the M1942 utilities, the jacket could be worn either loose, or tucked into the pants. Tankers wore the World War 2 composition helmet with M1944 dust goggles. A .45 pistol is worn with shoulder holster M7, the M1936 pistol belt, two-pocket .45 ammunition pouch and M1942 field dressing pouch.

2. MACHINE GUNNER, KOREA, SUMMER 1950

In addition to the weight of his weapon (.30 caliber Browning M1919A4 MMG), this Marine also carries his combat pack (M1941 haversack worn as light marching pack), M1943 entrenching tool, bedroll and sleeping bag. Several of his other accoutrements are unique to the Marine Corps. The canteen cover with crossover flaps is a USMC item from World War 2. The jungle first aid pouch was developed by the Army, but then dropped by them in 1945; the Marines, however, retained it up to the present day, now in a much updated version. Likewise, the grenade pouch (which came in one-, two-, and three-pocket versions) was an Army item retained by the Marines into the 1960s. As a machine gunner, this man also carries a .45 pistol in M1916 holster. The uncomfortable leggings were often discarded in combat, but not before the NKPA nicknamed the Marines 'Yellow-legs'.

3. RIFLEMAN, KOREA, SUMMER 1950

The Marines issued two types of World War 2 utilities as summer combat dress in Korea. This rifleman wears the M1942 pattern, made in cotton HBT (herringbone twill) material. The three-pocket jacket could be worn loose, as shown, or tucked into the trousers like a shirt. Personal equipment comprises the M1936 ten-pocket cartridge belt (each pocket holding one eight-round 'enbloc' clip for the M1 Garand), M1 bayonet in scabbard M7, jungle first aid pouch and M1941 pack and belt suspenders.

1. RIFLEMAN, KOREA, WINTER 1950–53

Winter combat dress, for most of the war, was based on the 'layering' principle, with a variety of garments worn one over the other. Typically, these might include woollen underwear, wool shirt and trousers, sweater, field jacket with liner, and the alpaca-lined, parka-type overcoat shown here. The parka's hood was supposed to fit over the helmet, but most people wore it as shown. The canvas and rubber 'shoepacs' created problems for the wearer: they made the feet sweat with any activity, then allowed moisture to freeze inside. Trigger-finger shell mittens, worn over wool glove inserts, protected the hands. Towards the end of the war a new range of winter clothing was introduced, replacing the item shown. The M1951 system remains in use to the present.

2. OFFICER, KOREA, SPRING 1951

This company officer wears an M1943 field jacket with liner over his utility uniform, probably with a sweater underneath. His wool scarf and fur cap are UN winter issue. He is armed with the .30 caliber carbine M2, with 30-round magazine. This weapon established a mixed reputation in Korea: its fully-automatic option and light weight made it initially popular, but it proved prone to jamming, especially in winter. Further 15-round magazines are carried in a pouch on the stock. The officer's .45 is worn on the pistol belt together with its magazine pouch, and the M4 bayonet in scabbard M8. A compass case is attached below the jungle first aid pouch. The M1943 combat boots are not Marine issue.

3. AUTOMATIC RIFLEMAN, KOREA, 1953

The Army and Marine Corps conducted joint research into body armor in the summer and fall of 1951, but chose different solutions to the problem. The original Marine M1951 armor vest (not to be confused with the different Army type designated M1952) was issued in the spring of 1952. There were several variants; this version, with asymmetrical front closure and breast pocket, is a later type (and drawn from one actually marked 'M1952'). The Army, having development problems with its own body armor, procured 63,000 Marine vests as an interim measure in 1952. The armored groin protector was also issued. It seemed useful during the later, positional phase of the Korean fighting, but eventually proved too awkward for more active situations.

1. FORCE RECON, CAMP LEJEUNE, 1955

In the 1950s the Marines decided they had a need for intelligence gathering beyond the normal tactical level. Their response was the establishment of special units reporting directly to the Fleet Marine Force commanders, Atlantic and Pacific. The units would have both parachute and scuba capability. This man wears the World War 2 reversible M1944 camouflage uniform of shirt and trousers, usually called 'the raider uniform'. The jacket shared certain features with the contemporary M1944 utility type—the two concealed map pockets, for example. A headscarf has been improvized for a helmet camouflage cover. While combat boots were usually worn, for some types of operations a lighter shoe was prefered. In addition to the M3A1 'grease gun' shown, the ordinary range of infantry weapons was employed. The Kabar knife has been a Marine tradition since World War 2.

2. SERGEANT, LEBANON, 1958

As they always do, the Marines made the 1958 landing in Lebanon in full combat order. This NCO, taken from a photograph, wears the newly issued M1955 armor vest. As compared to the previous M1952, it had a different, 'standard' front closure, and added to a very useful ripe ridge to the right side, to retain a slung rifle on the march. A reinforced and eyeletted band at the waist allowed equipment with M19101 horizontal hook fasteners to be attached. This NCO's pistol holster, M1910 field dressing pouch, canteen and bayonet are so carried.

3. OFFICER, UNITED STATES, 1958

At the end of the Korean War a new utility uniform was introduced into service. There were two versions, one made in HBT cloth and a later type made in ordinary heavy twill. Both were worn interchangeably. The jacket had a concealed map pocket located inside on the left side. The khaki belt and frame buckle have been Marine trademarks since World War 2, and are still worn. The characteristic utility cap (called a 'cover' as are all Marine headgear) is a Marine development of a World War 2 item once issued to both Army and Marine Corps. (The Army stopped wearing theirs during Korea.) Originally it was developed from a cap worn by civilian railroad workers. Officers wear pin-on rank insignia in the field, on both lapels and, optionally, on the cap.

1. SERGEANT, 1ST MARINE RECON BATTALION, VIETNAM, 1966

Initially, Marine Recon personnel wore standard utility uniforms in Vietnam. By 1966, however, locally-made camouflage uniforms were available. This NCO wears a set of the famous 'tiger-stripe' pattern, together with Vietnamese-made jungle boots (called 'Bata boots' after the principal manufacturer). A beret was the mark of élite forces in Vietnam, and Marine Recon personnel wore either a black or a tiger-stripe type. The weapon is a Stoner 63, which the Marines tested in the early 1960s.

2. RIFLEMAN, VIETNAM, 1965

When Secretary of Defense Robert MacNamara took office in 1961, he decided to reduce the number of common items in use by the different services. Starting in 1962, the Army OG 107 utility uniform began to be issued to Marines: it would take many years to completely replace the older type utilities. The black Army combat boots replaced the brown Marine type at the same time. The adoption of the M14 rifle and M6 bayonet also brought changes to Marine equipment. The M1961 rifle belt and pouches (each pouch holding one 20-round magazine) were introduced, still worn with M1941 belt suspenders, M1910 canteens, jungle first aid pouch and the Marine pack. A new pattern camouflage shelter half was used alongside World War 2 and plain OD Army types, never replacing either. The World War 2 grenade pouches were still in use.

3. GRENADIER, VIETNAM, 1966

The M79 40mm grenade launcher was another new weapon introduced in Vietnam. Its rounds were issued in cotton bandoliers, each holding six rounds in two plastic 'packs'. Originally two of these bandoliers were standard issue, but grenadiers soon learned simply to take as many as possible. A .45 pistol and Kabar knife were also carried. In addition to his own load, this man has been given two 7.62 mm ammo boxes to carry. With his pack, entrenching tool and hand grenade pouch (this time, a 'two'), they are strapped to a World War 2 packboard. A green nylon rain poncho with liner is carefully folded beneath the packstraps. The M17 protective mask was often used on operations—contrary to popular opinion at the time, both the US and North Vietnamese made use of CS gas in combat.

1. MACHINE GUNNER, VIETNAM, 1967

Together with other American troops in Vietnam, the Marines began to receive their first issues of jungle utilities in early 1965. There were several slightly different patterns. A special type of jungle boot was also developed and issued, among other things, it offered protection to the foot from enemy 'punji stake' foot traps. By this time the M1955 armor vest had been modified by the addition of two front pockets. Details varied from unit to unit; unmodified examples of the vest also continued in use. As a machine gunner, this man is also armed with a .45 pistol. The carrying of the Kabar knife, wedged behind the holster, is typical. Ammunition belts for the 7.62mm M60 machine gun are worn bandolier-fashion. An extra field dressing and a toothbrush for weapons cleaning are stuck in the helmet band, this time an Army issue type.

2. RIFLEMAN, VIETNAM, 1970

Camouflage jungle utilities were introduced in Vietnam in late 1967, initially only to élite units (Army Special Forces and LRRPs, Navy SEALS, Marine Recon, etc.). However, in late 1968 the Marine Corps decided to procure them for all their personnel in-country. The change took some time, but was virtually complete by the end of 1969. The matching wide-brimmed hat was seen alongside standard utility 'covers' or personally-acquired camouflage equivalents—as here. M16 rifle was introduced in 1966, often so quickly that some units did not initially receive its companion M6 Bayonet. The M16's 20-round magazines were not especially compatible with the M1961 pouches, and many Marines, such as this man, acquired the superior M1956 Army type. The Army belt suspenders, more comfortable than the Marine issue, were also a popular item. In addition to capacity and comfort, the Army equipment permitted the safe carrying of grenades, something that often had to be improvized with the Marine web gear.

3. HELICOPTER CREWMAN, VIETNAM, 1969

During the Vietnam War, Marine helicopter crews wore the same flying clothing as fixed-wing personnel: in this case, the CS/FRP-1 polyanamide fire-resistant coveralls, first issued in 1967. The SPH-3 Flying Helmet, especially developed for helicopter crews, was introduced in 1969.

1. GRENADIER, LEBANON, 1983

This Marine wears the latest, possibly the last variant of the M-1 helmet, with LC-1 suspension. The 'woodland' camouflage cover was introduced in the early 1970s. Over his BDUs he wears the new PASGT (Personal Armor System, Ground Troops) vest, which is replacing the older M1955 pattern. It is made of Kevlar, which has bullet-resistant properties; previous vests protected only against shrapnel. A helmet made of the same material, dubbed the 'Fritz' because of its Germanic shape, started being issued in 1984. The pack and LC-1 equipment together comprise the ALICE set, now in use by all US forces.

2. RECON MARINE, FMF-ATLANTIC, CAMP LEJEUNE, 1983

In the early 1980s the Army, Air Force and Marines adopted a new camouflage combat uniform. It was made in a half-and-half nylon-cotton mix, designed for maximum burn protection. Designated the BDU, for battledress uniform, it uses the 'woodland' colors, but with individual camouflage segments 1.6 times as large. The dyes are also specially treated to reduce the infra-red signature. The USMC decal is not used with this uniform. Other changes include a larger collar and smaller, unpleated pockets. Only Recon Marines use the Ranger-type hat. The DMS boots were introduced in the 1970s. Personal equipment is the LC-2 pattern, of nylon pistol belt, 30-round magazine pouches, 'Y' belt suspenders, etc. An M17 protective mask is worn at the hip. The Heckler 8 Koch MP5 SD3 is one of two silenced weapons available to recon units; the Ingram MAC-11 is the other.

3. ARMORED VEHICLE CREWMAN, 1983

In the late 1970s the Marines decided to adopt a camouflage utility uniforms for year-round wear, world wide. The uniforms themselves were taken from Vietnam-era stocks, and came in two camouflage schemes: the original 'leaf-pattern' colors and later 'woodland' scheme. The Vietnam type had slanted jacket pockets, but the postwar production replaced these with a smaller, squarer type. The Marine supply system did not distinguish between any of these, and all remain in use to the present day, with the square-pocket 'woodland' pattern gradually predominating. While subdued T-shirts are sometimes issued, the white version is still very much in evidence.

1   2   3

'Socialist realism' in war art: a
North Korean painting
showing 'valiant KPA soldiers'
in hand-to-hand combat with
'brutal imperialists' of the US
7th Division. [*US Army*]

'Socialist realism' in war art: a North Korean painting showing 'valiant KPA soldiers' in hand-to-hand combat with 'brutal imperialists' of the US 7th Division. [*US Army*]

On 25 June 1950, when North Korean troops crossed the border into South Korea to reunite the country under Communist rule through force, the only Americans on the peninsula were a handful of members of the Korean Military Advisory Group.

The US, remembering how giving into Nazi territorial designs failed to prevent World War 2, determined to resist Communist aggression wherever it happened. At the time, nobody foresaw that many Communist governments would fall apart eventually through their own lack of ability to deal with their citizens' needs and desires. Hence, it was determined to send US ground troops to help the South Koreans fend off the North Koreans. United Nations troops were also requested.

On 28 June an advanced group arrived; on 29 June, the first Army ground troops; on 8 July, the 1st Cavalry Division. Other units followed. In July, too, the President called up four National Guard divisions for active duty.

At the time, all of the US Army's ten divisions, nine separate regimental combat teams and the European Constabulary were considerably under strength in terms of men and equipment. Even by September many rifle companies were still at 25% of their authorized strength. In all, in 1950, the US Army consisted of 72,566 officers and 520,601 enlisted men; in 1952, at the war's height, it numbered 148,427 officers and 1,447,992 enlisted men.

However, observers noted that as late as November 1950 most US troops were poorly disciplined. They discarded their steel helmets in favor of more comfortable caps and threw away their bayonets and entrenching tools. The average soldier carried only one grenade and 16 rounds of ammunition. Most were not physically hardened enough for long route marches across rough terrain under heavy loads. Finally, most soldiers, it was found, simply lacked the motivation necessary to do their jobs well.

This lack of motivation was indicated by the fact that over half of the US soldiers taken prisoner died in their prison camps. In their defense, it should be noted that many wounded prisoners were shot in the head by the North Koreans rather than removed to camp hospitals. At the same time, however, not one member of the tough Turkish Brigade died in prisoner of war camps.

The Army found that morale was poor, too, among men who served in the lines too long, and set up a system of sending men off for brief periods of rest and relaxation (R & R) in Japan after some Korean service. Moreover, it designated that any man who had received 36 points was reassigned to the US. Each man in Korea received a basic two points a month, three a month for being in a combat zone and four a month for being on the front line. The average infantryman, therefore, spent only a year at the front.

The problem with rotation, however, was that it kept putting fresh, untrained troops, often conscripts, onto the front line. Many officers complained about the lack of combat skills only time in action can teach.

One final area of poor morale was among black troops who were assigned to all-black units. The all-black 24th Infantry Regiment broke at Techon 20 July 1950, getting the reputation as a 'bugout unit'. A professor at Columbia University, New York, who studied the problem said this was due to low black individual self-esteem and he recommended that Army units be integrated. In October 1951 President Truman ordered this done and a quota of 10% blacks in each Army unit was decided on.

The Army made other major changes in the way it was organized. On 5 May 1950, for example, it introduced the Uniform Code of Military Justice. This reduced the severities of discipline by introducing Article 15, under which a soldier charged with a minor crime need not be formally court-martialed but instead receive a punishment from his commander—the punishment being erased from his record after a short period.

While much US Army philosophy was changed by the Korean War, little in the way of new technology came

RIGHT: The commander of the
US 1st Marine Division, Maj.
Gen. Oliver P. Smith (left, in
the Marines' characteristic
HBT 'utilities' and
camouflaged helmet cover),
talks to US X Corps
commander Maj. Gen.
Edward M. Almond (right, in
M43 fatigues). Photographed
at Seoul in September 1950,
Smith would within two
months be leading the famous
fighting retreat of his division
from Chosin Reservoir. Just
visible at far right is 1st
Marine Air Wing commander
Maj. Gen. Field Harris, whose
Corsair squadrons provided
valuable support. [*USMC*]

RIGHT: The commander of the US 1st Marine Division, Maj. Gen. Oliver P. Smith (left, in the Marines' characteristic HBT 'utilities' and camouflaged helmet cover), talks to US X Corps commander Maj. Gen. Edward M. Almond (right, in M43 fatigues). Photographed at Seoul in September 1950, Smith would within two months be leading the famous fighting retreat of his division from Chosin Reservoir. Just visible at far right is 1st Marine Air Wing commander Maj. Gen. Field Harris, whose Corsair squadrons provided valuable support. [*USMC*]

1950–1953

US troops advance on Taegu during the offensive following the Inchon landings in autumn 1950; apart from the hessian helmet covers—and the 'brewed' T-34/85 tank of the KPA's 105th Armored Brigade—there is nothing to distinguish this scene from many taken in the latter stages of the Pacific War against Japan. [*US Army*]

out of the conflict. Most equipment there was the same as had been used in World War 2, and indeed most bore World War 2 manufacturers' dates.

Tactically, however, the US Army did begin to emphasize the use of firepower to avoid endangering its soldiers' lives, and artillery became of prime importance. By 1953, more shells had been fired in Korea than in all of World War 2.

The helicopter, too, came into its own in Korea. It saw service in moving people and equipment and as a mobile command post in clear view of an entire battlefield.

On the individual level, the Army began training more men in Ranger schools, with the intention of sending them among other combat units. There they would pass on both their skills and their motivations. And it began looking seriously at ways of using Army information personnel to indoctrinate its troops in monthly, hour-long information sessions.

Initially the North Koreans almost drove the Americans and South Koreans almost into the sea. But a landing in September far to the north, at Inch'on, caused the Communists to fall apart and they were driven almost to the Chinese border. Then the Chinese entered the war, driving back the Allies, who now included not only Americans but South Koreans, Britons, Turks, Benelux and other UN troops. On 4 January 1951 Seoul, South Korea's capital city, was again evacuated.

By 25 January the Allies had returned to the attack. But gains on the ground were small and both sides began talks about ending the war. Now looking like the Italian Front in World War 1, the conflict dragged on as the generals talked on. Finally, on 27 July 1952, the war ended with the lines virtually where they began.

The Communist forces, at the end, had gained nothing. The Allies could claim they had stopped Communist aggression, but little else. The American death toll was 38,000—a smaller number than the US's annual traffic death toll—but it was a war without a victory, a conventional war in the new nuclear age that decided nothing.

December 1951, and a US Marine squad return from patrol. They wear their helmets stuffed down over pile caps and—in the case of the foreground man, carrying the 'folded' M20 3.5 in. rocket launcher—over the hood of the parka. (The hood was supposed to accommodate the helmet, but was seldom worn that way.) The parka is identified as the light tan-colored World War 2 model by the skirt pockets: the M1951 model, issued towards the end of the war, had only the slanting pockets on the ribs. [*USMC*]

1. MAJOR, SUMMER KHAKIS, 1950

The term 'khaki' can cause confusion because Americans use it to mean a light tan, whereas to the British and others it means a darker shade more akin to the American olive drab. During the 1930s the practise of wearing khaki shirts and privately purchased trousers developed; and these became issue garments for enlisted men in 1938–40, along with the 'overseas cap', until then not authorized for wear in the US. This practical and comfortable hot-weather uniform was also widely worn by officers; it continued to be the main summer service dress after 1945, worn in rear areas such as Japan throughout the Korean War.

2. SOLDIER, SUMMER FIELD DRESS, 1950

Among the most important of the US Army's innovations during World War 2 was the use of fatigue clothing as hot-weather combat dress. The first fatigues used in this way were the M41 HBT (Herring-Bone Twill) work suits, which could be recognized by their hip-length jackets and shirt-type cuffs. These were occasionally to be seen in Korea; but were largely superseded by the two-piece M42 fatigues, which differed in having a longer coat with tab closures at the cuffs, a gas flap across the neck opening (almost always removed in practice), and unusually large 'bellows' pockets on the chest and high on the hips of the trousers. With these fatigues went a peaked field cap, whose short visor was lengthened after 1945. The HBT material was tough and hardwearing, but it was also heavy and slow to dry when wet. It presented a faintly 'striped' appearance, though this was only visible close up. The original color was a dark green (Army Shade 7) which quickly faded to a pale greenish gray. These garments became the basis for the Army's postwar summer combat dress.

3. CORPORAL, SUMMER FIELD DRESS, 1952

During the second year of the war the M42 HBT fatigues began to be replaced by a newer pattern. These appear to have been designed in 1947 but not manufactured until the early 1950s. The coat resembled that of the M42 set and had the same gas flap (again, almost invariably removed), but the cuffs were plain, and the pockets were of the normal patch type with squared-off flaps and 'docked' bottoms. The trousers had normal side and back pockets, and the buttons were of plain plastic instead of being the earlier '13 star' black metal pattern. The first batches of these new fatigues were made of the old HBT cloth, but later ones were of dark olive green (OG 107) cotton twill.

1. US Marine, Winter Dress, 1953

The US Marines wore their own HBT 'utilities' peaked field cap and camouflage helmet cover, and retained the early World War 2-pattern ankle boots and canvas leggings, which led the North Koreans to nickname them 'yellowlegs'. Their winter uniforms approximated more to the Army pattern, however, and included M43 jackets, trousers and pile caps, together with World War 2 parkas, and the unsatisfactory canvas and rubber 'shoepacks'. The M51 winter outfit was issued to both arms, although not until relatively late in the war. It was based on the same 'layering' principle as the M43. The field jacket and trousers were worn over frieze liners, which were white and dark green respectively; a green flannel shirt; and a loose-fitting white undershirt and drawers. For really cold weather a parka and overtrousers could be added. The parka resembled the World War 2 pattern except that it lacked a belt, had only the slanting upper pockets, and was olive green instead of the earlier light tan. The boots were of double-thickness rubber with a layer of felt between: perspiration was prevented from evaporating, but the insulation supposedly kept it from freezing.

2. Sergeant, US Army, Field Dress, 1951

The US Army retained its successful M43 field uniform after World War 2; the material was windproof cotton sateen in a distinctly greenish shade of olive drab. In summer the jacket could be worn over the HBT fatigues. In winter the jacket and trousers were worn over a woollen shirt, sweater and 'liner' (a woollen cardigan-style garment) in a browner shade of olive drab. The M43 peaked field cap had ear flaps, but the pile cap more commonly accompanied this uniform during the Korean winter. The World War 2 'double-buckle' combat boots were progressively replaced by plain lace-up ones, all in russet leather. This M43 uniform equipped the majority of US troops in Korea, as well as the re-equipped ROK troops and many of the UN contingents. However, it began to give way to an improved version known as the M51. The jacket differed only in having snap pocket closures instead of buttons; but the trousers had the side 'cargo' pockets previously used only by paratroops, and the shirt and sweater were dark green. The practise of adding a rigid liner to the M51 field cap produced the fashionable, képi-like 'Walker' or 'Ridgway' cap typical of the later 1950s and 1960s. This NCO wears the 1948-pattern miniature chevrons, just visible on the right, but many retained the older wartime ones until they were discontinued in 1951.

[For more US troops in Korea see pages 133 (Marines), 146–7 (Rangers) and 222 (Flak Jackets)]

US ARMY SPECIAL FORCES,

After the Korean War, and witnessing how the Communists had changed their tactics from set-piece affairs to terrorist wars as in Malaysia and Greece, some of the Army's top brass saw a need for the Army to have troops specially trained in organizing anti-Communist guerillas.

Therefore, in April 1952, they set up a Special Warfare School at Fort Bragg in North Carolina. According to Special Forces Captain Roger Donlon, who earned the Medal of Honor in Vietnam: 'In April 1952, when the Army decided to organize Special Forces, it . . . wanted paratroopers skilled in airborne assault, both day and night, and in infantry maneuvers, demolitions, amphibious landings, mountain and winter tactics, jungle fighting, and techniques of guerilla warfare. Over and above all that, they were to be organizers and teachers, capable of dropping into a strange land and building the natives there into an effective guerilla force.'

On 20 June 1952 the 10th Special Forces Group (Airborne) was formed at Fort Bragg by the commander of the World War 2 Office for Strategic Service Unit Detachment 101, Colonel Araron Bank. He recalled that the 10th's initial strength was 'one officer, one warrant officer and eight enlisted men. Our strength rapidly increased, and within approximately nine months we had a muster of over 1,000 personnel, of whom about 350 were officers.'

In September 1953 the 77th Special Forces Group (Airborne) was organized, drawing officers and men from the 10th. The latter was then posted to Germany. A 1st Special Forces Group (Airborne) was organized in Okinawa on 24 June 1957, largely from elements of the 77th.

In 1965 Donlon wrote: 'Men throughout the Army, in any of its branches, possess the same skills in Special Forces. But the Army has organized Special Froces as *the* unit of greatly skilled individuals. It has given them the triple mission of guerilla warfare, psychological warfare and counter-insurgency. The enlisted soldiers must be triple volunteers—for the Regular Army, for the Paratroopers, and for Special Forces. They are trained and cross-trained until nothing can faze them, from halting a sleeping sickness epidemic to holding off two battalions in the dead of night.'

President Kennedy, inspired by World War 2 airborne commander Maxwell Taylor's book *An Uncertain Trumpet*—which argued that the previous government's policy of 'massive retaliation' wouldn't work with guerilla wars—believed in having special units capable of any type of action. He therefore ordered the Special Forces program beefed up and four more Special Forces Groups were formed. They were designed for deployment in Africa, the Middle East, Central and South America and Asia.

Indeed some 58 Special Forces troops were sent to the Commando Training Centre, Nha Trang, South Vietnam, to help the local government in its guerilla war as early as 1957. Within a decade, the 5th Special Forces Group, activated on 21 September 1961 and assigned to South Vietnam, was advising and assisting over 80,000 local paramilitary, regional forces and popular forces soldiers. They were especially successful in organizing mountain tribes on the side of the South Vietnamese.

However, since their main goal was to organize guerilla units in hostile countries, rather than to defeat them in friendly ones, they were often misused. Special Forces units were put in fixed bases where the enemy could come to them when they wanted rather than being allowed to roam through a hostile environment. As such, they were actually more of an élite if regular

Vietnam veterans assigned to the 6th SFGA cross a three-rope bridge at Camp Mackall, North Carolina. The two in the rear wear tiger-stripes while the one in the center wears a Mike Force beret of the same pattern. [*US Army*]

Two HALO-trained A Teams don their A/P28S free-fall parachutes at Pope Air Force Base outside Ft Bragg, North Carolina. A Lockheed C-130 Hercules transport waits in the background. [*US Army*]

infantry force than a band of guerilla organizers.

The Psychological Warfare Center was renamed the US Institute for Military Assistance in July 1969. Recognizing Vietnam's lessons, Special Forces then received a mission of giving military support and advice to friendly states. Today, the Special Warfare Center is named the John F. Kennedy Special Warfare Center.

In the early 1970s Special Forces also received the duty of anti-terrorist activities. This assignment went to the new 1st Special Forces Operational Detachment Delta (SFOD D) in July 1978. Delta Force, as SFOD D was soon nicknamed, was the main combat unit in the ill-fated Iranian hostage rescue on 24 April 1980.

The 1st Special Operations Command (Provisional) (SOCOM) was established at Fort Bragg on 1 October 1982 to command all special operations forces.

Special Forces is organized unlike any other Army unit. Each group has a headquarters and headquarters company for administration and support and two to four line companies. The basic unit under each head-quarters is the Special Forces Operational Detachment (SFOD). Units under the SFOD are teams. The C Team, under a lieutenant colonel's command and with five other officers and 18 non-commissioned officers, con-trols two to five B Teams; each B Team, commanded by a major, has the same number of men as the C Team and controls a varying number of A Teams; the A Teams are the basic field units.

The 1958 A Team included a commander, an execu-tive officer, a team sergeant, four weapons specialists, four demolitions specialists, two radio operators, a

radio repairman and a medic. The larger 1965 A Team also received an operations sergeant, a heavy weapons leader, an intelligence sergeant, a light weapons leader, an assistant medical specialist, a demolitions sergeant and a combat demolitions specialist. This organization was changed again in late 1968.

Signal companies were added in 1960 and aviation companies in 1963, though these were disbanded in 1965, and service companies with aviation capacities were added in 1972. Today there are about 4,000 officers and men in the Special Forces.

Two members of the 5th SFGA planning a patrol during Exercise 'Polar Siege', Ft Richerson, Alaska, February 1964. They wear the OG 107 parka with fur-ruffed hood and three-finger Arctic mittens. Pinned to their shoulder is the old 'aggressor' insignia, a green triangle. By this time 5th SFGA had adopted an embroidered flash. [*US Army*]

1. Captain, FA Detachment Commander, 10th SFGA, Bad Tölz, West Germany, 1956

This officer wears winter semi-dress uniform, often refered to as 'pinks and greens' due to its appearance in bright sunlight. He wears the still-unofficial, German-made 'Munich' beret, which is of a lighter green than the later ones. Over the temple he wears the Group's 'Trojan Horse' badge. The Ranger and unofficial gold-yellow-on-teal-blue Airborne tabs are worn over the newly authorized Special Forces patch.

2. Master Sergeant, FA Detachment Sergeant, 1st SFGA, Ft. Buckner, Okinawa, Japan, 1960

The 'A' Team Operations Sergeant, as the senior enlisted man on the team, had the additional duty of 'Team Sergeant'. In a sense he was the first sergeant of the team and was, and is, often refered to as 'Top'. Over his right chest pocket he wears Nationalist Chinese master jumpwings: foreign jumpwings (or other qualification badges) are often worn by US personnel in this position when awarded by Allied units with which they have trained. Members of the 1st SFGA had numerous opportunities to obtain foreign jumpwings, and some individuals had different wings on virtually every uniform. The Army khaki uniform was available in issue cotton or privately purchased tropical worsted wool; often refered to as 'TWs', these were much favored by officers and senior NCOs.

3. Brigadier General William P. Yarborough, Commandant, US Army Special Warfare Center, Ft. Bragg, North Carolina, 1961

President John F. Kennedy, considered by many to be the 'patron saint' of Special Forces, visited FT Bragg on 12 October 1961 for a demonstration of SF capabilities. It was the first time that SF troopers appeared en masse wearing the green beret with official sanction. When the President stepped from his limousine to be greeted by Gen. Yarborough, he asked, 'Those are very nice. How do you like the green beret?' The general replied, 'They're fine, sir. We've wanted them for a long time.' Later, in a letter to Gen. Yarborough thanking him for SF's efforts, the President wrote, 'I am sure that the Green Beret will be a mark of distinction in the trying times ahead.' Little did he know of the future trials that SF would endure, and survive; but one of its longest battles, for the beret, had been won.

1. CIDG MOUNTAIN SCOUT, PLEI YT COMMANDO TRAINING CENTER, I CORPS TACTICAL ZONE, VIETNAM, 1963

The Plei Yt Commando Training Center was operated by Detachment A-751, US Army Special Forces, Vietnam. Black uniforms were normally issued to these troops, while olive green spotted camouflage ones were the normal issue to Strike Forces companies. Headgear varied greatly and included various color and camouflage pattern jungle hats and caps, and brown berets. LBE was minimal and usually consisted of World War 2 gear.

2. NCO, RECONNAISSANCE TEAM LEADER, MILITARY ASSISTANCE COMMAND VIETNAM, STUDIES AND OBSERVATION GROUP

This is a composite illustration of a typical USSF Reconnaissance Team (RT) member. During the eight years that MACV-SOG existed, widely varying mission uniforms and combinations of equipment were employed: they changed with time, experience, the requirements of the mission and other circumstances. The uniform pictured is jungle fatigues with black disruptive splotches spray-painted on. Although only used to a limited extent, it proved to be very effective in jungle shadows and at night. LBE items were similarly camouflaged. Olive green and camouflage jungle fatigues, jungle fatigues dyed all black, and the various patterns of tiger-stripes were also used. Olive green jungle fatigues were the most common, as the dark green color had the appearance of an NVA uniform from a distance. Uniforms were sometimes soaked in insect repellent and air-dried before a mission. All manner of headgear was worn.

3. NCO ASSISTANT RECONNAISSANCE TEAM LEADER, PROJECT DELTA, DETACHMENT B-52, 5TH SFGA, VIETNAM, 1964

Project Delta, like the other 'Greek-letter' reconnaissance projects, utilized various uniforms, equipment and weapons throughout its six-year existence. Tiger-stripes were the usual uniform for these projects. The cut-down-brim jungle hat was greatly favored by Delta, but headbands made from triangular bandages were also popular, especially if the individual did not have to be concerned with concealing light-colored hair. LBE was the usual M1956 gear with a lot of canteens: water was a constant problem for the RTs, as the enemy often patroled along streams.

1. Specialist 5, 2nd Mobile Strike Force Command, Detachment B-20, 5th SFGA, Vietnam, 1969

This man characterizes the enlargment and general upgrading of Mike Forces in 1968–69. He wears the newer style US size tiger-stripes which actually fitted Americans—who usually had to make do with 'large' Asian uniform sizes. On his pocket he wears the 2nd Mike Force patch; this was normally worn by the strikers, but some USSF also wore it: 2nd Mike Force USSF personnel had their own elaborate 'dragon' pocket patch, but these were not worn in the field. The standard helmet, with a Republic of Korea Army camouflage cover, is being worn due to the more conventional nature of their operations. His jungle boots have the 'Panama' soles, named for the area where they were developed; the cleated sole was designed to reduce mud build-up. The indigenous rucksack appeared in the early 1960s, and was modeled on the NVA version because of its practical design, ease of manufacture, and the fact that from a distance it would assist the wearer to appear as an NVA or VC. Most were made of a water repellent grayish green fabric, but olive green canvas ones were also made.

2. Sergeant First Class, 3rd Mobile Strike Force, Detachment A-302, 5th SFGA, Vietnam, 1966

This NCO, assigned directly to a Mike Force Company, is wearing an early pattern of the tiger-stripes, which began to be issued in the early 1960s. The small 'cigarette' pocket on the trousers, and also found on some shirt sleeves, was in fact intended for field dressings. His jungle boots are the early version without the reinforcing straps at the ankles. He wears a red, white and blue scarf, popular with many Mike Force units. In some Mike Forces different colored scarves—e.g. bright green—were presented as unit level awards to individuals.

3. CIDG Striker, Plei Mrong Camp Strike Force, I Corps Tactical Zone, Vietnam, 1964

The spotted pattern camouflage uniform was used from the late 1950s until fully replaced by tiger-stripes in the mid-1960s; it proved to be rather ineffective, as it was not green enough for Vietnam's lush jungles and it light color was conspicuous. Olive green and black uniforms of a similar design were also worn by the early Strike Forces.

1. CIDG STRIKER, COMPANY 331, CHI LINH CAMP STRIKE FORCE, III CORPS TACTICAL ZONE, VIETNAM, 1969

This Striker wears an older version of the tiger-stripes than figure 2. These are faded, but were originally a lighter shade to begin with. His jungle hat is standard indigenous issue, but has the brim cut down by the camp tailor, a common practice. His boots are the later black canvas, rubber soled 'Bata' boots manufactured by Bata Footwear of Canada. Some CIDG managed to acquire US-made, Asian size jungle and all-leather combat boots. The company scarf, originally red, white and blue, has faded with washing. The CIDG Camp Strike Force patch, authorized in 1968, was normally worn on the left shoulder, but Co. 331 wore it on a red patch on the chest pocket. He wears M1956 LBE and carries an ARVN rucksack.

2. NCO, WEAPONS SPECIALIST, CAMP STRIKE FORCE, 5TH SFGA, VIETNAM, 1969

This member of an A Detachment is wearing the later pattern tiger-stripe uniform with a locally purchased jungle hat. The not-too-popular blue and green striped scarf was worn by some members of Company A, 5th SFGA. It was extremely rare for any insignia to be won on these uniforms—primarily for security reasons, but also because they only lasted for a few operations.

3. STAFF SERGEANT, MEDICAL SPECIALIST, CAMP STRIKE FORCE, 5TH SFGA, VIETNAM, 1967

Except when actually conducting operations, when tiger-stripes were worn, SF troopers normally wore the standard jungle fatigues. All authorized insignia were worn on these uniforms. Even after 1968, when subdued insignia were introduced, full-color embroidered insignia were often seen. Worn over the right pocket are Vietnamese Special Forces (VNSF) jumpwings. Shown here are the more common Vietnamese pattern, but wings embroidered in US style were sometimes worn. VNSF jumpwings were awarded honorarily to USSF troopers, and US jumpwings were likewise awarded to VNSF personnel. Over his US jumpwings he wears the combat medic badge. All other team members were eligible for the combat infantryman's badge after serving at least 30 days as an advisor and being involved in at least two offensive ground actions.

1. **Sergeant, Demolitions Specialist, 6th SFGA, Ft. Greely, Alaska, 1970**
Rappeling is a basic skill for SF troopers. This man wears a wool shirt with field trousers, the trouser counterpart of the field jacket. Climbing boots (usually refered to as 'Chippewas' after the manufacturer), the M1951 field cap (commonly referred to as the patrol cap), and work gloves complete the outfit. Slung over his shoulders are an M14 rifle (not standard issue, but sometimes used in exercises) and a non-electric demolitions kit.

2. **Corporal Weapons Specialist, 77th SFGA, Uwharrie National Forest, 1955**
This weapons specialist is presenting a class to 'guerrillas' on the Soviet PPSh-41 sub-machine-gun. During this period the 77th was wearing a Canadian-made beret. He wears the herringbone fatigue uniform with an M1953 field jacket. In 1955 the World War 2 rank chevrons (previously worn until 1948) replaced the small and unpopular gold-yellow and dark blue chevrons.

3. **1st Lieutenant, A Detachment Executive Officer, 11th SFGA, Camp Drum, New York, 1972**
Operating the team's G-13 hand-cranked generator is one of the less popular chores that members are called on to perform; it is a standing joke within SF that this is one of the principal duties of the A Team XO. He wears an olive green cold weather parka and field trousers under a two-piece overwhite camouflage suit. The parka has a detachable fur-ruffed hood. The cold weather insulated cap is designed to be worn under the helmet; a woodland camouflage version was introduced in 1983. Three-finger mittens, often refered to as 'triggerfinger' mittens, and rubber insulated boots complete the outfit. The boots are also made in black; known as 'Mickey Mouse' or 'VB' (vapor barrier) boots, they are extremely warm—sometimes too warm, as they are completely airtight. For this reason there is an air release valve on the side to allow for equalization of pressure when in an aircraft.

1 [Right]. **Staff Sergeant, Ranter Instructor, Detachment A-41, 46th SF Company, Thailand, 1972**
Detachment A-41 (Ranger) was responsible for instructing the Royal Thai Army (RTA) Ranger School, a component of the

RTA Special Warfare Center. All of the team's personnel were Ranger-qualified; many of the NCOs had been instructors in the US Army Ranger Department, and were directly reassigned to A-41. The team was additionally tasked with clandestine missions in Laos and Cambodia. Olive green jungle fatigues were the authorized uniform, but often, for instructor duties and while conducting operations with Thai Rangers, its members wore standard-issue black Thai Ranger fatigues. These were not merely dyed jungle fatigues, but Thai-made with black fabric. Worn with this uniform was a black beret with the 46th SF Company flash topped by a Ranger tab. A green beret was still the standard headgear with other uniforms.

This soldier has a strobe light and the excellent Air Force survival knife attached to the STABO extraction harness. The Thai ceremonial dagger was not just for show: it was recognized as a sign of authority by Thais, and was in fact issued to SF personnel involved in advisory duties.

2. 1ST LIEUTENANT, EXECUTIVE OFFICER, DETACHMENT A-45, 46TH SF COMPANY, THAILAND, 1972

Detachment A-45 (Special Missions), like A-42, was a team directly under the control of 46th Company Commander and used for special assignments such as Operation 'Freedom Runner'; these were operations conducted with the Cambodian SF. These two teams also conducted special reconnaissance missions in support of the RTA 2nd and 1st SF Groups respectively. Other teams directly under 46th Company Commander's control were A-41 (Ranger), A-43 (SCUBA), and A-44 (HALO).

The lieutenant wears the standard RTA SF camouflage fatigues, which were popular among USSF personnel in the 46th Company. On the ground is a forest penetrator. This device is used on rescue hoist equipped helicopters. It has a weighted nose and folding blade seats that allow it to penetrate through interlaced tree branches. One to three men can be hoisted into the helicopter on the penetrator.

3. SURFACE-TO-AIR RECOVERY SYSTEM

The Fulton Surface-to-Air Recovery (STAR) system was developed jointly in the early 1960s by the Army and Air Force under Project 'Sky Hook'. It provides a means of recovering personnel or equipment with long-range aircraft from areas out of range of helicopters.

1. **NCO, Parachutist Rough Terrain System (PRTS), US Army Institute For Military Assistance, Ft. Bragg, North Carolina, 1982**

The ability of an A Team to parachute into an area considered to be unfavorable for parachute insertion is highly desirable, but somewhat risky. For years SF has used techniques and equipment developed by US Forest Service 'smoke jumpers' for this purpose. This includes the use of penetration suits and the conduct of rough terrain parachuting courses for landing in heavily wooded, rocky or mountainous areas. The old two-piece penetration suits were of heavy olive green cotton canvas (although white and orange ones have been used in training) with padding at the knees and elbows. There was a leg-bag on the right leg containing a 50-ft lowering rope. A football helmet with a wire mesh faceguard was used. In 1981 the requirement for a new suit was established.

2. **NCO, High Altitude-Low Opening Parachutist, 5th SFGA, Ft. Bragg, North Carolina, 1978**

This jumper is equipped with the MC-3 free-fall parachute assembly, which includes the military version of the sport Para-Commander Mark I canopy (pictured in the background). This is a highly manoeuvrable 24-ft canopy, available in olive green or a camouflage pattern. The reserve parachute is an olive green flat circular non-steerable canopy. The rucksack, a large LC-1 ALICE (Advanced Lightweight Individual Carrying Equipment) with an LC-1 frame, is strapped behind the jumper, rather than on the front as in the case of static line jumpers, to allow a more stable free-fall position. Additional team equipment can be dropped in a free-fall bundle with its own parachute and automatic opener.

3. **NCO, High Altitude-Low Opening Parachutist, 7th SFGA, Ft. Bragg, North Carolina, 1973**

The High Altitude-Low Opening (HALO) concept was developed by the 77th SFGA in 1957–58, and involves the principles of sport skydiving modified to meet the requirements of military free-fall. Its purpose is to provide a means of parachute insertion into the area of operations, while making it difficult to detect and/or destroy the aircraft due to its extremely high altitude of up to 40,000 feet. The HALO Course is conducted by the Special Warfare Center.

1. PFC, Student, SF Training Group, Simmons Army Air Field, Ft. Bragg, North Carolina 1968

This SF Student is prepared to jump from a C-119 transport into Camp Mackall for his Phase I Field Training Exercise. He wears cotton fatigues with full-color insignia: subdued insignia were not introduced until late that year. This was also before the rocker was added to PFC stripes. The trousers are a popular commercial version available in Post Exchanges and refered to as 'ranger' trousers due to the addition of the leg cargo pockets. On his M1 helmet is the old leaf pattern camouflage cover. On the reverse side of the cover is a spotted camouflage pattern of four shades of brown. The rucksack is the nylon, aluminium frame jungle model, which is attached to the jumper upside down. It was extensively used by SF units in the USA, but seldom in Vietnam, as its design limited the number of items that coud be attached to the utility belt. About 200 ft above ground the jumper will release the rucksack which will drop below him secured by a 15-foot lowering line; this prevents injury from the heavy rucksack on landing. His weapon is an M14, 7.62 mm NATO rifle.

2. PFC, Student, US Army Institute For Military Assistance Student Battalion, Pope Air Force Base, North Carolina, 1983

Today's SF Student, prepared for his Phase I ordeal at Camp Mackall; his jump aircraft will be a Lockheed C-130. He is clothed in the new woodland pattern Battle Dress Uniform (BDU)—see figure 2. page 167. A matching, non-reversible camouflage helmet cover is now issued. The rucksack is the large LC-1 ALICE pack with the later LC-2 frame. LBE is a mixture of the new nylon ALICE and cotton canvas M1956 gear. His weapon is an M16A1 rifle in an M1950 weapons container. The main parachute is an MC1-1/B, an olive green 35-foot parabolic circular steerable canopy (pictured in the background). The reserve is now olive green. Both the main and reserve parachute containers are now of nylon rather than the cotton canvas used for the T-10. This system also features a greatly improved harness.

3. CTU-2/A High-Speed Aerial Delivery Container

The CTU-2/A was developed in the late 1970s to provide a means of resupplying A Teams from high-speed aircraft.

1. SERGEANT FIRST CLASS, TASK FORCE IVORY COAST, SON TAY PRISON, NORTH VIETNAM, 1970

The raid on the Son Tay Prison on 21 November 1970 was probably one of the most expertly executed rescue missions in modern history; tragically, however, it proved a 'dry hole'. The 65 American prisoners of war being held there had been moved to other prisons shortly before the raid. The Army element of Task Force Ivory Coast were SF troopers selected from the 6th and 7th SFGAs and commanded by Col. Arthur 'Bull' Simons. They were inserted into the prison compound and surrounding area by Air Force HH-3 and HH-53 helicopters flown by Air Rescue and Recovery Service crews. The soldier portrayed here is not a specific individual taking part in the raid, but rather a composite example.

2. NCO, SPECIAL FORCES OPERATIONAL DETACHMENT, DELTA 'DESERT ONE' BASE, IRAN, 1980

Delta Force's uniform during the ill-fated hostage rescue attempt was quite different from the usual standards of military dress. This was due to the unit's unique mission requirements and the need to blend into the population, at least from a distance. The 'uniform' consisted of an M1965 field jacket (worn by many Iranian students and 'Revolutionary Guards'), dyed black; a dark-colored civilian shirt; blue jeans; wool navy watch cap; and some type of black boots. Issue combat boots were common, but 'Chippewa' climbing boots were favored by many. On the jacket sleeve was a tape-covered American flag: the tape was to have been removed when the force reached the US Embassy in Tehran the following night. He is armed with a 9 mm West German-made HK5A2 sub-machine gun; telescoping-stock HK5A3s were also used. Other operators carried XM177E2 and M3A1 sub-machine-guns, M16A1 rifles, and accurized M1911A1 pistols. The force was also armed with an M60 and an HK21 light machine gun, 7.62 mm, and a few M79 and M203 grenade launchers. LBE was not carried, as it would have made it too easy to spot an operator.

3. NCO, SCUBA DIVER, 8TH SFGA, PANAMA, 1972

SCUBA (Self-Contained Underwater Breathing Apparatus) operations as conducted by Special Forces units are primarily intended for infiltration into enemy-held areas.

1. MAJOR, B DETACHMENT COMMANDER, 5TH SFGA, EXERCISE 'BRIGHT STAR', EGYPT, 1982

The desert camouflage version of the BDU was developed in the late 1960s, but shelved as there was no pressing requirement for it at the time. It was introduced in 1982 for issue to units operating in desert areas. Units slated for Army Central Command (formerly Rapid Deployment Force–RDF) are among those issued with it due to their possible deployment to the Middle East. The uniform is of the same design and fabric as the BDUs. A wide-brimmed jungle-style hat of the same camouflage pattern is available, but a helmet cover was not; units usually fabricated some type of cover, using sand-colored cloth. Army personnel in Saudi Arabia in 1990, 'however, had 'Fritz' helmet covers of this material.

2. STAFF SERGEANT, A DETACHMENT RADIO OPERATOR, 10TH SFGA, FT. DEVENS, MASSACHUSETTS, 1983

The Battle Dress Uniform (BDU) was first issued in 1982. Its design is based on the jungle fatigues, but several of the more practical design features were not included, thus detracting from its value as a field uniform. It is infrared-absorbent, which gives it some protection from certain night vision devices. The BDU's thick 50% cotton/50% nylon fabric also proved to be too heavy for year-round wear. This became readily apparent during the 1983 Grenada invasion, when an emergency issue of jungle fatigues was made to some units. The Army reintroduced the design improvements as well as issue a lightweight tropical/summer version in 1985; these were basically the old jungle fatigues with the addition of the woodland camouflage pattern.

3. SERGEANT MAJOR, STAFF NCO, 1ST SPECIAL OPERATIONS COMMAND, FT. BRAGG, NORTH CAROLINA, 1984

The Army Green uniform was adopted in 1957 and has gone through a number of minor changes since. The gray-green shirt replaced the tan poplin model in 1976; the gray-green shirt, in conjunction with the Army Green trousers, may be worn without the coat. This uniform replaced the Army Khaki and Tan (tropical worsted) uniforms in 1985. 'Corcoran' jumpboots (a brand name that has become generic) are normal wear with service uniforms by all SF, Ranger and other airborne units.

THE VIETNAM WAR,

After World War 2 Vietnamese nationalists fought the French for a free and independent Vietnam. France could not prevail against the winds of nationalism and, after its horrendous defeat at Dien Bien Phu in 1954, agreed to let its colony go.

However, there were problems between the Catholic/Western-oriented and Buddhist/Communist populations. An international agreement was signed that initially split the country along the 17th parallel, giving the Communists the north and the other side the south, the idea being that a general election would be held later in the entire country which would be then reunited under one leader. Ngo Dinh Diem, who became South Vietnam's leader in 1955, refused to hold any elections, his position being supported by US officials who feared the entire country would turn Communist.

Many Vietnamese were angered by Diem's decision and organized themselves as the Viet Cong (VC, later NLF) for Vietnamese Communists. They launched a terrorist campaign designed to capture the countryside by killing government officials. The Americans provided military advisors to the South Vietnamese Army, and the first of these to die in action was killed in a VC assault on an outpost near Bien Hoa on 8 July 1958. He would be

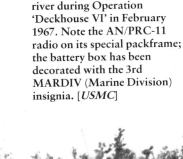

Marines of the 7th Fleet's SLF (Special Landing Force) cross a river during Operation 'Deckhouse VI' in February 1967. Note the AN/PRC-11 radio on its special packframe; the battery box has been decorated with the 3rd MARDIV (Marine Division) insignia. [*USMC*]

the first of nearly 50,000 US battle-deaths.

Diem also kept enemy successes secret. However, in late 1960 US diplomats and advisors finally realized the depth of the problem and persuaded President Kennedy to raise the amount of aid sent to Diem's government – though stopping short of asking for US troops to be committed. Still, the aid included a growing number of advisors, who were assigned into the US Military Advisory and Assistance Group, Vietnam. This group's designation was changed to the US Military Advisory Command, Vietnam (MACV) 8 February 1962, and placed under General Paul D. Harkins. By October 1963 MACV included 16,732 US officers and men.

Diem refused to commit troops to the large scale operations that MACV's officers deemed necessary, fearing the affect of heavy casualties among his supporters. MACV and US government officials had begun to lose trust in Diem as early as 1960 and, as reports of his family's corruption grew, he also lost support from many Vietnamese, notably the Buddhists. The Vietnamese and Americans began to look for ways of getting rid of Diem and his family, and in November 1963 Diem was overthrown. Kennedy was also killed days later.

Kennedy's successor, Lyndon B. Johnson, named Lieutenant General William C. Westmoreland to command MACV. Previously an artillery officer and airborne infantry divisional commander, Westmoreland's reaction to the war in Vietnam was a conventional one; indeed, most top American officers wanted a conventional war. Major General Harry Kinnard, who had been at Bastogne and now commanded the 1st Cavalry Division (Airmobile), noted: 'I had always thought that the correct US response – in a much bigger picture – should have been to march straight for Hanoi and force the other guy to fight on our terms. If we had gone into North Vietnam, we could have forced him to fight a conventional war, and we knew how to do that better than he did.'

Westmoreland asked for combat troops to guard MACV's growing number of land installations. When it appeared that North Vietnamese gunboats attacked the USS *Maddox* off their coast on 2 August 1964, Congress granted President Johnson the right to commit US ground forces to war in Vietnam. Today, it is difficult to tell if there actually was such an attack or not. It seems unlikely.

The first ground combat troops, some 3,500 Marines, landed on 8 March 1965. Reinforcements would not be far behind. The 1st Infantry Division landed at Cam Rahn that August, followed a month later by men of the 101st Airborne. The 1st Cavalry Division (Airmobile) arrived in September 1965. By now America was firmly committed to a land war in Asia.

All these units were officially permitted to begin

1962–1975

'offensive patroling' on 8 June. This was soon broadened to include 'search and destroy' missions, the first one of which was launched on 28 June. These were sweeps through the countryside in an attempt to perform the Army's traditional objective: 'find, fix, fight and finish the enemy'. There were variations of the search and destroy mission, known as 'raids', 'search and clear', and 'clear and hold'. The latter missions were, however, somewhat rare, for, as Kinnard later said: 'With an air assault unit [as most combat units were organized in Vietnam] you don't give much of a damn about terrain. You can go anywhere. The focus is on the enemy. You go where he is.'

The American troops were based in heavily fortified camps. They would board helicopters at these bases, head out into the country and set down in some pre-determined point. From there, they would march towards another pre-determined point in an attempt to pin down and destroy enemy forces.

These tactics, depending basically on attrition, were badly flawed. The lighter equipped and armed enemy troops could easily escape the heavier equipped and armed Americans and their allies. Or, if they wanted, they could stay just long enough to inflict morale-

With face camouflaged, and wearing a 'tiger-stripe' uniform and 'Jones hat', a reconnaissance soldier wades a stream; even his M-16 is 'tiger-striped', apparently with paint. He is a member of the Aerorifle Platoon (ARP), 2/17 Cavalry, 101st Airborne Division; ARPs undertook short-range reconnaissance, evaluated air strikes, and provided security for downed aircraft. He is festooned with cotton bandoliers and grenades. A pilot's survival knife is taped to his harness, and above it an empty film can, probably to hold matches. The knife is a poor choice of weapon, due to its short blade and sawtooth back. A field dressing pocket has been sewn to the left sleeve of the jacket, and note the yellow chamois leather work glove, a fairly common item. The rucksack is the ARVN two-pocket model. [*US Army*]

Soldiers of the 1st Infantry Division's 61st Infantry Platoon (Combat Tracker) with one of their Labrador retriever dogs, near Lai Khe Base Camp in October 1969. Magazines for their CAR-15 SMGs and M-16 rifles are carried in cotton bandoliers and in the newly issued M1967 lightweight ammunition pouches. Note bag-type 'two-quart canteens' slung from belts, right foreground, and profusion of smoke grenades. This photo shows some of the ways the 'boonie hat' could be worn; and the left hand man wears a locally-made leaf-pattern 'Jones hat'. The sergeant (E5) team leader, sipping from his canteen, wears on his hat a 'peace sign' made from a grenade ring and trip-flare wire. The unit's élite status is marked by a shoulder title worn above the 'Big Red One' shoulder patch. [*US Army*]

A heavily-laden 'grunt' lugs an M-60 machine gun up a steep slope during a search-and-destroy mission in May 1969. His waist and pack are festooned with ammo belts; a belt-fed machine gun requires some exposed 'ready' ammunition to be carried, but in strong sunlight their glitter can be seen too clearly for tactical safety. A canteen is clipped to the rucksack. Note the towel round his neck and the matchbooks in his helmet band. [*US Army*]

Heavily-equipped soldiers of Co. 'C', 1st Bn., 18th Infantry, 1st Division, man a machine gun position on their perimeter during an action near Tan Uyen in August 1969. [*US Army*]

damaging casualties on the Americans. In 1967, for example, it was reported that 88% of all engagements were actually initiated by the NLF rather than by the Americans. Moreover these tactics, while definitely killing enemy soldiers, did not deny them access to the civilian population, from whom they drew supplies and men. These tactics suited the NLF in that they met their own objective, which was to draw the Americans away from pacification projects and engage them in inconclusive battles.

Still, even the NLF had to admit they were losing men. So it was that the North Vietnamese Army (NVA) sent its first combat units south in May 1965 to support the NLF.

These Vietnamese were there for the duration, unless killed or badly wounded. The Americans, on the other hand, didn't have one army in Vietnam for 13 years; they had 13 armies there for one year each. For every man 'in country' had to serve there 365 days before being sent back to the US. Thus each soldier's main objective was simply to survive one year. Specialist Four David Clark, a radio operator in A Company, 8th Cavalry, 1st Cavalry Division, was quoted by a *Life* magazine reporter after coming back from a mission in October 1970 as saying: 'It was all right. Main thing was we got through without getting anyone hurt. We didn't get anything done, but I don't care.' The motto of the 101st Airborne Division was 'Stay Alert–Stay Alive'. True, but hardly heroic.

These short tours of duty were 'criminal', Kinnard later said. 'I was brought up in World War 2 and you stayed in your unit until you were killed, wounded or the war was over. There was no other way out. I think that it should have been that way in Vietnam. Between the losses to combat, malaria and tours, there's no question that the quality of the 1st Cavalry was going down . . .' as the war continued.

The United States began to lose local civilian support as it declared open warfare on anything that moved during its search and destroy missions through countryside considered in enemy hands. Major General Julian J. Ewell even gained the nickname of the 'Delta Butcher' as his 9th Infantry Division sought to earn high 'body counts', the US measure of success in a war without lines. 'We really blew a lot of civilians away,' one of his officers was later quoted as saying.

By late 1967 the Communists felt confident enough to engage in fixed battles, starting by besieging a Marine force of some 3,500 men at Khe Sahn. The US was determined to hold the position, and it soon gained almost all of their attention. But as they became mentally pinned down there, the NVA launched a major offensive on 30 January 1968–the Tet Offensive, named after the Vietnamese New Year holiday.

Some 30 out of 44 provincial capitals were in their control by 5 February, while their men even managed, guns blazing, to get into the US Embassy grounds in Saigon. In Hue, once Vietnam's capital, they held on long enough to gather thousands of South Vietnamese

'Tunnel Rats' of the 56th Engineer Demolition Team, 25th Infantry Division, display captured enemy equipment during Operation 'Wahiawa' in May 1966. They wear M-56 equipment over M1952 armor vests and OD T-shirts. These early model vests were later modified, losing their shoulder straps and receiving an uncomfortable three-quarter collar. The central man has a white plastic C-ration spoon tucked in his equipment. A mixture of M-14 and M-16 rifles is evident; the captured weapon is the ChiCom Type 53 carbine. [*US Army*]

sympathizers and brutally murder them. In most areas, however, they were quickly driven off with heavy losses.

By 26 February the Tet Offensive was over. It was, as far as the men in the field were concerned, a major South Vietnamese victory, but the picture was different back in America. The nation's civilians began taking to the streets to protest the war, and some of its politicians began to agree with them. Westmoreland was named the Army's Chief of Staff in Washington, and on 13 May 1968 peace talks began in Paris.

To satisfy the American public President Nixon began withdrawing troops, starting with some 35,000 in December 1969 and followed by another 50,000 in April 1970. Yet this still left 300,000 US combat and 180,000 US support troops in the country — and Nixon ordered these men, and their allies, on a large-scale raid into Cambodia to destroy North Vietnamese supplies and attempt to capture their headquarters. Although many supplies were found and destroyed, the headquarters escaped and the American public was outraged by this extension of an already unpopular war.

Nixon was forced to continue withdrawing American troops. America's final ground troops, a defense force around the Da Nang air base, where the very first American ground troops had been deployed, left for the US on 11 August 1972. Only embassy guards remained.

Though a peace treaty was signed on 27 January 1973 the actual war continued, and on 2 January 1975 the NVA began an attack on a Phuoc Bihn, which fell that May. Other cities fell like playing cards, with Da Nang in enemy hands by 31 March and Qui Nhon by 1 April. Finally, on 1 May 1975, NVA tanks drove down Flower Street in Saigon with no resistance. America had lost its first war — exactly 200 years after it began the fight for nationhood.

The repercussions in the Army were many. Some observers blamed the Army, with its emphasis on individual advancement above overall goals in its big-business structure. Others failed to see the basic fact that the military, not civilians, controlled the field war, focusing on the lack of civilian support. They did not realize that the defeat was indeed fundamentally a military one, caused by an inexperienced force lacking in dedication and using badly flawed tactics.

1. 1ST LIEUTENANT, INFANTRY, US MILITARY ADVISORY COMMAND VIETNAM, 1965

The standard fatigues worn in the early stages of the war before the issue of special tropical clothing. Note straight shirt pockets and the lack of thigh pockets on trousers. The high-lacing black combat boots were also standard at that time. The helmet has a camouflage-printed cover, slit for the attachment of foliage and with a green elastic band round it for the same purpose. The basic web set is worn–pistol belt and braces, with holster for .45 caliber automatic and first aid pack only. Thread versions of the silver rank bar and gold rifles branch badge are worn on the shirt collar points, and name and 'U.S. ARMY' tags on the right and left breast respectively, the former in white, the latter in yellow letters on black. The MACV sleeve patch replaced the old blue MAAG (Military Assistance Advisory Group) patch with white stars.

2. 2ND LIEUTENANT, INFANTRY, US ARMY, 1965

This newly arrived officer wears the walking-out or 'Class A' summer uniform authorized throughout the year in Vietnam. The olive sidecap is trimmed with mixed gold and black cord; enlisted men had black trim, and generals wore gold trim. Officers wore rank insignia on the left, and on the right this man wears a patch indicating service with an airborne command.

This officer wears the sky-blue infantry shoulder cord indicating that he has successfully completed a unit army training program while in an assigned infantry unit. The green epaulette loops indicate that he commands a unit 'whose mission is to combat the enemy by direct means or methods'. Rank and branch of service badges are worn on his right and left collar points respectively. His name tag is white on black plastic, pinned above the right pocket. Above the left pocket are parachute wings, and an Expert Infantryman badge; this latter was awarded to men who passed a series of proficiency tests.

The two medal ribbons beneath these qualification badges are the Good Conduct and Armed Forces Expeditonary medals; the first was awarded only to enlisted men after three years of excellent service–this officer thus served in the ranks before being commissioned, which helps explain his rather formidable appearance in such a junior rank. The Armed Forces Expeditionary Medal was awarded for service in an operation for which no campaign medal was struck, such as in Cuba (1962–1963) or in the Congo (1964).

1. SPECIALIST 4, HQ COMPANY, 864TH ENGINEER BATTALION (CONSTRUCTION), 1965

One of the first American units to land in Vietnam, the 864th received early-pattern fatigue uniforms, including sun helmets. Dark patches on the old fatigues indicate the previous owner's commissioned rank. Note the leather and canvas double-buckle boots, the sunglasses case on belt, and the unit and rank insignia.

2. 1ST LIEUTENANT, 18TH INFANTRY, 1ST DIVISION, 1965

This man has the later pattern tropical fatigues, with tilted pockets fastened by hidden buttons, and a fly front. The leather and nylon jungle boots are obviously brand new–after any time in the field the dust or mud rendered them an overall tan, thus the slang name 'boonie buffs'. Metal insignia of rank and arm are worn on the collar here, and the 1st Division's 'Big Red One' patch is worn in unsubdued form, in red on olive green. The camouflaged helmet cover has an elastic band round it for the attachment of foliage, into which, typically, this officer has forced his plastic bottle of insect repellant.

Basic web equipment is worn, with one ammo pouch on his left front and a smaller first aid pouch on the right; a green smoke grenade is taped to one suspender, a Kay-bar to the other, and a fragmentation grenade is worn on the side of the ammo pouch. Note the olive plastic canteen stopper. His weapon is the CAR-15, of which one forthright officer later wrote: '. . . it was short and sharp and looked good on television or in movies or in pictures for the old family album, but it was, in fact, one hell of a lousy weapon. It misfired, jammed, and just plain did not operate–but it did look good.'

1. PRIVATE, US MARINE CORPS, 1968
The standard fatigue shirt has the sleeves cut short and rolled. Marine units tended to lag behind the Army in the issue of new patterns of equipment; this man carries the M14 rifle, and the old pre-war metal canteens, and wears black leather boots. An extra ammunition bandolier is slung around him. The helmet cover–typically for a Marine, worn without the elastic band–has been 'felt-tipped' with an indication of his home town and state. Less restrained decorations were widely observed.

2. 2ND LIEUTENANT, US MARINE CORPS, 1968
The visored cloth fatigue cap, of characteristic Marine shape, bears the gold rank bar above the stencilled black Corps badge. Gold rank bars are worn on each collar point of the old-style fatigue shirt, and US Navy pilot's wings are worn on the left breast. Noted the wristwatch worn through the buttonhole; and the black leather holster for a .45 caliber automatic on the right hip.

1. MAJOR, ARTILLERY, US SPECIAL FORCES, 1966

This major wears the green beret with the intermediate tropical fatigues with exposed buttons. The gold leaf of this rank is pinned through the black, white-bordered beret patch of the 5th SF, with the red and yellow diagonals adopted while serving in Vietnam. The green unit commander's loops on the shoulder-straps appear in the photograph from which this illustration is taken to bear the Special Forces crests. Yellow thread rank and artillery branch badges on olive backings are sewn to the collar points. Yellow and black 'RANGER' and 'AIRBORNE' flashes are worn on the left shoulder above the teal blue SF patch. The name tag is black on olive, the U.S. ARMY tag yellow on black, and white cloth parachute wings are sewn about the latter.

The weapon at this early date is the .30 caliber M2 carbine with 'banana' magazine, and a .45 caliber automatic is worn on the belt in its standard brown holster. The brass bracelet on the right wrist is one of those presented as a sign of friendship by the Montagnard peoples among whom the SF often operated, in the course of an elaborate ritual. Cheap Vietnamese-made copies were often bought and worn by men who had never even seen a 'Yard'.

2. CHIEF WARRANT OFFICER W2, 1ST CAVALRY DIVISION (AIRMOBILE), 1970

Helicopter pilots like this man were often warrant officers especially trained for this specific duty. The gold rank bar with three brown rectangles is worn on the right collar, the warrent officers' eagle on the left. The 'subdued' divisional patch is on the left shoulder. He carries his flying helmet, and wears one of the several slightly differing versions of 'flak jacket' in service. Helicopter crewmen were sitting targets for ground fire, and generally wore them; ground troops in the bush found them extremely hot and burdensome and often left them in camp, depending on the type of opposition they faced. Photographs indicate that US Marine infantry tended to wear them more regularly than Army personnel. This pilot wears a typical civilian revolver holster rig with a privately acquired 'six-shooter'.

3. TROOPER, ARMOR, 1969

Typical informal wear for US personnel—bare torso, bush hat decorated with beadwork and slogans, towel, and fatigue trousers with jungle boots.

1. STAFF SERGEANT, 101ST AIRBORNE DIVISION, 1965

The 101st was among the first major units to deploy to Vietnam, and the sergeant's appearance is typical of this period. His M-1 steel helmet is covered with a reversible camouflage cover held in place by an elastic camouflage band; the band also holds a plastic bottle of insect repellent. He wears the early model jungle uniform, with exposed buttons and full-color insignia and nametapes. His newly procured 'jungle boots are the early pattern, without ankle reinforcement.

2. TANK CREWMAN, 11TH ARMORED CAVALRY REGIMENT, 1968

Armor crewmen in Vietnam wore the same uniforms as everyone else. Personal equipment was dictated by the nature of their duties. Poor visibility from inside the vehicles often required the crews to expose heads and upper torsos during operations, so flak vests were common wear (ordinarily these were worn by Army troops only in static positions). This man has the later version of the Army M1952, without shoulder straps and with a three-quarter collar added. Although steel helmets were prefered, the vehicle's communications system required some personnel to wear the CVC (combat vehicle crewman's) helmet, made of fibreglass and offering little protection from enemy fire. The M1944 goggles worn with it were also issued to drivers of ordinary wheeled vehicles. As personal protection this man carries a .45 pistol in a shoulder holster. He is currently examining the contents of a captured NVA rucksack.

3. SPECIALIST 4 GRENADIER, 1ST INFANTRY DIVISION, 1968

This soldier wears the later-style utilities (made in rip-stop cotton) with an OD towel as a sweat rag. His M-56 equipment has some additions reflecting his duties as a grenadier. The M79 40 mm grenade launcher was a new type of infantry weapon and its ammunition was originally issued in special cotton bandoliers, each holding six rounds in two 'packs' of three (each 'pack' further secured in a plastic holder). The original issue of two bandoliers proved totally inadequate, and further rounds were carried in ammo pouches and empty Claymore mine bags. He holds a captured ChiCom Type 56 LMG, a copy of the Soviet RPD; this was the standard NVA and VC Main Force LMG by this period.

1. US MARINE MACHINE GUNNER, HUE CITY, TET OFFENSIVE, FEBRUARY 1968

Adapted from a photograph, this Marine M60 gunner wears an intermediate type of jungle utilities with concealed buttons. Over this he wears a nylon US Navy rain jacket, and the Marine M1955 armor vest. His personal equipment includes the marine jungle first aid kit and two OD plastic canteens in M1910 carriers. As a machine-gunner he is also issued a .45 pistol and a Kabar knife in lieu of a bayonet. All of these are attached directly to the bottom of the vest, which has a row of grommets for this purpose.

2. US MARINE RIFLEMAN, 1ST BATTALION, 7TH MARINES, SPRING 1969

Starting in late 1968, the new 'Leaf-Pattern' camouflage uniform was adopted by the Marine Corps. Unlike the Army, the Marines were allowed to 'mix and match' camouflage with regular jungle utilities during the transition period. This rifleman has the modified M1955 armour vest, with two crude pockets sewn on the front. He is equipped only for a short patrol. M16 magazines are carried in a bandolier and an old Claymore bag, and the pockets of the vest. M1910 canteen carriers were becoming scarce by this time, but this man has found one to carry an OD plastic canteen.

3. US MARINE RADIOMAN, OPERATION STARLITE, AUGUST 1965

Operation STARLITE, conducted against the 1st VC Regiment in the 'Street Without Joy' region of I Corps, was the first major Marine operation of the war. This lance-corporal's uniform and equipment are typical of the period. He wears the Marine HBT utilities, of 1950s vintage, and the characteristic Marine utility cap. The Marine globe-and-anchor insignia is stencilled on both. Rank insignia are displayed as metal pin-on devices on both shirt lapels. In common with most US troops at this time, he has yet to receive jungle boots and so wears his black leather issue. His reversible helmet camouflage cover is worn 'brown side out' in the coastal sand dunes; a camouflage band has been improvised from a strip of inner tube. His personal equipment includes the M1961 rifle belt and ammunition pouches, especially designed for the M14 rifle. The rest of his equipment is of much older vintage and the AN/PRC-10 radio is an obsolescent model dating from the Korean War, but then still in used by the Marines.

1. **STAFF SERGEANT, US ARMY SPECIAL FORCES, RT ZETA, MACV-SOG, 1968**
Reconnaissance Team Zeta was one of a number of similar teams conducting covert cross-border operations under the auspices of the Military Assistance Command Vietnam's Studies and Observation Group (MACV-SOG). It operated in the tri-border region of Laos, Cambodia and Vietnam under the direction of Command and Control, Central (CCC), based at Kontum, RVN. A mixture of indigenous personnel and American Special Forces were employed. This SF trooper wears a private-purchase 'tiger-stripe' camouflage uniform; this version is a Thai pattern probably obtained on a Bangkok R&R. Headgear is an ARVN camouflaged 'Jones hat' with brim removed.

As load-bearing equipment this man wears a STABO rig, manufactured at the unit level from nylon aircraft harness. It doubled as an extraction harness. Attached are an Air Force strobe light in its case and a PAL RH-36 knife. The standard M1956 pistol belt, worn as part of the harness, holds four M1956 universal pouches and two two-quart canteens. The pack is an ARVN two-pocket rucksack with integral 'X'-frame, which holds an AN/PRC-25 radio with a plastic bag fastened around the handset to keep moisture away from components. Two M26A1 fragmentation grenades are ready at the belt; additional grenades are carried in two Claymore bags slung over the rucksack, and two standard canteens are attached at the sides. The weapon is an M16 fitted with a Human Engineering Laboratories M4 silencer and an AN/PVS-2 starlite scope.

2. **US ARMY LRRP, 74TH INFANTRY DETACHMENT (AIRBORNE) (LRRP), 173RD AIRBORNE BRIGADE, 1968**
This man wears the ARVN camouflage beret, which along with the camouflage 'Jones hat' and M1951 Patrol Cap was the usual combat headgear of all Allied élite forces. 'Leaf-pattern' camouflage utilities are worn with M1956 pistol belt and suspenders and four universal pouches. These held a total of 16 M16 magazines, and a further 14 were often carried in two bandoliers tied around the waist. At 19 rounds per magazine (a full 20 might cause malfunction) this gave a total of 570 rounds for the weapon—in this case an XM-177, universally known as a CAR-15. This was the SMG version of the M16.

1. HELICOPTER PILOT, 1ST AVIATION BRIGADE, 1970

This Army captain, returning from a decoration ceremony, wears the two-piece flying suit ('Shirt and Trousers, Flyer's, Hot Weather, Fire Resistant Nylon OG 106'). Especially developed for Army aviators, it was made of Nomex, a fire-resistant synthetic, and was first issued in late 1969. Sleeves were tightly tailored to discourage personnel from rolling them up (some did anyway), and it included a multipilicity of pockets. Most of the insignia worn here are of subdued pattern, as per regulation. These include the pilot's nametapes, branch (infantry) and rank insignia, and the Army Aviator's badge above the left pocket. Full-color insignia (reserved for 'best dress') include the shoulder patch of the 1st Aviation Brigade (left shoulder), the 121st Aviation Company on the left pocket, and this unit's RAZORBACKS platoon patch on the right. The last two items are examples of unofficial unit insignia. The man also wears the full color patch of the 4th Infantry Division on his right sleeve, indicating a previous combat tour with that unit. His black Stetson hat is an affectation of some Cavalry and Aviation units in the early 1970s; it was strictly for ceremonial purposes, and was not worn in the field, as some film-makers would have us believe.

2. HELICOPTER CREWMAN, 1ST CAVALRY DIVISION (AIRMOBILE), 1968

Before the introduction of Nomex uniforms, Army helicopter crews flew in standard fatigues. Ordinary ground troops' body armor was worn. In late 1968 the Army introduced new types especially for aircrews. This man, an Sp5 crew chief of the 229th Assault Helicopter Battalion, wears the version for gunners and crew chiefs. Usually called the 'chickenplate vest', it comprised front and back plates of aluminum oxide ceramic armor, moderately effective against high-velocity small arms projectiles. A version for helicopter pilots and co-pilots (who had armoured seats to sit in) comprised only the front plate. Later models used lighter and stronger ceramics which reduced the weight slightly from this model's 25 lbs. The crew chief also wears the Army APH-5A Flyer's Helmet with integral headphones and boom mike. His weapon is the famous 'Swedish K' (Kulsprutpistole M45 'Carl Gustav'), a 9 mm weapon originally introduced into Vietnam in the early 1960s by the CIA.

1

2

US FORCES IN THE AMERICAS,

In the 1980s the United States' primary military involvement was in Latin America, where Communists continued to take advantage of corrupt and cruel dictatorships to ferment rebellion. On the little Caribbean island of Grenada, however, Maurice Bishop overthrew the country's first independent government in March 1979 and then invited Communist countries to assist him. He also organized the People's Revolutionary Armed Forces (PRAF), which grew larger than the neighboring island nations' armed forces. And work began on a large airport which could possibly be used by Russian or Cuban bombers.

Then, in 1983, Deputy Prime Minister Bernard Coard, who desired even closer ties with other Marxist countries, had Bishop and many of his supporters placed under arrest and shot. In October members of the Organisation of Eastern Caribbean States (Dominica, St Lucia, St Vincent, Montserrat, St Kitts-Nevis and Antigua) decided to invade Grenada and replace the Marxist government with a more peaceful one. Since their armed forces were too small to do this, they appealed for help to the US, Barbados and Jamaica, and US Navy Vice Admiral Joseph Metcalf III was named overall invasion forces commander.

Metcalf and his staff devised a complex operation. The 75th Infantry (Rangers) would seize the Port Salines airport with a company-sized parachute drop while the rest of a battalion would disembark from planes as they slowly rolled down the runway; Marines would land on the northern part of the island; SEALS, the Navy's elite commando force, would capture Government House, free the Governor-General and seize Radio Free Grenada's transmitter; the Army's Delta Force would capture Richmond Hill Prison and take up positions around the airport before the Rangers arrived.

Grenada's PRAF consisted of two infantry battalions, along with another seven militia infantry battalions which were almost worthless in action. The defense could also draw on around 700 Cubans, most of whom were construction workers with only basic military training, and 38 armed Soviet, 17 Libyan, 15 North Korean, 12 East German, and three Bulgarian military 'advisors'. The island had a minimal air defence system made up of 20 ZSU 23 anti-aircraft guns which, in fact, saw little action. Most of the defenders' weapons were hand-me-downs from Cuba of World War 2 vintage. They had eight BTR-60PB armored personnel carriers, most armed only with machine guns, and two BRDM-2 armored vehicles.

Delta Force and the SEALS were parachuted onto the island on 23 October. A Cuban worker spotted the Delta Force at the airport shortly after 2am and the garrison was quickly alerted. They surrounded and pinned down Delta Force until the force could be covered from the air by an AC-130 Spectre gunship and brought out by Rangers. At least six Delta Force troops were killed while another 16 were wounded.

The Delta Force whose goal was the prison were

The 4th Platoon, 2nd Amphibious Assault Company regroups at LZ 'RACETRACK' on Wednesday 26 October 1983. Generally known as the 'amtrack', the LVPT-7 is the standard USMC personnel carrier; it can carry 25 passengers as well as a crew of three, and is armed with a .50 caliber turret-mounted machine gun. A UH-46D of HMM-261, workhorse of the Grenada campaign, waits behind it. [USMC]

1983 & 1989–1990

brought in on helicopters of Task Force 160, an élite aviation unit. Since the helicopters were unable to land in the rough terrain, the men began to repel by ropes, coming under heavy fire as they dropped. As many as five helicopters were knocked from the sky. The mission was a failure and the survivors quickly retreated. Marines captured the empty prison the next day.

Meanwhile, the main assaults began. On the morning of the 25th, Rangers arrived at Port Salines to find the runways blocked by construction equipment, so they decided to drop the entire group by parachute instead of simply one company. Rigging had to take place in the air, and normal jump procedures were abandoned. Jumping at low altitudes with heavy loads, the Rangers also came under fire that was heavier then expected. The first two aircraft veered off at the last minute, so the first Rangers to jump, at around 6am, were from the third.

The first men to land started up bulldozers and began to clear the runways, which was done in around 30 minutes. Other Rangers moved against Cuban positions which were as close as 400 yards from the drop zone. Finally, around 10am, they declared the airport area safe and called for relief, as per plans, from the 82nd Airborne Division.

Around 2pm the first men of the 82nd began to land – much to their surprise under fire from a Cuban barracks near the airport that had not yet been captured. While one of the stated reasons for the invasion had been to free American students at a Grenadan medical school, it was not until late in the afternoon that the Rangers were able to capture one of the school's campuses and free the students there.

All night Cuban and PRAF troops prepared their defenses and sniped at the Americans. The next day, the 82nd advanced to link up with the Marines, but stiffened resistance held the advance to a crawl, despite heroic uses of air power.

By the end of the second day the 82nd had come only four miles from the airport, and defenders still held Calivigny Barracks and Fort Frederick. Rangers landed by helicopter to capture the barracks, while gunships plastered Fort Frederick (and, unfortunately, a nearby mental hospital). Both were then quickly captured.

Late on the 27th it was declared that 'all major military objectives on the island were secured' – a task that required some 5,000 paratroopers, 500 Rangers and 500 Marines as well as special and support units. Although the armed forces gloried in their success, in truth the operation was something less than magnificent; intelligence was poor and joint forces planning produced an overly complex plan.

The Army's next involvement in the Americas was in Panama, where Panamanian Defense Forces (PDF) General Manuel Noriega voided free elections that had not endorsed him as President in May 1989. His

handpicked government named him 'Maximum Leader', and he then declared Panama and the United States were in a 'state of war'. His supporters began harassing US servicemen along the Panama Canal.

In the early hours of 20 December 1989 almost 20,000 US soldiers, sailors, and Marines invaded the little country. The 6th Mechanized Battalion and a battalion of the 87th Infantry captured the headquarters of the PDF. One battalion of the 75th Infantry captured Panama City's airport, while a second battalion captured Rio Hato, where Noriega's most loyal units were based. Troops of the 82nd Airborne blocked the way into Panama City from the east, while two Marine companies, a rifle company and a light armored infantry company cut off the route from the west. Troops of the 82nd Airborne and 7th Infantry Divisions captured the electrical power station at Sierra Tigre, the Madden Dam on the Canal, and the Gamboa Prison, where Noriega's political prisoners were detained.

The next day President George Bush was able to tell his fellow Americans that the invasion was 'pretty well wrapped up', and only minor sniping continued as the legitimately elected civilian Panamanian government was sworn into office. Yet the major object of the exercise – the kidnap of Noriega to face drug-smuggling charges back in the US – was not accomplished, and an embarrassing New Year stalemate followed. Eventually, on 4 January 1990, the deposed 'President' gave himself to the US forces and was flown to Miami to stand trial. As in Grenada, better intelligence and less force might well have brought richer dividends for the US.

A US Army Ranger from 1/75th Ranger Battalion leads two handcuffed PRA infantrymen into captivity at Point Salines. Slung over his shoulder is one prisoner's folding stock AKM, and in his right hand he carries their web gear of Soviet origin. The captives wear Cuban fatigue uniforms and boots, while the helmets are the latest Soviet type. Many of the units which served in Grenada and then saw action in Panama during 1989 also participated in 'Operation Desert Shield' from August 1990 as a force defending Saudi Arabia against potential attacks from Iraq, who had conquered Kuwait.
[*US Army*]

1. GRENADIER, 2/325TH INFANTRY (AIRBORNE), 82ND AIRBORNE DIVISION

The 82nd Airborne Division was the first unit to recieve the new Kevlar helmet, developed as part of the PASGT System. Because of its Germanic shape it was immediately dubbed the 'Fritz' by the Army. Any problem with its appearance was quickly forgotten on Grenada; the new helmet was credited with saving the lives of at least two paratroopers. The 82nd received a special paratroop model of the 'Fritz', with a different internal suspension from the model issued to ground troops. The rest of this grenadier's equipment is the standard ALICE nylon web gear, with 40 mm grenade rounds carried in Vietnam-era plastic slip-on carriers. (The standard method of carrying these rounds is the nylon vest shown opposite, but the 325th also used the type shown here.) Extra rifle ammunition is carried in cotton bandoliers secured across the body. A LAW anti-tank rocket is secured to the soldier's pack. The carrier for the protective mask at the man's waist is worn secured for jumping with a strip of tape; after arrival on the island, many paratroops did not bother to remove the tape. BDU sleeves are rolled up in the approved Army fashion, which leaves the camouflage pattern outermost.

2. SNIPER, 1/508TH INFANTRY (AIRBORNE), 82ND AIRBORNE DIVISION

In the US Army the maroon beret was first introduced (unofficially) for Airborne troops in the mid-1970s. Permission for its wear was withdrawn in 1979, but reinstated a year later. As with other units authorized a beret (Special Forces and Rangers), it is worn with a shield-shaped 'flash' in the unit colors. Centered on the flash officers wear metal rank insignia, and enlisted men the distinctive metal unit crest. Not all 82nd troops wore BDUs in Grenada; some still had the older cotton woodland uniform. The standard Army sniper weapon is the 7.62 mm M21 rifle, used with the Redfield Accutrack riflescope offering a variable capacity of 3 to 9 power. This man also carries a pair of M19 general field use binoculars.

The uniforms were the same in the Panamanian campaign as on Grenada, save that invasion troops wore small regular colored (red, white and blue) US flag patches, edged in yellow, on their right sleeves. Some troops also wore white rags tied round their upper left arm as a kind of field sign.

1. RANGER, 2/75TH RANGER BATTALION
In addition to his normal ALICE equipment, this 2/75TH rifleman wears the unique ammunition vest issued only to this battalion. Developed by a private contractor, who arranged a gratuitous issue to the unit, it was designed to carry various types of magazines and grenades. Apparently several different patterns were provided for testing. In the field, the metal pin-on rank insignia normally worn on the collar (see figure 2) are often omitted. Four M59 fragmentation grenades are carried attached to ammo pouches, and an M7 bayonet in scabbard M8A1 is attached to the LC-2 pistol belt.

2. RANGER, 2/75TH RANGER BATTALION
In common with other Rangers, this man wears jungle boots, Vietnam-era hot-weather fatigues, and the all-nylon web gear designated the ALICE System. Individual components are designated in the LC (lightweight combat) series. The standard set comprises belt suspenders, LC-2 pistol belt (with quick-release buckle improved over the LC-1 type), field dressing pouch, two ammunition pouches and two plastic canteens in carriers. His weapon is the M203 rifle/grenade launcher, which combines a pump-action 40 mm grenade launcher with the standard M16 rifle. Its rounds are carried in a special grenadier's vest; made of nylon mesh and cotton duck, it holds 24 rounds. In addition to M67 grenades carried on ammo pouches, a snap ring, used in rappeling from helicopters, is also attached. Instead of the PASGT armor vest the black hardcore second chance type is worn; in general, on Grenada, it was used only by vehicle drivers who had remained aboard the C-130s and came in afterwards. The plain OD M1951 patrol cap, with its distinctive 'crush', is now unique to the Rangers: the rest of the Army uses the same cap but in woodland camouflage.

3. RANGER, 1/75TH RANGER BATTALION
The little-known 90 mm M67 recoilless rifle was developed in the early 1960s as a company anti-tank weapon. In most of the Army it has since been replaced by guided missiles; however, because of its light weight, it remains in use with the Ranger battalions. Their gunners had an excellent chance to demonstrate its effectiveness at Point Salines! Remaining A/T rounds and the ever-present light anti-tank weapon (LAW) are carried in this man's ALICE pack. His personal weapon is a CAR-15.

183

1. US MARINE MACHINE GUNNER, 2/8TH MARINES, 22ND MAU

The Marines taking part in 'Urgent Fury' were dressed in the new camouflage battledress uniform, usually refered to as 'BDUs'. This was adopted by the Army and Marine Corps in 1981 to replace all other field clothing in use. Made of a 50/50 nylon-cotton fabric for greater burn protection, the uniform was the subject of criticism even before Grenada. Some odd features of its styling, as well as the fabric itself, made it hot and uncomfortable in warm climates. A lighter weight Tropical BDU uniform has since been developed. With it is worn standard ALICE gear and the new PASGT (Personal Armor System, Ground Troops) body armor. Made of Kevlar, the vest provides protection against both bullets and shrapnel; older US body armor protects against shrapnel alone. Metal pin-on rank insignia is displayed on the flap. As a machine gunner, this man is also issued a .45 pistol and Kabar knife. The pistol's spare magazine pouch is also attached to the vest, a common practice.

2. US MARINE RIFLEMAN, 2/8TH MARINES, 22ND MAU

Stripped to his olive-green T-shirt (now used only by the Marine Corps), this Marine shows a rear view of the LC-2 webbing. The rectangular pouch at the rear of the belt is the jungle first aid kit; while part of the ALICE system, it is used only by the Marine Corps. Not all Marines were issued jungle boots, and this man has the ordinary DMS (direct moulded sole) type.

3. DRAGON A/T GUNNER, 2/505TH INFANTRY (AIRBORNE), 82ND AIRBORNE DIVISION

The wire-guided M47 Dragon missile is the Army's medium-range anti-tank weapon; launcher, base and sights fold neatly into this configuration for carrying. Seen from this angle, the gunner also presents a good view of the ALICE medium pack. Shown attached to its right side is the standard two-quart canteen. Helmet camouflage policy varies in the 82nd by battalion: some units use only the woodland cover while others, 2/505th among them, specify additional strips of burlap to help break up the helmet's outline. Similarly, strips of tape are used to camouflage the stock and foregrip of the rifle. This soldier has also carried out a standard, although unauthorized modification to his M16, improvising an assault sling from the standard issue.

1. RANGER, 2/75TH RANGER BATTALION

Both the 1/75th battalion, from Ft Stewart, Georgia and the 2/75th battalion, from Ft Lewis, Washington, jumped at Point Salines, using T-10 parachutes rather than the newer MC-1. Because of the low altitude from which they jumped, the 2/75th were ordered to discard their reserve parachutes. Current procedures call for rucksacks to be carried upside-down beneath the reserve 'chute. Apparently, due to the speed with which they 'packed' in the crowded C-130s, many men elected to jump with their equipment rigged as shown.

2. SPECIAL FORCES OPERATIONS DETACHMENT DELTA

In the early 1970s the role of the Special Forces was expanded to include anti-terrorist activities, and most of these jobs were given to a new 1st Special Forces Operations Detachment Delta (SFOD D) in July 1978. In 1980 several helicopter companies in Ft. Cambell, Kentucky, were formed into the 160th Task Force and trained to carry SFOD D when needed. The two units saw action in Grenada, where their casualties were unexpectedly high.

There was supposedly wide variation in weapons and personal equipment. This trooper wears the plain OD (Olive Drab) jungle fatigues without insignia (both plain and slanted pocket types were wore) with standard jungle boots. Load-bearing equipment includes a STABO extraction harness and LC-2 pistol belt. Attached to the harness is a Gerber Mk II knife and an Air Force strobe light. Worn on the belt itself are two standard canteens and a third, two-quart canteen carrier, employed as a pack. It contains a flare projector, certain components of an MRE ration (Meal, Ready to Eat), half of a two-part survival kit, etc. A standard Army flashlight completes the soldier's equipment. His weapon is the folding-stock Uzi 9 mm SMG with improved Sionics sound suppressor.

3. HELICOPTER PILOT, 82ND COMBAT AVIATION BATTALION, 82ND AIRBORNE DIVISION

This UH-60 Blackhawk pilot is wearing the standard flying equipment issued to all Army aircrew, including the CWU-27 flight suit, GR-FRP-1 gloves and the steel-toed boots used in all flying operations. The helmet worn is the SPH-4C, originally introduced in the late 1960s for both fixed and rotary-wing aircrew.

THE US ARMY TODAY

A drill sergeant demonstrates bayonet moves to a trainee. Both wear the battle dress uniform (BDU). [*US Army*]

After Vietnam the US Army was a defeated organization, full of self-doubts, and its leaders soon saw the need for reshaping it. The draft was eliminated in 1973 and the Army became an all-volunteer force, but with that the quality of enlisted personnel fell off; in many headquarters companies during the draft as much as 75% of the enlisted personnel had been draftees with higher educational levels than volunteers. Drug and alcohol use was high. Discipline was poor.

The Army initiated a program to improve non-commissioned officer (NCO) skill levels to those existing prior to Vietnam. Benefits were improved and, during the slow economic times that followed the Vietnam War until the early 1980s, a better class of volunteer began to arrive.

This became vital since so much of the Army today is computerized, using highly advanced technology. For example, each field artillery battery uses a Battery Computer System (BCS) to provide fire control and ballistic computation capability. Enlisted soldiers now operate the world's first automatic hostile-weapon-locating system, Firefinder. They may have to use a Ground/Vehicle Laser Locator Designator (G/VLLD) which finds the range, azimuth and elevation to enemy targets and speeds up artillery fire. Some men work TACJAMs, the Army's ground-based, highly mobile tactical communications jamming systems. Even the Army's pay system is now completely computerized.

To get soldiers with these above-average abilities, the Army began to make better use of women volunteers. In 1973 women officers were allowed to command men in any but combat or tactical units; the same year they became eligible for flight training; in 1976 women cadets were accepted at the US Military Academy; and finally, in October 1978, the Women's Army Corps was folded and 'WACs' became 'soldiers'.

There are now over 83,000 women in the Active Army, working in 318 out of the 368 enlisted Military Occupational Specialties (MOSs), 70 of the 90 warrant officer specialties, and 198 of the 207 commissioned officers specialties (combat jobs are still forbidden). Women play a larger role in today's US Army than in any other army in the world. The Army even authorizes maternity camouflage fatigues.

The US Army of the 1990s comprises the Regular Army, the Army National Guard and the Active Army. The Regular Army consists of a permanent, professional group of volunteers who make the military their careers. Army Reserve Components include the state National Guards, which report to state governors in times of need as well as to the Army, and the Army Reserve, which is the Army's general reserve force. Almost half of the Army's combat forces are provided by reservists. The Active Army is made up of the Regular Army and any Army reservists on active duty at the time.

The Army's slightly fewer than 780,000 active person-

An M1 Abrams main battle tank moves down a range road. Its low profile can be appreciated when compared against the height of the tank commander. [*US Army*]

nel, the limit set by Congress, are organized into different branches of service, as they first were in 1775. Officers begin in one branch and stay there until they retire or become general officers. Most enlisted men change their branches as they are reassigned into different types of units; some senior NCOs, such as first sergeants, remain in their designated branches.

There are 23 branches, both combat and combat service support. Combat branches include Infantry, Air Defense Artillery, Field Artillery, Armor, Aviation and the Corps of Engineers. Combat service branches include the Signal Corps, Military Police Corps, Chemical Corps, Military Intelligence, Adjutant General's Corps, Finance Corps, Quartermaster, Ordnance, Transportation, Chaplain Corps, Judge Advocate General's Corps, Medical Corps, Dental Corps, Veterinary Corps, Medical Service Corps, Army Nurse Corps, and Army Medical Specialist Corps. There is also a Warrant Office Corps. In addition two branches, Staff Specialist (Corps) and Civil Affairs, exist only in the Army Reserves.

Air Defense Artillery is charged with eliminating an enemy air threat, largely with HAWK, Roland and Chaparral guided missiles. The Army Air Defense Artillery School is located at Fort Bliss, Texas.

Armor is given the job of developing and conducting 'mobile warfare'. Successor to the Cavalry, its chief weapon is the M1 Abrams main battle tank. There are four Active Army armored divisions, the 1st Cavalry and

A tripod-mounted AN/TVQ-2 ground-vehicle laser locater-designator is aimed at a target to guide either a Hellfire missile or Copperhead 155 mm projectile. [*US Army*]

the 1st, 2nd and 3rd Armored Divisions. The two Army National Guard armored divisions are the 49th ('Lonestar') and 50th ('Jersey Blues'). The Armor School is located at Fort Knox, Kentucky.

Aviation, the Army's newest combat branch, is formed into combat aviation brigades (CABs), which are assigned at corps and division levels. Its primary weapons are AH-1S Cobra and AH-64 Apache attack

The HMMWV (high mobility, multipurpose wheeled vehicle), or 'Hum-Vee', is one of the principal vehicles used by the 9th Division (Motorized), but is also replacing the $\frac{1}{4}$-ton 'jeep' utility vehicle in most other combat units. Available in a number of versions, this model mounts an M220A1 TOW missile system. [*US Army*]

A ground-mounted M220A1 TOW missile system is prepared for firing. Mounted above its main tracker (sight) is an AN/TAS-4A thermal-imaging night sight. [*US Army*]

As an instructor looks on, an infantry trainee fires a 40mm M203 grenade launcher mounted on an M16A1 rifle. Though seemingly awkward to fire, it is an extremely accurate weapon out to 380 yards. [*US Army*]

helicopters. The school is at Fort Rucker, Alabama.

The Corps of Engineers does the Army's building and destruction jobs. It has a full range of equipment from M9 armored combat earthmovers to rock-crushing machinery. The US Army Training Center (Engineer) is at Fort Leonard Wood, Missouri.

Field Artillery has both self-propelled and towed cannon in its arsenal. The M119 105mm and M198 155mm towed howitzers are its primary towed guns, while the M109A2/A3 155mm self-propelled howitzer is the main self-propelled gun. The Field Artillery School is located in Fort Sill, Oklahoma.

Infantry is the oldest formal US combat arm. Most of the Army's infantry has been assigned to divisions. Active Army infantry divisions include the 1st (Mechanized), 2nd, 3rd (Mechanized), 4th (Mechanized), 5th (Mechanized), 6th (Light), 7th (Light), 8th (Mechanized) and 9th (Motorized), plus the 25th (Light), 82nd Airborne and 101st Airborne (Air Assault). As the threat of a European war declines with the breaking up of the Soviet Union's sphere of influence, some of these divisions may be demobilized to cut costs.

Army National Guard divisions include the 26th ('Yankee'), 28th ('Keystone'), 29th (Light–Blue and Gray'), 35th (Mechanized–'Santa Fe'), 38th ('Cyclone'), 40th (Mechanized–'Grizzly'), 42nd ('Rainbow') and 47th ('Viking').

Mechanized infantry rides into battle in Bradley fighting vehicles or the older M113 armored personnel carrier. The men are armed with Dragon anti-tank missiles; M249 Squad Weapons, which are 5.56 caliber machine guns, Stinger air defense missile systems, M16A2 rifles with 30-round magazines, MK19-3 40mm automatic grenade launchers, and M9 9mm automatic pistols. Company artillery support comes from M224 60mm lightweight and M252 81mm mortars. The US Army Infantry Center and School is at Fort Benning, Georgia.

The Chemical Corps is responsible for nuclear, biological and chemical warfare. Chemical and biological material is tested at Dugway Proving Ground, Utah, and chemical munitions are made at the Pine Bluff Arsenal, Arkansas.

Military Intelligence handles intelligence, counter-intelligence, cryptologic and signals intelligence, electronic warfare, operations security, order of battle, interrogation, aerial surveillance, imagery interpretation and related activities. The Army Intelligence Center and School is located at Fort Huachuca, Arizona.

The Military Police Corps not only provides post security and law enforcement, but also conducts combat operations against enemies behind the front lines and helps men and equipment reach the front lines smoothly. The MP School is at Fort McClellan, Alabama.

The Signal Corps is responsible for the Army's communication systems. The US Army Signal Center and School is at Fort Gordon, Georgia, with the US Army Information System Command at Fort Huachuca.

The Adjutant General's Corps handles personnel and administration. This includes everthing from library management to heraldry, from internal review and audits to the physical disability evaluation system. The school is at Fort Benjamin Harrison, Indiana.

The Chaplain Corps is in charge of conducting religious services and advising commanding officers on morale and religion. The US Army Chaplain Center and School is at Fort Monmouth, New Jersey.

Infantrymen attending the Light Leader Course—an especially rigorous course for light infantry NCOs and junior officers—rappel from a UH-60A Blackhawk helicopter. [*US Army*]

The Finance Corps controls the computerized Joint Uniform Military Pay System (JUMPS) at the US Army Finance and Accounting Center, Fort Benjamin Harrison. The Finance School is at the same Indiana post.

The Judge Advocate General's Corps conducts court martials and advises commanders on military justice and discipline enforcement. The Judge Advocate General's School is located on the campus of the University of Virginia, Charlottesville, Virginia.

Ordnance is in charge of developing, making, acquiring and supporting Army weapons systems, ammunitions, missiles, and ground mobility matériel. The Office, Chief of Ordnance, is located at the Aberdeen Proving Ground, Maryland.

The Quartermaster Corps performs various logistical support activities ranging from supplying clothing and food to graves registrations, laundries and petroleum product testing. Its school is located at Fort Lee, Virginia. The Transportation Corps moves the Army's men and equipment on land, sea and air, and the US Army Transportation School is located at Fort Eustis, Virginia.

The Warrant Officer Corps is made up of warrant officers whose job skills and knowledge are too specialist in scope to require a commissioned officer but too important to trust to an enlisted man. Warrant officers fill some 90 jobs in 13 career fields: administration, aviation, communications/electronics, criminal investigation, graphics, health care delivery, intelligence, marine operations, mechanical maintenance, services, supply, weapons maintenance and utilities maintenance.

The Army Medical Department actually has six corps under it, with headquarters at the US Army Health Services Command, Fort Sam Houston, Texas. The Medical Corps includes the Army's physicians, the Dental Corps is made up of dentists, the Veterinary Corps comprises veterinarians and the Army Nurse Corps includes the Army's nurses. The Medical Service Corps provides medical scientists and specialists such as pharmacists, optometrists, biochemists, physiologists, podiatrists and audiologists. It also handles medical administration, lab work and experimental and practical environmental work. Finally, the Army Medical Specialist Corps includes dietitians and occupational and physical therapists.

Infantrymen wearing ALICE load carrying equipment coordinate with a supporting M901 ITV's commander. ALICE stands for All-Purpose Lightweight Individual Carrying Equipment. [*Emerson Electric Co.*]

1. DRILL SERGEANT
Outfitted in the universally-worn battle dress uniform (BDU), this DS wears the drill sergeant's trademark, the 'Smokey Bear' hat, or officially 'hat, drill sergeant, male, enlisted'. Modeled after the M1910 campaign hat (used until 1942), its style led to the drill sergeants' nickname of 'Smokey Bear' – never uttered by trainees in their presence. He wears the Expert Infantryman's Badge and the cloth version of the metal Drill Sergeant Identification Badge.

2. PHYSICAL TRAINING SUIT
Introduced in 1987, the physical training suit replaces a reversible gold-black version – the Army's colors; matching short-sleeve undershirt and running shorts are also available. These are not issued, but purchased from Quartermaster Sales. Running shoes are also privately purchased.

3. BASIC TRAINEE
Basic trainees wear a helmet liner with their company designation stencilled on the side; M1 steel helmets are also worn. On graduating to Advanced Individual Training, they are permitted to wear camouflage covers to set them apart from basic trainees. The brown AS 436 undershirt has completely replaced the olive green OG 109 for wear with all field or Class C uniforms.

4. FEMALE DRILL SERGEANT
With the increase in female volunteers in the mid-1970s, female DSs were authorized their own distinctive hat.

LIGHT INFANTRY FIRE TEAM, 7TH INFANTRY DIVISION (LIGHT), FT. ORD, CALIFORNIA

A rifle squad consists of two four-man fire teams, designated Alfa and Bravo, and a squad leader. One team provides a base of fire while the other maneuvers, and then roles are switched. The staff sergeant squad leader, positioned between the two teams, directs the squad by verbal orders and arm and hand signals. The squad move with the fire team in wedges, with the rear team covering the lead. During contact the teams will alternate, bounding past each other and providing covering fire. One of the platoon's two 7.62 mm M60 MG teams may be attached to a squad and positioned near the squad leader. These troops are equipped with the Integrated Individual Fighting System, consisting of the individual tactical load-bearing vest and the new large field pack. They also wear the Personal Armor System for Ground Troops (PASGT) helmet, commonly called the 'Fritz' due to its similarity to the German 'coal scuttle' design.

The team comprises: 1. The rifleman, armed with an M16A1 rifle and carrying a one-shot 66 mm M72A3 light anti-tank weapon (LAW); 2. The squad automatic weapon (SAW) gunner, carrying a 5.56 mm M249E1 SAW with a 200-round belt in the assault magazine; it will also accept M16A1 magazines; 3. The team leader, a sergeant, leading by example, i.e., his men freeze when he halts, fires when and where he does: he is armed with an M16A1 rifle; 4. The grenadier, armed with an M16A1 mounting a 40 mm M203 grenade launcher.

VOLSTAD

VOLSTAD

1. M224 60MM LIGHTWEIGHT MORTAR, 82ND AIRBORNE DIVISION, FT. BRAGG, NORTH CAROLINA

Light, airborne, air assault and Ranger rifle companies' mortar sections are equipped with this excellent weapon to provide immediate indirect fire support. Its 3,500 m range, coupled with greatly improved M720 HE rounds, makes it almost as effective as the 81 mm M29A1 mortar. This mortarman is armed with the new 9 mm M9 pistol (Beretta 92 SB-F) in an M12 holster.

2. STINGER ANTI-AIRCRAFT MISSILE SYSTEM, 2ND ARMORED DIVISION, FT. HOOD, TEXAS

The Stinger missile system, proved effective in Afghanistan and Nicaragua, is replacing the M41 Redeye as the small unit portable air defense weapon. It is issued as a round of ammunition in a disposable launch tube requiring no maintenance or testing. The 2nd Armored Division traditionally wears its 'Hell on Wheels' patch on the left chest – as Patton once stated that he wanted the division to be close to his men's hearts! A .45 caliber M1911A1 pistol is carried in the M11 shoulder holster.

3. M47 DRAGON MEDIUM ANTI-TANK/ASSAULT MISSILE SYSTEM, 8TH INFANTRY DIVISION (MECHANIZED), WEST GERMANY

The wire-guided Dragon's 1,000 m range and high hit probability provides rifle platoons with an unprecedented tank-kill capability. The missile is issued as a round of ammunition in its disposable launch tube. The Dragon is fitted with an AN/TAS-5 night tracker (sight) which detects a target's thermal (heat) signature. Its replacement, the Advanced Anti-tank Weapon System-Medium, is under development. This Sp4 is outfitted with the All-Purpose Lightweight Individual Carrying Equipment (ALICE), adopted in 1974 and still standard.

1. EXTENDED COLD WEATHER CLOTHING SYSTEM, 10TH MOUNTAIN DIVISION (LIGHT INFANTY), FT. DRUM, NEW YORK

The Army began to issue test models of Gore-Tex cold weather clothing in the early 1980s, but it was not until 1986 that the ECWCS was adopted for issue to light infantry, Ranger and SF units. Gore-Tex is a water and windproof laminated membrane fabric which 'breathes', preventing moisture build-up and overheating. The AN/PRC-119 radio began replacing the AN/PRC-77 in 1988; it is a member of the Single Channel Ground and Airborne Radio System (SINCGARS-V) family.

2. SNOW CAMOUFLAGE, 25TH INFANTRY DIVISION (LIGHT), CAMP KAMI FURANO, JAPAN

Troops training with the Japanese Self-Defense Forces wear a white ski mask-type cap, which can also be used as a helmet cover. The US Navy-issue navy blue watch cap is also authorized. The overwhite parka, trousers and mitten shells are merely a single layer of cotton fabric to provide snow camouflage when worn over the cold-wet and cold-dry uniforms.

3. COLD-WET UNIFORM, 2ND INFANTRY DIVISION, SOUTH KOREA

This uniform is designed to protect against the wet snow, slush, rain, mud and changing temperatures of a cold-wet environment. It includes long underwear, olive green OG 108 wool shirt and trousers, woodlands pattern camouflage field jacket (which replaced the M65 OG 107 in 1987) and liner, and OG 107 field trousers. It was planned to issue camouflage field trousers, but this has not been undertaken. The black rubber insulated boots are exceptionally warm and waterproof. He carries an M1911A1 pistol in an M2 holster.

4. COLD-DRY UNIFORM, 6TH INFANTRY DIVISION (LIGHT), FT. RICHARDSON, ALASKA

The cold-dry uniform protects against the temperature extremes, snow, ice and high winds found in far northern and Arctic regions. It consists of the cold-wet uniform, with the addition of Arctic parka and trousers, both with insulated liners. The camouflage-pattern insulated cap replaced the OG 107 type in the early 1980s. The white insulated boots are the same as the black model, but with an extra layer of insulation.

1

2

3

4

1. **RAIN SUIT, 5TH INFANTRY DIVISION (MECHANIZED), FT. POLK, LOUISIANA**
This M60 machine-gunner wears the standard rain suit over his BDUs. The green overboots replaced a higher and heavier black model in the early 1980s. Though still wearing an M1 helmet, he has been issued a PASGT helmet cover.

2. **DESERT NIGHT CAMOUFLAGE UNIFORM, 24TH INFANTRY DIVISION (MECHANIZED), EGYPT**
Participating in the 'Bright Star' Exercise with the Egyptian Army, this soldier is outfitted with the desert night camouflage parka and trousers, which serve two purposes: providing warmth for cold desert nights (liners are provided), and limiting detection by infrared night vision devices.

3. **LIGHTWEIGHT BATTLE DRESS UNIFORM, 1169TH ENGINEER GROUP, NAPO PROVINCE, ECUADOR**
Army Reserve National Guard (ARNG) and US Army Reserve (USAR) engineer units rotate to various South and Central American countries for three weeks annual training, to construct roads and take part in other civic action projects. The efforts in Ecuador are particularly grueling due to the extremely difficult terrain and climate. This second lieutenant wears the ripstop fabric BDUs, similar to the old tropical uniform (jungle fatigues). These began to be issued in 1986, since the standard BDUs are far too heavy for warm-hot climates. They replaced the OG tropical in 1987.

4. **DESERT BATTLE DRESS UNIFORM, 101ST AIRBORNE DIVISION (AIR ASSAULT), SHARM EL SHEIKH, EGYPT**
Battalions of the 82nd and 101st Airborne Divisions and the 197th Infantry Brigade rotate to the Sinai on three-month tours as America's contribution to the United Nations' Multinational Force and Observers (MFO). They wear the MFO patch on their right shoulder and a US flag patch on the left, below their unit patch. All MFO troops wear a 'burnt orange' beret with a small version of the MFO patch. The desert BDUs, introduced in 1982, have a slight drawback in that they were patterned for American deserts and do not sufficiently blend with those of the Middle East. A desert-pattern hat, of the same style as that worn by figure 3, is also issued. The same uniform saw service in Saudi Arabia, where the unit was part of Operation Desert Shield against Iraq in 1990.

1. M25A1 TANK PROTECTIVE MASK, 11TH ARMORED CAVALRY REGIMENT, GERMANY

Armored fighting vehicle crewmen are issued this mask, which utilizes a hose and M10A1 filter canister rather than the M17A2's internal filters. It includes an integral microphone permitting hook-up to the vehicle's intercom and radio system. An M5 hood is available, but was deleted here the more clearly to show the mask. The M24 aircraft mask is similar, but can be attached to the aircraft's oxygen supply. The M24 and M25A1 can be worn with the flight and combat vehicle crew helmets.

2. M40 PROTECTIVE MASK

After several unsuccessful attempts to develop a replacement for the M17A2, the M40 mask was decided upon. Among its improvements are added comfort, which means longer endurance and increased efficiency while in MOPP 4. The improved chemical protective overgarment features the woodlands camouflage pattern.

3. BOMB DISPOSAL CLOTHING SYSTEM

This suit is intended for Explosive Ordnance Disposal (EOD) personnel, and consists of a fire-resistant Nomex fabric shell lined with 16 plies of Kelvar ballistic fabric. Nomex/Kevlar spats protect the lower legs and feet. The face shield is made of a polycarbonate/acrylic material mounted on a foam-filled fiberglass chest plate. The effectiveness of the standard PASGT helmet is increased by addition of a bonnet of the same materials and layering as the suit.

4. MOPP 4

Mission-Oriented Protective Posture 4 translates to full nuclear, biological, chemical (NBC) protection; MOPP 1 is the field uniform with mask only, MOPP 2 adds the gloves and hood, and MOPP 3 includes the protective suit. The protective overgarment has a charcoal-impregnated polyurethane foam lining offering six hours of protection from chemical agents. The M17A2 protective mask, coupled with the M6A2 hood, provides excellent defense against NBC contamination. It includes a voicemitter and an integral drinking tube, which when attached to a canteen's M1 NBC cap permits the wearer to drink. The M17 mask did not have this capability. The M248A1 decon. kit (attached to the mask carrier) is used to decontaminate skin and individual equipment. M9 chemical detection tape is affixed to the suit.

VOLSTAD

1

2

3

4

1. CWU-27/P FLYER'S COVERALL, 6TH CAVALRY BRIGADE, FT. HOOD, TEXAS

This one-piece suit replaced a two-piece model in the late 1970s. The CWU-27/P, like most aviators' clothing, is made of fire resistant Nomex; both sage green and OG 106 versions are issued. A new Nomex BDU-style and pattern suit has begun to be issued. The individual's aviator wings, rank, and name are embossed on a Velcro-attached leather name tab. The steel-toed flyer's boots use 'D' rings rather than eyelets (to prevent burns caused by metal eyelets) and are lined with glove leather.

2. MA-1 INTERMEDIATE FLYER'S JACKET, 1ST ARMORED DIVISION, GERMANY

Made of Nomex, the MA-1 jacket features a reversible international orange lining to aid search and rescue efforts. In garrison officers wear full-color rank on their caps so they can be more easily identified.

3. N-2B COLD WEATHER FLYER'S JACKET

The nylon satin N-2B is issued to aviators operating in extremely cold regions. His GS/FRP-2 flyer's gloves are of Nomex and leather. He carries an individual cold climate survival kit.

4. SPH-4 FLIGHT HELMET AND SRU-21/P SURVIVAL VEST

The SPH-4 features a retractable sun visor, boom microphone and connector permitting all crewmen to enter the aircraft's intercom and radio system. The red and white reflective tape can be applied in several standard patterns; camouflage-pattern tape is also used by some units. The SRU-21/P vest has numerous pockets for a large number of survival items, a survival knife scabbard and revolver holster can also be attached. He holds an AN/PRC-90 radio, used to communicate with search and rescue aircraft.

1 [Right]. TANK BATTALION COMMANDER; 32ND GUARDS MOTORIZED RIFLE REGIMENT, FT. IRWIN, CALIFORNIA

Actually a captain and tank company commander of the 1st Battalion, 63rd Armor, 177th Armored Brigade, he plays the role of an OPFOR major and tank battalion commander. He wears the OG 507 durable press utility uniform (fatigues), which were no longer authorized after September 1987, but are still used by the '60th Guards Motorized Rifle Division'. A black beret is locally authorized for the unit, and displays his actual rank, the OPFOR star, and OPFOR branch of service insignia. The OPFOR shoulder patch is also worn.

With the ending of the Cold War it is questionable if OPFOR will continue to wear copies of Soviet-style dress in the 1990s–or even remain in existence.

2. OPPOSING FORCES SOLDIER; 60TH GUARDS MOTORIZED RIFLE DIVISION, FT. IRWIN, CALIFORNIA

This OPFOR soldier of the National Training Center's role-playing 'Soviet' unit is actually a member of the 1st Battalion (Mech.), 52nd Infantry, 177th Armored Brigade, outfitted in the OPFOR uniform issued through Training Support Centers. It features a 'Soviet' look-alike plastic helmet shell on a US helmet liner, Soviet-style branch of service collar tabs, and slip-on rank shoulder straps, here representing a junior sergeant. Note that OPFOR insignia, while similar to their Soviet equivalents, are of a different design. He is rigged with XM60 MILES (Multiple Integrated Laser Engagement System) gear, a system of laser detectors which registers 'hits' and near misses from a laser transmitter coded to distinguish the range and killing power of specific weapons, fitted to the rifle or other weapons, including tanks. When 'hit', a buzzer sounds and a light flashes from the alarm carried on his suspenders.

3. MECHANIC'S COVERALL; NATIONAL TRAINING CENTER SUPPORT BATTALION, FT. IRWIN, CALIFORNIA

This armored vehicle mechanic wears unit-issue OG 106 coveralls and steel-toed safety shoes. 'Class X' BDU's, i.e. worn and stained, are also used by maintenance personnel.

4. TANK COMMANDER; 194TH ARMORED BRIDGADE (SEPARATE), FT. IRWIN, CARLIFORNIA

Participating in a National Training Center rotation, this TC wears the lightweight BDUs. A special Nomex tanker's suit has also been developed along with a micro-climate cooling system ensemble, which cools the individual rather than attempting to cool the entire vehicle interior. The DH132 combat vehicle crew helmet is issued to all crewmen of armored fighting vehicles including commanders and drivers of APCs, IFVs, and SP artillery; it includes a vehicle intercom and radio microphone.

1, 2. INFANTRYMEN, 1990s

While much of the gear used by these soldiers is now in the process of being issued, some of it is not yet in wide use. It includes the lightweight BDUs, PASGT vest and helmet, Gargoyles 'Eye Armor' protective glasses, new combat boots, Individual Integrated Fighting System Tactical Load-Bearing Vest, and M9 multipurpose bayonet.

Figure 1, a mechanized infantryman, carries an M231 firing-port weapon as used in the Bradley fighting vehicles; outwardly similar to the M16A2, it is internally and functionally different. Bradley infantrymen are also armed with M16A2s for off-vehicle use; he also carries a Swedish-designed 84 mm AT4 multipurpose weapon, the replacement for the M72A3 LAW. Fluorescent 'cat's eyes' are displayed on his helmet band, allowing squad members to follow each other at night. Figure 2, a light infantryman, is armed with the much improved M16A2 rifle; and carries the new M22 7 × 50 binoculars, which incorporate laser protection filters.

3. SNIPER'S 'GHILLIE SUIT', 7TH INFANTRY DIVISION (LIGHT), FT. ORD, CALIFORNIA

The word 'ghillie' comes from the outfits used by Scottish gamekeepers or ghillies, who trained British snipers in World War 1. Snipers make their own suits by gluing protective canvas panels to the shirt and trousers fronts–they crawl a lot. Netting is sewn to the back, and burlap strips and camouflage garnishing are attached. A tropical hat is likewise camouflaged, and a veil added to conceal the face and drape over the rifle. His jungle boots are painted green. He is armed with a 7.62 mm M21 sniper rifle, an accurized version of the M14, fitted with a 3–9 × -power-adjustable ranging telescope; he carries the new M22 7 × 50 binoculars, incorporating laser protection fitters. The M21 will be replaced by the Remington 7.62 mm M24 bolt-action rifle with a 10 × scope. When crawling, the rifle is protected in a camouflaged 'drag bag'.

1. OFFICER'S ARMY GREEN UNIFORM, 1ST INFANTRY DIVISION (MECHANIZED), FT. RILEY, KANSAS

The AG44, 344, or 444 'Greens' are now the all-season standard service uniform since the Army Tan and Khaki uniforms were phased out in 1985. This Class A uniform, i.e. with coat, is worn on and off duty, and while traveling. The Class B version, i.e. without coat, may be worn with either long or short sleeve AG415 or 428 gray-green shirts; the long sleeve must be worn with a necktie. The enlisted version is similar, but without the black cuff and trousers braid. The green shoulder tabs indicate a Combat Leader, here a lieutenant-colonel of the 5th Field Artillery. There is also an optional white version of this uniform.

2. ENLISTED ARMY GREEN UNIFORM, FOURTH US ARMY, FT. SHERIDAN, ILLINOIS

This Sp4 wears one of many possible combinations of the female AG344 or 434 classic ensemble, which may be configured with and without coat, AG415 or 428 long and short sleeve gray-green shirts, and slacks or shirt. Over the name plate is the crest of the Signal Corps.

3. ENLISTED PULLOVER SWEATER, 7TH TRANSPORT GROUP, FT. EUTIS, VIRGINIA

This 11th Transport Battalion Sergeant 1st Class wears the optional-purchase pullover, modeled after the British 'woolly pully', also worn by females. The same type of shoulder marks are worn on the gray-green shirts; officers' have a thin gold stripe at the base. The AG garrison cap is normal wear for enlisted men. An optional black cardigan (button front) sweater is also authorized.

4. OFFICER'S WINDBREAKER

This captain wears another optional item that is seen with gray-green shirts or the pullover sweater. The female beret may also be worn with the classic uniform in lieu of the service cap worn by figure 2. A black single-breasted raincoat (with zip-out liner), replacing the AG rain- and overcoats, is worn with the Army Green and Blue, and Army White and Blue Mess uniforms.

VOLSTAD

1. **GENERAL OFFICER'S ARMY BLUE UNIFORM**
While the uniform is similar to other officers' 'Blues', general officers wear a different pattern of service cap and dark blue trousers.

2. **ENLISTED ARMY BLUE UNIFORM, GUARD, TOMB OF THE UNKNOWN SOLDIER, ARLINGTON NATIONAL CEMETERY, VIRGINIA**
'Blues' are issued only to enlisted personnel whose duties require their wear, as in the case of this guard of the Honor Company, 1st Battalion, 3rd Infanty ('The Old Guard'). However, his uniform bears several distinctions that set it apart from the 'normal' Army Blues: authorized wear of sunglasses, Honor Guard tab, Tomb of the Unknown Soldier Guard identification badge, no name plate or rank insignia (for uniformity–NCOs do wear their gold-on-dark-blue stripes), dress belt, and special padded shoes. Only the most select soldiers are chosen for the honor of guarding this shrine 24 hours a day, 365 days a year.

3. **OFFICER'S ARMY BLUE UNIFORM**
Neither slacks nor or the black beret are authorized with the female 'Blues', worn here by an Ordnance Corps first lieutenant. Male officers wear light blue trousers similar to enlisted men's, including the same width braid. Unit shoulder patches are not worn on 'Blues'.

1. OFFICER'S ARMY WHITE MESS UNIFORM

'Mess Whites' are worn at social functions from April until October. Another uniform class based on this is the Army White Evening Mess, worn with a formal dress shirt and white vest and bow tie. For a long time an 'officer's only' uniform, it was authorized for enlisted wear in the mid-1980s, along with the 'Mess Blues': enlisted personnel wear simplified cuff braiding with small gold rank insignia within. Female versions include black and white knee-length and full-length black skirts.

2. OFFICER'S ARMY BLUE EVENING MESS UNIFORM

This Medical Corps captain, identified by branch of service color lapel facings, wears the evening mess version of this most formal of uniforms, authorized for year-round wear. The 'Mess Blues' female version uses a knee-length skirt.

3. GENERAL OFFICER'S ARMY BLUE UNIFORM AND CAPE

Wearing the generals' version of figure 1's uniform, this figure demonstrates the principal differences—the sleeve ornamentation and trouser braid. Generals' capes are lined with dark blue while other officers' are lined with their branch color. Males' capes are knee length and females' finger-tip length.

201

US INFANTRY EQUIPMENT,

Company H, 44th Indiana Infantry Regiment, *c.* 1863 – a study of typical field infantry of the Civil War. The officer, second from the left, wears a shoulder sling as part of his sword belt. The first sergeant, next to him, wears a common private's belt and kit, as do the other men in the company. [*National Archives*]

Many Continental sergeants carried halberds, such as this British example, as symbols of their rank. The poles were generally six feet long. In the field, however, muskets were preferred. [*Philip Katcher*]

Just as the Army's organization has evolved, so the infantryman's combat load has been rationalized throughout the years to keep pace with weapons and manufacturing technology. Until 1866, with the acceptance of a breech-loading infantryman's longarm, cartridges have been nothing more than loose powder and a ball or balls wrapped in paper. To load his weapon, the infantryman tore the paper with his teeth, poured the powder down the gun-barrel and then rammed the ball down.

These cartridges were both fragile and non-waterproof. To keep them safe, therefore, infantrymen needed some sort of cartridge box. The first cartridge boxes were little more than leather pouches wrapped around a wooden block. The block was bored with holes, one for each cartridge, which kept the cartridges from rattling around and breaking open, while the leather flap kept the cartridges dry.

Most of these cartridge boxes were slung from the left shoulder to the right hip with a leather or linen sling. The 1798 model, however, as were some earlier ones, was worn on a waist belt, with a narrow strap passing up the chest and around the neck to keep the boxes secure.

In 1808 an improved model which incorporated a tin tray under a removable wooden block appeared. This box was later improved with an inner flap for added rain protection. It lasted until it was replaced with a box designed for the M1842 musket in that year. The new box used two tin containers instead of the wooden block and a small pouch on the inside front for rifle tools, rags and cleaning patches. An oval brass plate with the letters 'US' was attached to the flap. The M1850 box was similar, but had only one tin container. It was also made for use on a waist belt, rather than a shoulder belt. The

M1855 box returned to the two tin containers and had provisions for either a shoulder belt or a waist belt.

The last issued cartridge box was also the only one designed for fixed ammunition with brass cases. The so-called McKeever box first appeared in 1874 and held 20 cartridges in web loops sewn in the leather box. Later variations to this box include the M1876 0.45 caliber box, the M1880/1881 box, which used Mills web cartridge loops and bellows, and a final M1903 model for the M1903 rifle.

Most soldiers preferred to carry their fixed ammunition in loops sewn to their waist belts to inside cartridge boxes. The first of these were homemade by or for each soldier, but the Army accepted this method with the issue of the canvas web M1876 belt. It was followed by a series of slightly different belts, beginning in 1880.

The bayonet is the other basic attachment for each musket, and these were carried in scabbards attached to belts. Shoulder belts of leather or linen, passing from the right shoulder to the left hip, were worn from 1775 until the late 1830s, when waist belts gained favor. From 1808 until they were no longer used, shoulder belts were marked with a round beltplate worn on the center of the chest.

The first bayonet scabbards were leather with a brass tip and, after 1828, a brass throat. In 1862 a steel scabbard was introduced and this became standard issue in 1870.

With the introduction of percussion caps in 1841, some provision for their storage also had to be made. The first troops armed with these weapons had small pockets inserted on their jacket waistbands, but later a small leather pouch with an iron nipple pick and sheepskin lining was introduced. This was worn by

1775–1910

soldiers on the right front hip, beside the beltplate.

The equipment associated with the weapon was designed and issued by the Ordnance Corps, while other personal infantryman's equipment was designed and issued by the Quartermaster's Department. The two staff branches of service did not work together at any time to provide equipment that worked together to form a system.

The soldier's clothing and, at times, spare ammunition, was carried in his knapsack. The first American knapsacks were provided to Maryland, Pennsylvania, New Jersey and Virginia Continental troops. They were worn slung over the right shoulder and under the left arm, with a red-painted flap and two bags inside strapped together. One was to serve as the knapsack, the other as the haversack.

Later in the Revolution a painted linen or duck knapsack worn square on the back was adopted. It lasted until 1808, when the Lherbette patent knapsack, which had an inside divider and a separate bag for wet clothing, was used. These were painted blue with the red letters 'U.S.' in a white oval on the flap.

The Lherbette knapsack was finally replaced by the M1833 model, which had a rectangular wooden internal frame to keep it stiff and straps on the top to retain the soldier's gray blanket. That in turn was replaced by the M1853 knapsack, treated with black paint for waterproofing and with straps passing down from the shoulder straps to hook into the M1855 rifleman's belt.

During the Civil War most soldiers prefered to wear their clothing rolled inside their blankets, waterproof groundsheets, and shelter halfs. This roll was slung, horseshoe style, from the left shoulder and under the right arm. This field knapsack became officially adopted, though a number of knapsacks were later experimented with until the M1910 equipment was officially issued.

The soldier's food was to be carried in his haversack. The first haversacks were simply linen or canvas bags worn on a shoulder strap and fastened with three buttons. A black tarred version fastened with a leather strap appeared in the late 1850s, but was replaced in the 1870s by a khaki canvas model with a separate leather shoulder belt.

This M1850 copper flask was designed to hook on to the outer straps of the M1841 rifle pouch and belt. It is known as the 'peace flask' because of the clasped hands in the center of the design. The spout is a replacement; the original had adjustments to produce different measures of powder. [*Philip Katcher*]

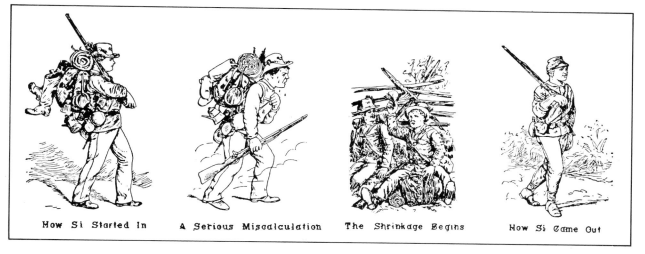

How Si Started In   A Serious Miscalculation   The Shrinkage Begins   How Si Came Out

The realities of the soldier's load remain the same to this day . . . what is perceived to be needed, as opposed to what is actually required. [*From Corporal Si Klegg and His 'Pard' by Wilbur F. Hinman, published by N. A. Hamilton and Co., Cleveland, Ohio, 1888*]

1. OFFICER, 1780
Both these infantrymen are clad in the uniform prescribed in 1779. The lieutenant, dressed in the buff facings of New York and New Jersey, wears his sword belt over his coat (although it was often worn under it, with a plain frame buckle). His sword belt plate is taken from one worn by the commander of the 3rd New York Regiment. He is armed with a spontoon and a typical light sword.

2. INFANTRYMAN, 1780
The private, who wears the red facings of Pennsylvania, Delaware, Maryland or Virginia, has a leather bayonet scabbard mounted in a white linen shoulder belt. The cartridge box is taken from an original in a private collection, and is the prefered box of the Continental Army; it contains only the wooden block, without a tin underneath. Two different types of typical musket slings are also shown; a third type used a brass buckle without a tongue. The private's weapon is a British Army Short Land Pattern Brown Bess.

3. BAYONET BELT & CANTEEN

4. CARTRIDGE BOX DETAILS

5. ALTERNATIVE MUSKET SLINGS

1, 2. OFFFICER & INFANTRYMAN, 1813

Although whitened buff-leather was pre-fered, most soldiers of the American War of 1812 received black leather belts. Wood canteens were also typical, but tin canteens of this kidney-section shape were issued in the Northwest Army in 1812, and have been dug up at Fort Meigs, Ohio. The knapsack is the Lherbette patent model, adopted in 1808. The private's weapon is an M1808 contract musket. The captain's silver shoulder belt plate is rectangular, with lipped corners, and with a central national eagle for a design.

3. HAVERSACK & CANTEEN

4. LHERBETTE PATENT KNAPSACK

1, 2. INFANTRYMAN & OFFICER, 1832
The Black Hawk War (April–September 1832) found a small but well-equipped army. The cartridge box was an improved M1808; the ornate flap adopted in 1832 is shown in detail. The grenadier company sergeant's weapon is an M1816 musket. The captain wears a waist belt with an M1821 belt plate, worn at those times when waist belts were worn instead of the regulation shoulder belt, until replaced in 1851.

3. 1808 CARTRIDGE BOX WITH 1832 FLAP

1, 2. INFANTRYMAN & OFFICER, 1847

The waist belt had been made regulation for enlisted men by the Mexican–American War. The cartridge box shown in the detailed sketch was designed for the M1842 musket; it could be worn only on a shoulder belt. The implement pouch was used for musket tools and patches. Notice the maker's name, Dingee, stamped on the inner flap. The corporal's weapon is the M1842 musket while the first lieutenant is armed with an M1840 foot officer's sword worn from the regulation shoulder-belt with its rectangular plate.

3. SHOULDER BELT & BAYONET SCABBARD

4. M1842 CARTRIDGE BOX

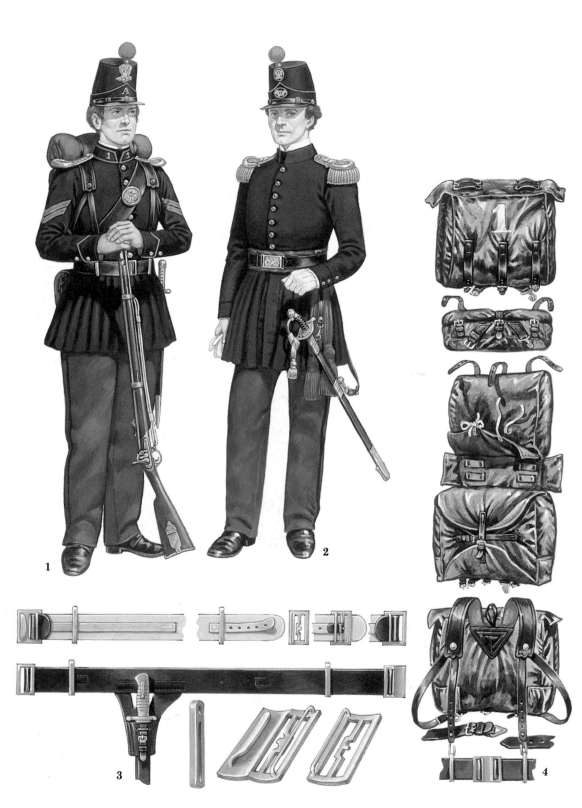

1, 2. INFANTRYMAN & OFFICER, 1857

The French influence was very noticeable in the appearance of the Army that went to Utah to ensure that Morman citizens there obeyed US laws. The corporal wears the M1853 knapsack hooked, as it was designed to be, to the M1855 rifle belt. Steps in attaching the buckle to the M1855 rifle belt are shown in the detailed sketch. The corporal wears no percussion cap pouch since the M1855 rifle came with the Maynard primer, a device using a roll of paper caps within the lockplate mechanism, instead of copper caps. The captain is also in dress uniform, armed with the M1850 line officers' sword.

3. M1855 RIFLE BELT DETAILS

4. M1853 KNAPSACK

1, 2. OFFICER & INFANTRYMAN, 1863

The field dress of the American Civil War infantry was plain but serviceable. The percussion cap pouches worn on the corporal's and first lietenant's right front hips contain, as shown, an iron nipple pick. This particular model is an early one, with a shield-shaped outer flap; later examples had the flap and closing strap cut as one piece. The corporal's weapon is an M1861 Colt contract rifled musket. The first lieutenant has an M1851 Colt 'Navy' revolver in his holster. His sword is the M1850 line officers' model.

3. HAVERSACK & CANTEEN

4. REVOLVER, HOLSTER & BAYONET SCABBARD

5. CAP POUCH

6. M1855 CARTRIDGE BOX

1, 2. OFFICER & INFANTRYMAN, 1876
As though preparing for a guard-mount in the same year as the Battle of the Little Big Horn, the corporal wears a dress belt with a McKeever box, although the cartridge belt was preferred for field use. The backs of two types of McKeever boxes are shown; one slips over the belt, and the other was designed to be used with the braces of several experimental infantry equipment systems, such as the M1872 infantry equipment. The corporal's weapon is an M1873 rifle. The first lieutenant wears the M1860 staff and field officer's sword, made mandatory for all infantry officers in 1872.

3. OFFICER'S BUCKLE

4. M1860 OFFICER'S SWORD

5. McKEEVER CARTRIDGE BOX

1, 2. Officer & Infantryman, 1898
Several variations of the M1887 web cartridge belt were in use during the Spanish–American War. The 'H' type belt plate was the first type; but to meet the sudden demand for gear for thousands of volunteers during the war, the Army adopted a simpler system using a simple brass wire fastening belt buckle, as shown in detail. The steel bayonet scabbard was worn hooked over the top of the belt as shown. During this period, too, the men started wearing their canteens and haversacks on opposite sides instead of the canteen on top of the haversack. The private's weapon is an M1898 (Krag-Jorgenson) rifle. The captain's M1896 0.36 caliber revolver is carried in a holster first issued around 1897.

3. Canteen Cup & Haversack

4. Early M1887 Woven Cartridge Belt

5. Officer's Buckle (Cast Brass)

6. Brass Wire Fastening (Late Pattern Belts)

7. M1897 Holster

US Marines patrol 'Sandbag City', the Marine compound at Beirut Airport in the Lebanon, November 1983. They are wearing Kevlar flak jackets designated Body Armor, Fragmentation Protective Vest, Ground Troops (PASGT) – personal armor system for ground troops – integrated into the IIFS system. [*USMC*]

With the adoption of a clip-fed rifle, the M1903, the army adopted the M1903 web cartridge belt with nine pockets, each holding two clips. A first-aid packet was also hooked to the center rear of the belt. An M1909 canteen, M1905 bayonet and M1908 haversack were later hooked to the same belt.

Since these banged about and were uncomfortable to use, a new system that combined all these elements was introduced in 1910. It placed the haversack square on the back, with the bayonet hanging off the left side and, later, a mess kit (called a 'meat can') and entrenching

Troops of the 96th Infantry Division advances on Leyte Island, 1944. The kneeling man wears the M1928 haversack, jungle first aid kit, and two canteens as authorized for Pacific Theater troops. [*US Army via Shelby Stanton*]

tool hanging on the back. A blanket roll, including the soldier's poncho and extra clothing rolled inside a shelter half, was strapped like an upside down 'U' around the haversack top and sides.

The bayonet and entrenching tool were returned to the waist belt with the M1928 haversack. Indeed, throughout its 40-year-history, every element of the M1910 system was extensively altered, even though the basic system remained.

In 1936 a new system incorporating the waist belt, a new field bag and suspenders was adopted for officers. This system, allowing the field bag, or 'musette bag' as it was known, to be detached (unlike the M1910 haversack, which could not be used without the belt), became the prefered system among World War 2 combat troops.

To meet demands for greater carrying capacity, the Army introduced cargo-and-combat packs in 1944 and 1945. An 'assault pack' was issued to troops landing at Normandy in 1945, containing a pack, a haversack and four smaller pouches sewn onto a waistcoat-like affair, but due to its weight and bulk, most soldiers threw these packs away shortly after landing and picked up other issue equipment. A rubber-lined pack was also introduced in 1943 for Pacific jungle use. These packs meant the official end of the musette bag, though it still saw use for some years.

This brings up an important point. With the introduction of interchangeable equipment in 1910, different types of equipment have been in use within the same unit at the same time years after they were officially discarded. In 1963, for example, one supply sergeant found a mess kit in his Strategic Army Corps (STRAC) battery stores and kept it for himself since it was marked the year he was born – 1916.

In 1956 a whole new system was introduced which

1910–1990

used clips rather than double hooks in an effort to prevent equipment bouncing. Its major components were the double-ended adjusting waist belt; a field pack; two universal small arms ammunition pouches; suspenders; an entrenching tool carrier; a first-aid/compass case; a canteen, cup and cover; and a sleeping bag carrier. The bayonet scabbard was attached to the entrenching tool carrier.

The M1956 web was replaced with the M1967 nylon modernized load-carrying equipment (LCE). This was developed for use in Vietnam, where heat and humidity would not affect its nylon. The equipment itself was essentially the same as the M1956 equipment, although patented closing systems replaced earlier snaps and it included a new folding entrenching tool.

In 1974 the All-Purpose Lightweight Individual Carrying Equipment system (ALICE) was introduced. It looked like the LCE kit but used a hard plastic entrenching tool cover and a variety of different packs for different purposes.

The latest combat equipment, the Integrated Individual Fighting System (IIFS) was first fielded in 1988. It is based around a tactical load-bearing vest (TLBV) not unlike the World War 2 assault jacket and bears ammunition, grenade pouches and a pistol holster. It accepts a small 'patrol pack' for short missions or a larger 'alpine pack' for longer ones. The TLBV is designed to be worn tight to allow free movement.

For the future the Army is working on a complete combat suit, now called PITMAN, which will protect its wearer from 0.50 caliber bullets, lasers, land mines, chemical and biological poisons and nuclear radiation. An internal air conditioner will cool the soldier, while he would be able to eat through a tube in his helmet. A battery-powered device will run a locomotive system that makes the spacesuit-like device move on command, while passive sensors will alert the wearer to any nearby enemy. Finally, PITMAN will be equipped with a plethora of arms, including anti-tank and anti-helicopter weapons.

The drive towards complete body armor like PITMAN first began with the adoption of the M1917 steel helmet. This was replaced in 1941 by the M1 helmet which had a separate liner and steel 'pot', and in 1982 the M1 was replaced by a helmet made of aramid fiber called Kevlar, nicknamed the 'Fritz'.

In 1987 the Army also began the issue of ballistic-laser protective spectacles. These eye-glasses, which can be made to any wearer's prescription, are bronze-tinted and protect against shrapnel, bullet fragments and even laser beams.

Although many volunteers wore 'bullet-proof' steel chest-plates during the Civil War, the Army did not officially issue body armor until World War 2. The US Army Air Force then began issuing armored vests to

The individual tactical load bearing vest (ITLBV) worn over the PASGT armor vest with the Kevlar (aramid fiber) 'Fritz' helmet, pictured in 1987. The helmet's nickname comes from its similarity to those worn by the Germans in World War 2, and it provides 35% more protection than the M1, introduced in 1941. [*US Army*]

aircrews. Foot soldiers, however, did not receive body armor, in the form of flak jackets, until 1952 in Korea.

The M1951 armored vest reduced battle casualties by as much as 30% among Marines, and thereafter M1955 and M69 flak jackets were widely issued in Vietnam—although, due to the heat, many were left behind in the field. In 1968 the Army began issuing 'Variable Body Armor', made of a ballistic nylon cloth with a ballistic filler of needle-punched nylon felt and anatomically shaped ceramic/GRP composite armor plates, for use in Vietnam.

An assault support patrol boat settles by the stern after being hit by enemy fire in the Mekong Delta in June 1968. Wearing standard M-1952 and M69 jackets, the crew return fire while attempts are made to keep the craft afloat. [*US Navy*]

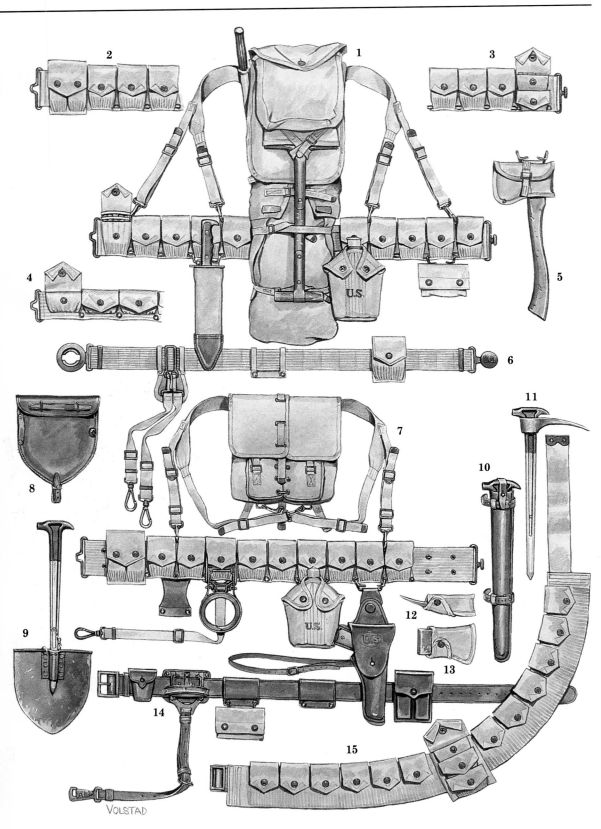

M1910 Infantry & M1912/14 Cavalry Equipment

1. A rifleman's M1910 infantry equipment included the haversack and pack carrier with the long pack roll, on which are attached the shovel carrier and M1905 bayonet. the dismounted cartridge belt carried the bolo, original style dismounted canteen cover and first aid pouch.

2. Left end of the M1910 mounted pistol cartridge belt with the two-cell magazine pocket.

3. Right end of the M1910 mounted revolver cartridge belt, with two pockets on both ends.

4. Left end of the M1910 four-pocket revolver cartridge belt.

5. M1910 hand axe and carrier.

6. A composite M1910 garrison belt (not an actual configuration). Only the officer's and staff NCOs' belts were fitted with the sabre sling. The bayonet sliding frog was worn only on enlisted men's belts. Two cartridge pockets were fitted near both ends of the enlisted men's and the mounted orderlies', scouts' and machine gunners' belts. The band and musicians' belt had no fittings.

7. Cavalryman's M1912/14 equipment (configured for dismounted use) included the left and right side M1912 ration bags assembled as a knapsack, M1914 cavalry belt with M1912 magazine pocket, tool frog, rifle belt ring (lowered) and rifle strap, M1910 dismounted canteen cover, and M1912 holster with an M1911 pistol.

8. M1912 E-tool (entrenching tool) carrier, also used to carry a pick or hatchet head, and horse shoes and nails.

9. M1912 E-tool assembled with a picket pin handle.

10. M1912 picket pin and carrier.

11. M1912 pick assembled with a picket pin handle.

12. M1912 pick head in its cover.

13. M1912 hatchet head in its cover.

14. Cavalryman's M1912 garrison belt with a rifle cartridge pocket (five loose rounds), rifle belt ring (raised) and rifle strap, two sliding frogs for the M1910 first aid pouch and the M1912 holster (not pictured), and the M1912 leather magazine pocket.

15. M1914 cavalry bandoleer.

(NOTE: *When identifying items attached to belts, the order of description is: the pack, suspenders, and the items attached to the belt from the reader's left to the right*).

World War 1 M1917/18 Equipment

1. M1918 dismounted cartridge belt with a 20-round extension magazine carrier, M1917 trench knife, M1910 canteen cover, and first aid pouch. This depicts the belt back made of duck rather than the M1910's woven webbing.

2. Mk I trench knife, sometimes incorrectly refered to as the M1918.

3. M1917 mounted canteen cover. The M1910 mounted cover was similar, but had a web strap.

4. M1912 pistol belt with an M1917 revolver cartridge pouch, and M1917 revolver holster with a Smith & Wesson or Colt M1917 revolver.

5. M1918 pistol magazine pocket on an M1912 pistol belt.

6. This 1918 rifleman is outfitted with the M1910 wire cutter and carrier and armed with an M1917 Enfield rifle and M1917 bayonet.

7. The M1918 shotshell pouch carried 28 × 12-gauge shells for trench guns (Model 1897 pictured).

8. This 1918 automatic rifleman has the M1918 automatic rifleman's belt and is armed with the M1918 BAR, and M1911 pistol in an M1916 holster. His modified M1910 haversack is without the carrier and long pack roll.

9. Both sides of the M1918 assistant automatic rifleman's belt had two each BAR magazine and rifle cartridge pockets.

(NOTE: *When identifying items attached to belts, the order of description is: the pack, suspenders, and the items attached to the belt from the reader's left to the right*).

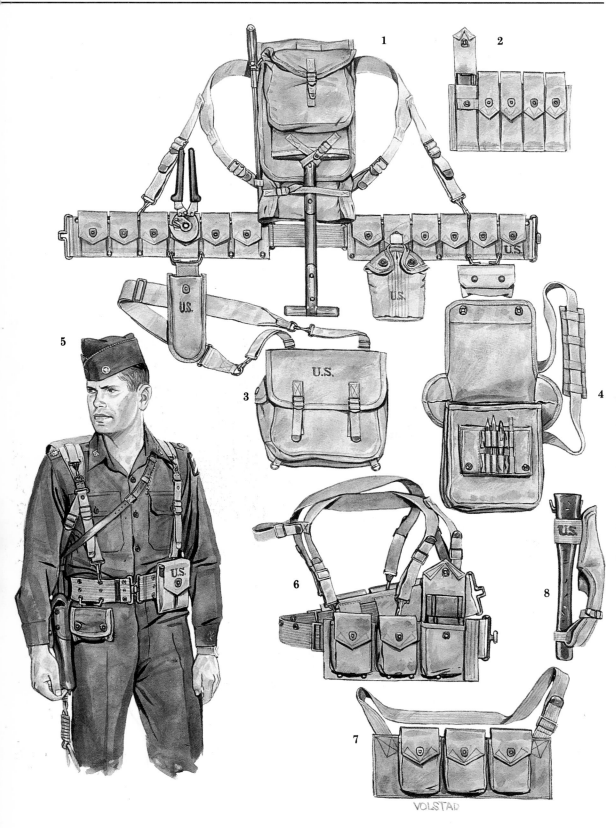

EARLY WORLD WAR 2 IMPROVED M1910 EQUIPMENT

1. By the beginning of World War 2, little of the rifleman's 'M1910' equipment was actually M1910. The M1928 haversack, with a short pack roll, has an M1910 E-tool and carrier and M1942 bayonet (M1903 series and M1 rifles) attached. The M1938 12-pocket dismounted cartridge belt is fitted with the M1938 wire cutter and carrier, M1910 canteen cover, and M1924 first aid pouch.

2. Thompson M1928A1 sub-machine gun magazine pocket holding five 20-round magazines.

3. M1936 field, or musette, bag fitted with the carrying strap used on many other bags.

4. M1938 dispatch bag, often called a map case.

5. This 1942 infantry officer is outfitted with typical dismounted officer's field gear: M1936 field bag attached to M1936 suspenders, M1936 pistol belt, engineer compass case, M1923 magazine pocket, M1 (formerly M1916) holster with M1911A1 pistol, and (not visible) M1924 first aid pouch, M1910 canteen cover, and M17 binoculars case.

6. M1937 automatic rifleman's belt with its special suspenders.

7. M1918 right-side automatic rifle ammunition bearer's bandoleer.

8. M1910 pick-mattock rigged in its carrier.

(NOTE: *When identifying items attached to belts, the order of description is: the pack, suspenders, and the items attached to the belt from the reader's left to the right*).

VOLSTAD

Late World War 2 Improved M1910 Equipment

1. The rifleman's 'M1910' equipment had evolved even further by 1945. The M1945 combat field pack has its cargo pack attached below. The M1 bayonet (M1 rifle) and M1943 E-tool and carrier are attached to the pack. The M1923 dismounted cartridge belt is fitted with the M1910 canteen cover (with a black enamelled canteen issued only in 1942), and British-made first aid pouch. A Mk IIA1 fragmentation grenade is attached to the suspenders.

2. M1941 mounted canteen cover.

3. Sub-machine-gun magazine pocket for three 30-round M1928A1, M1-series (Thompson), and M3-series ('grease gun') magazines.

4. An individual armed with an M1 carbine might be equipped with an M1936 pistol belt, two or more 15-round carbine magazine pockets (the left pocket is the early web version and the right is the later duck model), three-pocket grenade carrier (the two-pocket was similar), M4 bayonet (not issued until very late in the war), jungle first aid bag issued in the Pacific, and M1942 first aid pouch.

5. A 15-round carbine pouch converted for 30-round magazines by adding a flap extension; 30-round pouch production did not keep pace with M2 carbine production.

6. Early pouch for two 30-round carbine magazines.

7. Large pouch for four 30-round carbine magazines.

8. Shotshell ammunition case for 12×12-gauge shells.

9. General-purpose ammunition bag with M1936 carrying strap.

10. The jungle pack, later redesignated the M1943 combat pack, was also issued in an OD version.

(NOTE: *When identifying items attached to belts, the order of description is: the pack, suspenders, and the items attached to the belt from the reader's left to the right*).

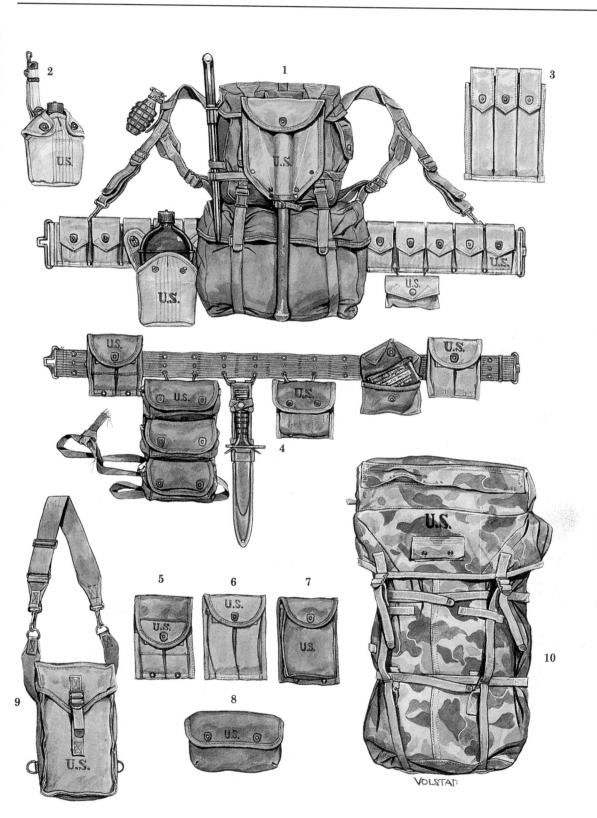

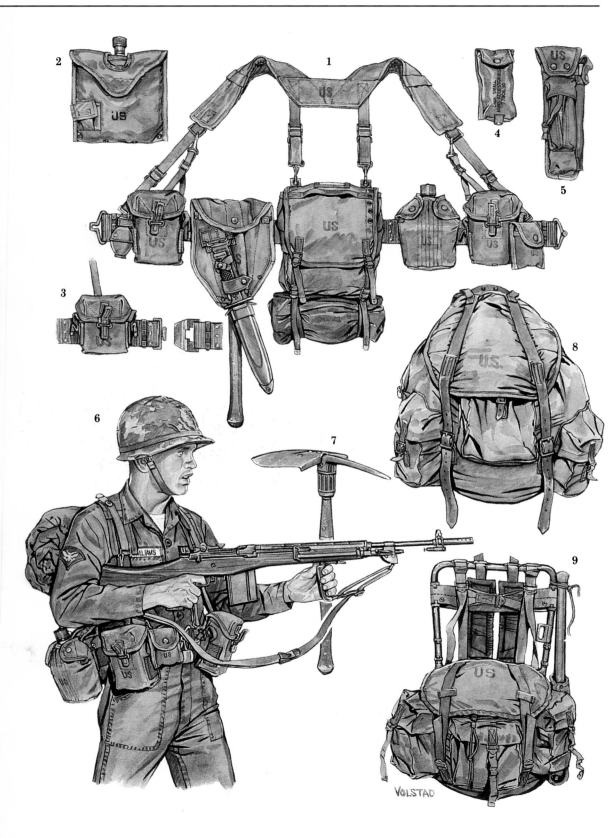

M1956 Load-Carrying Equipment (LCE)

1. A rifleman's M1956 equipment consisted of a combat field pack with a poncho secured under it, suspenders, pistol belt, two universal small arms ammo pouches, E-tool carrier with the M1943 or combination E-tool, and M6 bayonet (M14 rifle), canteen cover (metal ones remained in use well into the 1960s) and first aid pouch. An M26 fragmentation grenade is secured to an ammo pouch.

2. The early two-quart plastic bladder canteen and cover.

3. The quick-release pistol belt buckle, with an M16A1 pouch attached.

4. The small arms accessory case was made of synthetic rubber-coated nylon.

5. The M16A1 rifle XM3 bipod carrying case also accommodated cleaning items and rod.

6. This 1965 rifleman, armed with an M14E2 AR, is outfitted with standar M1956 gear, but with the M1961 combat pack. His canteen is attached to eyelets on the right side of the pack flap. He is carrying the unpopular M1956 sleeping bag carrier with an M1949 mountain sleeping bag.

7. A combination E-tool.

8. The M1951 mountain rucksack replaced the 1941 model and was itself replaced by E9.

9. The lightweight rucksack with frame. Since the E-tool was seldom used by Special Forces, this was a common method of carrying it.

(NOTE: *When identifying items attached to belts, the order of description is: the pack, suspenders, and the items attached to the belt from the reader's left to the right*).

M1967 Modernized Load-Carrying Equipment (MLCE)

1. A rifleman's M1967 MLCE gear consisted of basically the same items as the M1956 gear, but made of nylon. The combat field pack, with the lightweight poncho secured, is attached to the shoulders rather than the belt. Two M161A1 ammo cases, M7 bayonet (M16-series rifles), E-tool carrier, plastic canteen and cover, and first aid pouch complete the equipment. An M68 impact-detonated fragmentation grenade is secured to an ammo pouch.

2. The still-standard two-quart plastic collapsible canteen and cover.

3. The five-quart flotation bladder canteen and cover.

4. The one-quart arctic canteen and cover.

5. The M18A1 Claymore anti-personnel mine bandoleer, or simply the 'Claymore bag', was often used in Vietnam to carry magazines, grenades, and other items in its two compartments.

6. This 1968 fire team leader carries typical Vietnam M1967 MLCE. The pack, with a poncho and poncho liner, and an M1956 E-tool carrier attached, is fastened to the belt. Additional M16A1 magazines are carried in seven-pocket bandoleers. M18 colored and AN-M8 HC white smoke grenades are attached to the gear.

7. A partly folded collapsible E-tool; test models were OG.

8. The nylon tropical rucksack, with an 18-in. M1942 machete in a plastic sheath.

9. The indigenous rucksack was used by the Civilian Irregular Defense Group (CIDG) and some US LRRP and Ranger units, since a comparable US-made model was not available until F8 was introduced.

(NOTE: *When identifying items attached to belts, the order of description is: the pack, suspenders, and the items attached to the belt from the reader's left to the right*).

VOLSTAD

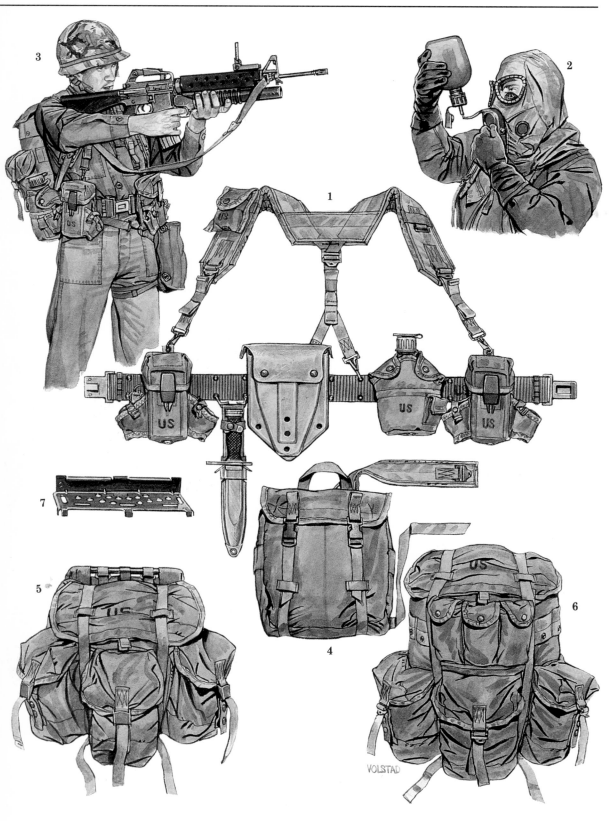

ALL-PURPOSE LIGHTWEIGHT INDIVIDUAL CARRYING EQUIPMENT (ALICE)

1. A rifleman's ALICE gear consisted of suspenders, equipment belt, two small arms ammo cases, M7 bayonet, plastic E-tool carrier (with collapsible tool), LC-2 canteen cover (with the plastic canteen and an M1 NBC drinking cap), and first aid pouch. An M67 fragmentation grenade is secured to an ammo case.

2. Outfitted in a chemical protective suit, this soldier demonstrates the use of the M1 NBC drinking cap with the M17A1 protective mask and M6A2 hood.

3. This 1976 grenadier is outfitted with normal ALICE gear. He has the ALICE medium combat pack, without a pack frame, and an M17A1 protective mask carrier. He is armed with an M16A1 rifle with a 40 mm M203 grenade launcher attached.

4. This simple two-compartment combat field pack was developed for use by the Contras in Nicaragua in the early 1980s and subsequently adopted by the Army for limited issue.

5. Medium combat field pack with the early LC-1 frame.

6. Large combat field pack with the later LC-2 frame.

7. Pack frame cargo support shelf, here the black LC-1; the LC-2 is the same, but OG.

(NOTE: *When identifying items attached to belts, the order of description is: the pack, suspenders, and the items attached to the belt from the reader's left to the right*).

INTEGRATED INDIVIDUAL FIGHTING SYSTEM (IIFS)

1. This rifleman's IIFS gear is made up of the ALICE belt attached to the individual tactical load-bearing vest (ITLBV). On the belt are the first aid pouch, M9 multipurpose bayonet (M16-series rifles), plastic ALICE E-tool carrier and canteen cover.

2. Front and backside views of the 'ambidextrous' Kevlar M12 holster for the M9 pistol (Beretta 92SB-F 9 mm) and magazine pouch.

3. The general officer's leather version of the M12 holster with a leather magazine pouch, attached to the leather general officer's belt.

4. Carrier for the M249E1 squad automatic weapon's belted 200-round magazine.

5. MX-991/U flashlight used since the late 1950s.

6. M2 compass moulded plastic case used by artillerymen, mortarmen and forward observers.

7. This 1988 light infantryman is outfitted with IIFS gear and armed with an M16A2 rifle. He wears the patrol pack (detached from the large field pack) and an M17A2 protective mask carrier, on which is attached an M258 individual decontamination kit.

8. The field pack, large, with internal frame (FPLIF).

(NOTE: *When identifying items attached to belts, the order of description is: the pack, suspenders, and the items attached to the belt from the reader's left to the right*).

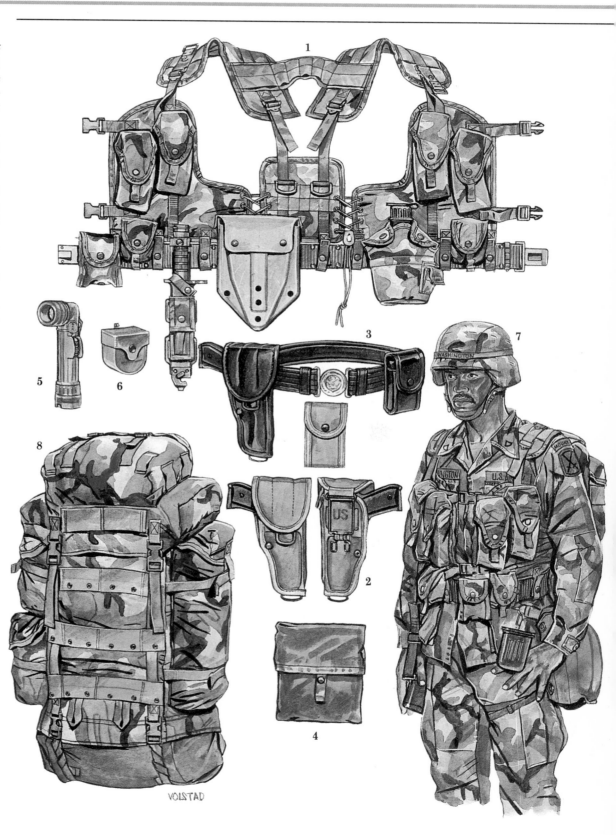

1. USAAF B-17 FLYING FORTRESS WAIST GUNNER, EUROPEAN THEATER OF OPERATIONS, 1944
Over his electrically heated flying outfit, this .50 caliber Browning gunner is wearing a 'flak suit' comprising flyer's armor vest M1 providing front and back protection; flyer's armor apron M4, attached to the front of the M1 vest by three quick release fasteners; and helmet M4, consisting of segments of Hadfield steel in overlapping cloth pockets.

2. USAAF B-29 SUPERFORTRESS PILOT, PACIFIC THEATER OF OPERATIONS, 1945
By 1945 'flak suits' were in widespread use by the US Army Air Forces. This bomber pilot is encased in flyer's armor vest M2; flyer's groin armor M5, with a skirt over each thigh and a center-piece upon which he sits; and helmet M5.

3. US MARINE, KOREA, 1953
One of several significant tactical and technical innovations instituted by the US Marine Corps during the Korean War was the 'flak vest' in the form of the vest, armored, M1951, as shown on this rifleman.

1. US MARINE, VIETNAM, 1968

This Marine hurling a grenade is depicted in the battle of Hue during the Tet offensive of 1968. His vest, armored, M1955 is adorned with typical slogans—against the regulations, which allowed only name and number to be inscribed on flak jackets and helmets.

2. TANK COMMANDER, VIETNAM, 1968

Over his jungle fatigues, this tank commander of the 11th Armored Cavalry Regiment is wearing an M69 flak vest surmounted by a combat vehicle crewman's (CVC) helmet with integral communications; composed of plastic resin-coated ballistic nylon, it gives almost the same protection as the M1 helmet.

3. INFANTRYMAN, VIETNAM, 1969

The US 9th Division fought a grim and grueling campaign among the Rung Sat swamps and the Mekong Delta waterways in 1969. As a point man on patrol, this 'Old Reliable' is wearing variable body armor; M1 helmet; and the experimental quick-drying 'delta boots' to offset dermatophytosis (trench foot)—another example of special protective clothing devised for the combat soldier.

1. ARMY AVIATOR, VIETNAM, 1970
Laying down suppressive fire, a crewchief leans far out of his Huey helicopter, protected from enemy fire by ceramic body and composite-steel leg armor. The body armor was commonly called 'chicken plate' as a reflection on the wearer's courage. The inset view shows the front of the earlier 'T65-1 frontal torso armor', with a crude bulls eye painted on it as an act of bravura; and the rear of the standard item embellished with typical graffito of the period.

2. PARATROOPER, GRENADA, 1983
Armed with an M203, a trooper of the 82nd Airborne Division near the Grenada Beach Hotel at Grand Anse during Operation 'Urgent Fury'. The Personal Armor System for Ground Troops (PASGT) embraces both the flak jacket and the 'Fritz' helmet, which are covered with 'woodland' camouflage material.